Episodes

from a

Twenty-Year Vacation

Keith Lowry

Episodes from a Twenty-Year Vacation
Text & Cover copyright © by Keith Lowry 2019

All rights reserved. © 2019 by Keith Lowry
No part of this book may be reproduced or transmitted in any form or by any means, electronic or mechanical, including photocopying, recording or by any information storage and retrieval system, without written permission of the publisher.

This is a work of semi-fiction. Characters have fictitious names and modified identifying characteristics.

Paperback - ISBN 978-3-9819790-0-8
e-book   - ISBN 978-3-9819790-1-5

By the same author

Höttlland

Höttlland, Part II A Life after Deaths

CONTENTS

CHAPTER 1 - The Road to Who Knows Where 1
CHAPTER 2 - Daze, Months & Years 6
CHAPTER 3 - Cornwall via Israel 11
CHAPTER 4 - Out of the woods & into the forest 17
CHAPTER 5 - Back in Rhein- Main 25
CHAPTER 6 - Ga Ga land 33
CHAPTER 7 - Oder in der DDR.. 40
CHAPTER 8 - Shepherd School....................................... 55
CHAPTER 9 - Eiskapades 59
CHAPTER 10 - On tour in the USA 69
CHAPTER 11 - Bunte Mischung....................................... 83
CHAPTER 12 - Toilet Paper 98
CHAPTER 13 - The saga begins 102
CHAPTER 14 - Elmer Fudd Live...................................... 108
CHAPTER 15 - The Yukon Quest 115
CHAPTER 16 - The Jet Car 135
CHAPTER 17 - Hunting Höttl 139
CHAPTER 18 - The Ugly Stepsisters 145
CHAPTER 19 - Quite the Night at the Opera 152
CHAPTER 20 - Women and children first? 165
CHAPTER 21 - Healing Waters 168
CHAPTER 22 - Through the Mill..................................... 174
CHAPTER 23 - Medicinal Magic 178
CHAPTER 24 - Bad Beer & Bologna................................ 182
CHAPTER 25 - Dracula 187
CHAPTER 26 - The Pied Piper 228
CHAPTER 27 - The Golem 233
CHAPTER 28 - Surviving the Hindenburg....................... 246

CHAPTER 29 - The Legend of Sparta 250
CHAPTER 30 - Long lost Brother 276
CHAPTER 31 - Sparta in Sicily 283
CHAPTER 32 - Safe Food in Salzburg 294
CHAPTER 33 - Nuggets on Tour 302
CHAPTER 34 - To the Core 320
CHAPTER 35 - Lobster Boy 326
CHAPTER 36 - Behind the scenes 332
CHAPTER 37 - Island Fortress 337
CHAPTER 38 - Heated Moments 351
CHAPTER 39 - Face Value 361
CHAPTER 40 - Chasing Cheetahs 372
CHAPTER 41 - A Dude in Paris 378
CHAPTER 42 - Ditto in Rome 389
CHAPTER 43 - On the phone with Hitler 403
CHAPTER 44 - Terrible Tale of Twins 408
CHAPTER 45 - A Death Wish 415
CHAPTER 46 - A Memorable Exit 419
CHAPTER 47 - Land Mines 426
CHAPTER 48 - Denouement in Davos 451
CHAPTER 49 - Cacoethes Scribendi 455

CHAPTER 1

The Road to Who Knows Where

"Nobody abandons a career in the federal government."

Those were the first words out of my boss's mouth after she waved me into her office and solemnly closed the door. I took my seat opposite awaiting her second salvo, aware that she was prepared to pull out all the stops, if for no other reason than to avoid a departure that might reflect badly on her management style. There was cause for concern, as on previous occasions she'd shown a disturbing tendency to slip into panic mode whenever something upset our tranquil office atmosphere. Hoping to avert such a tantrum I began my volley with "How many ways to be".

"And just what is *that* supposed to mean?" she said with a scowl.

"Back in school, when the guidance counsellor asked what we saw ourselves doing after graduation, I was always suspicious of those who could deliver a definitive answer."

"But you're not sixteen anymore," she interrupted.

"True enough, but if I have to work for another thirty years or so, I need to make sure it's at something I like. My résumé already looks like a small town's telephone book. All I can tell you at this point is, after eight months on the job, this one doesn't feel right."

It was the wrong tactic. Visibly irritated by my explanation, she squirmed to recross her legs. Leaning forward with clasped hands, she blurted out her response.

"Do you think I like *my* job every day? Do you think I *like* having to work full time simply because my husband decided he wanted the freedom to 'explore another side to himself' in the company of a younger woman? Do you think every job is stimulating, gratifying... *fun*? If you do, I'm afraid you're in for a very rude awakening, young man. Do you have any idea how many people out there would die to have your job?"

At that moment I wanted to tell her, "*Then I suppose they'd be perfectly qualified,*" but wisely left it a passing thought. What arose in its place was the temptation to mention Kierkegaard's perspective that: "*Man is protected by the secure and limited alternatives his society offers. If he does not stray from the path, he can live out his life with a certain dull security.*" But again, a little voice in my head warned it was not the time or place for philosophy.

To be honest, I could never quite figure out how a career in the federal civil service had come to be perceived as being within the "upper echelon" of sought after pursuits. Perhaps if there had actually been something to do in my job, matters might have turned out differently. As it was, things were rather slack - and when I say slack, I'm talking comatose. Each morning I would dutifully show up at the office at eight a.m. to spend the first half hour perched on the corner of a desk chatting with Suzanne, the office receptionist. Conversations were often interrupted as various colleagues from other departments poked their head through the doorway, hoping to make a lasting impression with the young, attractive secretary. Withdrawing to the desolate confines of my office, I would then begin the daily struggle of finding things to do. Phoning friends was effective for awhile, but calls were soon cut short with a, "Sorry gotta go... some of us have to work for a living, you know."

With eighty percent of the staff at head office in their late fifties, dropping by colleagues in other sections also not high on my list of diversionary tactics. Getting to the one person who was my own age took some finesse. As sauntering down the hallway with your hands in your pockets was a dead giveaway, I soon developed what I came to call the LBM, or Look Busy Mode. Simply by placing a manila folder under my arm, cocking my head slightly forward with a look of urgency and walking with a determined pace, I could literally go anywhere unmolested. As it happened, the tour in question took me past a row of glassed-in cubicles, where numerous grey-haired seniors could be seen jawboning each other. Many, I'd been told, had acquired their jobs through post-World War II appointments where experience had apparently not been a requirement. Although never close enough to hear actual discussions, their slouching body language suggested they weren't debating policies, but rather, much like myself, how to avoid another day of crushing boredom.

Having somehow bridged the gap until nine-thirty, I would then head off to the basement cafeteria, where I was joined by Suzanne and a striking dark-haired twenty-one-year-old who worked as the telex operator. The three of us would stand in line chatting for several minutes, before squeezing into a booth to catch up on the latest scuttlebutt, nursing our coffees under the covetous gaze of office intriguers. Within a few weeks, coffee breaks that had started off at fifteen minutes inched their way towards the half hour mark, conveniently shortening the span until lunchtime.

"You're having lunch with the wrong people," my boss had announced one afternoon while Suzanne was off in the "powder' room."

"What?" I answered with a frown.

"Lunch… You lunch with Suzanne and that young telex girl. You need to develop contacts if you want to get ahead here. I'm afraid you're not making the right decisions… career wise, if you know what I mean," she added with a smirk.

"*Career*-wise?" I repeated, aware that most of the people she was suggesting I dine with, were yearning to trade places with me in the cafeteria.

Although my accuser and would-be benefactor had no inkling of it at the time, that brief exchange had delivered the first nail in the coffin. As the same weary cycle continued to unfold day after day after day, it got to the point where I began to feel that the office motto could have easily been an adaptation of Churchill's famous utterance, "Never have so many, done so little, for so long, for so much pay as we in Public Affairs." Finally, after eight long months of this routine, an internal clamour forced me to acknowledge the job had evolved into little more than suicide in slow motion.

As her fiery monologue dragged on that morning, whatever lingering doubts I still had about the wisdom of abandoning a federal job began to evaporate. Despite her efforts to present my decision as a horrendous mistake, she was simply laying out a future I couldn't bear to face. Thanking her for her remarks, I took my leave, promising I would "think it over."

"How'd it go?" Suzanne whispered once the door had

been shut.

"Compared to what?" I said, wrinkling my forehead. "Not well, from her viewpoint. If she happens to ask where I've gone, just tell her I'm taking the longest lunch break in history."

Shortly before the loss of my job, or more accurately, my extrication from it, another halyard tying me to Winnipeg had been severed in a divorce court. The result of frivolous youth, that entanglement had commenced with the decision to marry at the tender age of twenty-one, in an era when people still believed marriage was an institution. Following five years of less than domestic bliss, during which time we both bore the brunt of each other's uncertainties, it was abundantly clear to me that only some people belong in institutions. For awhile thereafter, feelings about matrimony tended to drift towards the Hitler school of thought, which was basically to get married one day and shoot yourself the next. That option however, was eventually dismissed as being somewhat flawed, leaving me with the conclusion that while marriage might be good for some, for me it was not a pre-requisite for validating commitment.

In any event, although grateful for having removed myself from a job that had had all the markings of an insufficient destiny, within a few weeks of leaving, the inevitable question of "Now what?" slipped into place. With that query momentarily unanswerable, the notion that loomed forth to displace it was simply, "Why squander your life away in your hometown when you can do it London, Paris and Rome?"

CHAPTER 2

Daze, Months & Years

Something felt different the instant the first blotches of Europe became visible through the clouds. The surge of excitement so common to previous landings was missing, replaced by the ominous feeling that sometimes being prepared for everything just isn't good enough.

Despite the pleasures offered by anonymity, the first months in Frankfurt were mired in hardships, a situation not helped by the fact my German was limited to "Ein grosses Pils, bitte"(a large beer please). As a result, the simplest of daily tasks morphed into monumental chores, whether in a department store, post office or bank. Faced with such daunting challenges, I did what any sensible person would do. I ran away.

"What's a Canadian doing in Germany?" quickly became the standard query in my albeit constrained conversations with travel companions. Unable to explain it to myself, let alone to strangers who picked me up hitchhiking, it was easier just to say, "I was deported because I refused to play hockey." That is until the looks on numerous faces made it clear I was being believed. The solution was simply to develop another response.

"Fresh buns every day."

"I'm sorry... I don't understand you," was the common reply.

"If I were to tell you I came to Germany solely

because I like to cross the street each morning and buy fresh buns, you'd think me a bit odd. But being able to do that is just one of the hundreds of things that make up a culture."

There seemed little point in telling most inquisitors I'd simply become tired of North American culture; that predictability had set in with such a deadly force, I could describe what a dozen friends were doing at any given moment. Hoping to avoid such a fate, I had gone in search of something else. Having felt an affinity for the continent ever since my first visit in 1972, Europe had seemed the logical choice.

On the few occasions where conversations did progress that far, they were usually concluded with silence or a look of utter bewilderment.

"But Canada is paradise."

The zenith of this widespread empathy for the "poor Canadian," came one cold winter morning in the hills north of Frankfurt. I happened to be hitchhiking through the countryside, itself an oddity at that time of year, when I was picked up by a man and his teenage daughter. Both seemed eager for the chance to display their presumed prowess in English which made for pleasant company over the course of our short journey together. As our mutual paths drew to an end in downtown Frankfurt, I saw the man mutter something to his daughter in hushed German. Halting a short while later to let me out, he turned to shake my hand and wish me a good day. As his daughter proceeded to do the same, she awkwardly pressed a twenty-mark bill into my palm.

"What is this?" I asked.

"Please take it," her father insisted. "We would like you to have it."

"But why?" I answered, holding the bill aloft as if it was something I'd never seen before. "I don't need any money."

"Please…"

Evidently something in our exchange had convinced them I must be disturbed, destitute or both. Anyone who could leave the dream country of Canada undoubtedly needed all the help he could get. Bundled up against an icy breeze, waving goodbye as they merged back into traffic, I thought, *"Talk about paradise… in what other country do they pay you to hitchhike?"*

※

Over the next month, as my touring extended into southern Germany, additional encounters came to the fore, some more enjoyable than others. One day that had pluses and minuses, started off as I drove through the snow-covered hills of the Black Forest, marvelling at its dark and brooding beauty. Later that evening I stopped for dinner in a small town. Pushing aside the heavy curtains hung inside the door to keep out the cold air, I was startled when the entire noisy crowd suddenly fell silent as all heads turned to assess the "Fremder" (stranger) in their midst. As the waitress gave me a thorough once over from head to toe, I was tempted to ask, "What are *you* staring at, you fool?" Instead, I chose to simply nod and make a feeble attempt at "Guten Abend." (Good evening) With the crowd slowly resuming its chatter, the waitress directed me to a seat in the corner.

"Excuse me," I asked another rather husky-looking waitress who came to take my order. "Could you please tell me what this is?" I said pointing to an item in the leather-bound menu. Why I'd bothered asking is beyond me, as I didn't understand a single word of her explanation. Assuming that most German food is edible, I went ahead and ordered a "Knödel." When it was finally placed in front of me, my sole thought was that I hope it didn't taste as bad as it looked. Despite the absence of a handy dictionary, I was certain "Knödel" must be German for "cooked tennis balls."

In any event, touring south western Germany also provided the opportunity to slip across the border into France, not only to see how little of my high-school French I'd retained, but also to experience the solemnity of World War I military cemeteries. Knowing both grandfathers had spent time in similar circumstances, albeit much further north, I wandered through the trenches in the mountains above Munster , filled with an eerie vision of what it must have been like to have spent weeks, if not months under such conditions.

※

By the time I returned to Frankfurt, I was convinced it was time to start looking for work.

"Where do they *find* these people?" I moaned, slamming the office door behind me and gaining the attention of a dozen sets of glazed eyes in the dimly-lit hallway. "There must be a secret factory where they make these less than civil serpents, training them how to scowl, grumble, and be unfriendly, presumably to discourage clients from ever wanting to return," I said to no one in particular. But despite repeated visits to the dreaded "Ordnungsamt," the possibility of a Canadian obtaining a work permit looked bleak, even if I could find a job opening. After three months of fruitless searching for positions that didn't exist for a non-German speaker, the only alternative was to head for a land where my mother tongue would not be a disadvantage. Fortunately, friends I'd met in Israel two years earlier, graciously offered me accommodation in London. It was a cool, rainy morning in March when I arrived in the southern suburb of Tooting Bec. Shivering in a classic red phone booth near their residence as I debated whether six-thirty was too early to land on their doorstep, I was struck by a sudden surge of doubt about the decision to come to England. Reassurance arrived however, when I noticed a large psychiatric hospital just across the Common, conveniently located in case the looming edge I'd felt in Germany decided to move any closer.

CHAPTER 3

Cornwall via Israel

Despite having to adapt to yet another new reality, the move to England was a good one. Things started to fall into place immediately. A random conversation with my two hosts on the second evening of my stay revealed the possibility of becoming an Irish citizen, solely because Ireland had been the birthplace of my paternal grandfather. Suddenly the door to the entire Common Market stood tantalizingly ajar. A phone call to the Embassy the next morning prompted a flurry of letters to government offices in Dublin and Winnipeg. Three weeks after the final document had been posted, I stood in the front doorway of my friends' flat signing for a new future, courtesy of a grandfather who'd left the Emerald Isle some 70 years earlier. But rather than use my new-found status to hop the next ferry back to the continent, I decided I was deserving of a break. For no other reason than the appeal of traveling as far west as possible, Cornwall became my chosen destination. Having left most of my meagre possessions in London, the next two weeks were spent exploring the rugged Cornish coastline between St. Ives and Land's End, with the sheer grandeur of the endless Atlantic as a backdrop.

Despite having to put up with snoring neighbours in youth hostels for fourteen nights, it was with reluctance that I prepared to make the trek back to Germany. I had just started hitch-hiking to catch the train from Truro when, whether by chance or fate, I was picked up by an

Australian ex-pat behind the wheel of an old Citroen 2CV. Over the course of a conversation that couldn't have lasted much more than fifteen minutes, he let it be known that he and his buddy were looking for workers to help renovate an old farmhouse they had recently purchased. That thought kept playing over and over in my head during the long train ride to London, so that by the time we pulled into Paddington Station that evening, a decision had been reached. After recovering my belongings from the flat in Tooting Bec, I returned to Cornwall within the week, to start what was to become one of the most challenging and enjoyable summers of my life.

※

The collection of stone buildings that formerly constituted a small pig farm was located on the crest of a hill overlooking the Atlantic coastline and portions of the town of St. Ives. The Australian and his partner, an Englishman from Ilkeston, intended to convert the property into a series of artist co-ops as well as their own living quarters. Hired as part of a mini-construction crew, I was to spend the next six months doing hard labour in their courtyard, the most onerous task being banging nail holes into slate shingles destined for the enormous roof. The work, however, was made tolerable by the unseasonably warm weather that summer and the enticing views of the sea. The second my eight-hour shift was up, I'd be off into town, heading directly for Porthmeor Beach, where weather permitting, the next three to four hours would find me in aquatic heaven, boogie-boarding until I could barely walk. Recovery would often take place on a grassy knoll above the beach, where I'd stuff myself with a daily dosage of fish and chips, while leisurely watching the sun head for Canada.

As anyone who has visited Cornwall knows, public transport is not the optimum way to explore the county. To overcome that obstacle, a month after my arrival I became the proud owner of a genuine Morris Mini. Complete with tuned-up engine and miniature racing slicks, it was the ideal vehicle for navigating the network of narrow, winding roadways that criss-cross the Cornish countryside. Each and every time I dropped into the driver's seat I felt like Stirling Moss, scooting over hilltops and around blind corners at excessive speeds, yet always able to stop on a dime. Even the simple act of fetching groceries was cause for excitement.

With my mobility secured, weekends became expeditions to explore the backroads, quaint villages and hidden coves, all of which Cornwall has in abundance. On one of these adventures, I set off one Saturday morning with no particular destination in mind, heading southwest on the coastal road through the undulating green landscape between St.Ives and Pendeen. On a whim, I pulled into a small roadside parking lot carved out of the thick carpet of bracken. Following my nose down a steep, rather treacherous incline, I stopped at a ledge some sixty feet above the crashing waves. There, gazing out over an endless pleated ocean, I was filled with a strange and pleasurable sensation of no longer knowing where the ground ceased and I began, or where I stopped and the sky began. Laying on that ledge, I was able to trace the trail back to the simple twist of fate that had brought me there.

*

The encounter in question began some three years earlier at the central bus station in Tel Aviv. There, amidst the throng of dark-haired travellers, my attention was drawn to a woman with short blonde locks. The silent satisfaction that arose from seeing her board the same bus as me was heightened even more when two hours later, she clambered off at the same stop in the middle of nowhere. Walking along a deserted highway bordered on both sides by groves of grapefruit trees, for the first while I kept a respectful distance behind her. Eventually, the absurdity of acting as if another person wasn't there prompted an overture.

"Excuse me," I asked, quickening my pace to catch up alongside. "Are you heading for the hostel at Kara Deshi as well?"

She was, and for the next seventy-two hours, Gundula, a name it would take a string of embarrassing requests to remember and pronounce correctly, became my traveling companion, hiking through the Golan Heights, exploring luscious, vine-clogged forests, and sharing mutual stories of our journeys through Israel.

On our last evening together, we sat on the shoreline looking out across the calm waters of the Sea of Galilee, my presence having helped her fend off the amorous advances of the camp's maintenance director. Gundula was scheduled to sail to Cyprus the next day before catching a plane home to Germany. As my own plans to return to Jerusalem were flexible, I decided the Holy City could wait and accompanied her to Haifa the next morning. After spending several hours languishing in the sun on the harbour front, what might have been a potentially awkward goodbye was buffered when another German woman, booked on the same ship, barged her way into our conversation just outside the train station. With my train to Jerusalem set to leave well before her ship, I bid Gundula a somewhat perfunctory adieu: wishing her well before turning to walk away. No more than a dozen steps into the terminal, I suddenly stopped and returned to where she was still sitting on the stone steps. There was no way of knowing at the time, that the simple, spontaneous gesture of bending down to give her a hug, would produce such a series of repercussions, starting with a stopover visit to her in Frankfurt before heading home to Canada. This was followed by her six-month visit to Winnipeg later that fall. Both encounters helped solidify our relationship, adding fuel to my long-smouldering urge to return to Europe for good.

※

Including my brief exile in Cornwall, the relationship with Gundula lasted three tempestuous years. Following a six-week trip through France, Spain and Morocco in the winter of 1986, we returned to Frankfurt to go our separate ways, a parting made easier by the fact both of us had already drifted into the sphere of new partners. Certain I wished to remain in Germany, but tired of drifting through a series of dead-end jobs since my return from Cornwall, I concluded it was time to find something more fulfilling. Although now armed with an official German "Arbeitserlaubnis," (work permit) thanks to my Irish citizenship, my limited language skills still ruled out certain jobs. Responding to an ad in the local paper that called for a native English speaker, I accepted a position with a large international advertising firm housed in Frankfurt's chic west end. I did so with trepidation; having never fully vanquished my general dislike of advertising, born during my days at college. As premonitions tend to do, this one didn't take long to materialize. Before the end of my first day, I found myself in the office of the personnel director. Ostensibly there to sign my contract, I could not refrain from divulging the truth.

"I'm afraid my career in advertising has been cut short by an industrial accident," I told her.

"I'm sorry, I don't quite understand," she replied in a thick Oxford English accent common to many Germans.

"I accidentally thought I could work in this industry."

In a brief re-enactment of my former boss's pleas, the woman tried to persuade me that I was making a mistake. But it was to no avail. Once out on the street, I literally sprang into the air and clicked my heels, happy in the knowledge I wouldn't be forced to "write for the wrong reasons".

CHAPTER 4

Out of the woods & into the forest

Several months after my career in advertising had been scuttled, I was back in the Black Forest, this time with my new partner, Isabelle.

"I don't know if this will be worth the effort," I said, as we slid into the exit lane, headed for an address I'd picked out of a regional phonebook when we'd stopped for gas a half hour earlier. "This town looks pretty small. It's probably a one-man band guy working out of his basement."

"It's only three kilometres off the autobahn," Isabelle admonished. "Besides, we've come this far. We might as well follow it through. You never know."

It was with a sense of curiosity and nervousness that I rang the doorbell at the glassed-in entrance of what looked to be a renovated old schoolhouse.

"Guten Tag," I began, after the door was opened by a young German in her early twenties. "I am a Canadian and I am looking for work in video," I continued in exceedingly bad German.

Completely befuddled by my overture, she stood there for a moment, before turning to call out in exceedingly good German what I'm convinced was, "Rainer, there's something, ... er, someone here at the door who wants to talk to you."

Through a combination of good timing and sheer luck, the small production company *was* looking for a camera assistant. Located a mere twenty kilometres from the city of Strasbourg, the job offered the extra benefit of being able to explore and enjoy French culture during my free time.

The owner of the firm, Rainer, was as suspected, pretty much a one-man operation. Having built up a virtual monopoly over the years supplying industry image films for much of southwest Germany and Switzerland, Rainer himself didn't need an assistant. That honour had fallen to his girlfriend's brother Friedhelm, who at the time was taking on jobs Rainer was either too busy or unwilling to accept. As my background had been in educational television, slipping into commercial television was uncharted territory and it took a while to adapt to a format I had previously shunned. One advantage to this work was that it provided access to aspects of life I'd never known, offering my first glimpse of what I would come to call "a window on how the world works."

By this time, I had been involved with video in one form or another for nearly 10 years, having started back in the Stone Age where the Sony Port-a-pac had been in widespread use. For those unfamiliar with it, the Port-a-pac was a recording unit whose camera produced grainy, black-and-white images, that were sent to a separate reel-to-reel tape recorder carried over your shoulder.

Five of those ten years had been spent in a provincial government community development program that worked with closed-circuit television. With the mandate to "encourage people in rural and remote areas of Manitoba to use the resources within themselves and their communities to resolve important issues," the program had produced videos that were used as catalysts for discussion groups at various locations around the province. Despite its noble intentions, after several years of operation, the program got bogged down in internecine squabbles, not to mention political priorities. As a relative innovative and autonomous program, it became a target for elements within the government bureaucracy who were eager to rid themselves of a group considered far too radical for their liking. With the election of a new conservative government in the spring of 1977, we were among the first to be turfed.

While losing my job at twenty-seven was not a particularly uplifting experience, the five year stint as a production co-ordinator had provided me with exposure to all aspects of television production. Of more concern at the time of its demise, was the thought that the program might have spoiled me for future endeavours. Political intrigues aside, during its short lifespan, it had demonstrated television's power to educate and reform.

After almost a full year of coasting, the opportunity then arose to make my own film. Despite being told that "formidable odds" were stacked against me, I submitted a proposal to the Canada Council, the federal government arts-funding agency, to make a documentary that would explore "what motivates people to abandon their artistic career goals." Aimed primarily at high schools students in the early throes of selecting a career, *Nothing But The Second Best* would show viewers the reality of life in the arts - the sacrifices, the struggles and the joys. It was meant to encourage students to pursue their artistic interests while still young, so they would not regret not having done so later in life. To put it another way, to stick a burr under the complacency that comes with uncertainty or procrastination, by posing the question, "what will you do if you don't?"

Aware that for every "successful" artist, there were 10,000 struggling ones, I purposely chose not to interview "famous" artists, but rather focused on people from all walks of life. Interestingly enough, when asked what they had wanted to do when they were about to leave high school, almost everyone mentioned a dream they had failed to pursue.

Given a rather meagre budget, which was used to cover production costs as well as general living expenses, I was obligated to beg, borrow and barter for assistance from friends and sympathetic companies. Editing, for example, a torturous endeavour in those days, was conducted on the midnight shift, toiling from twelve until six in the morning when a friend's studio was not in use.

By the time Part I was completed in the fall of 1981, I was burned out and desperately in need of a break. Before any consideration could be given to tackling Part II, fate intervened when an old federal government colleague invited me to visit at her new posting in Germany. What was planned as a three week visit turned into a six month stay, during which time a month-long trip to Israel and Egypt ultimately led to the fateful morning in Haifa. (For the record, Pt. II was completed in the summer of 1982 with the aid of a Manitoba Arts Council grant. Both films were subsequently sold to school divisions across Canada.)

❖

My first shoot on European soil took place at a family-owned factory situated in one of the Black Forest's many wooded valleys. Despite my thirty-eight years on the planet, it was the first time I'd ever been inside a modern factory - in this case a manufacturer of screwdrivers - not exactly enthralling, but interesting nonetheless. Although filled with a range of highly automated computer-driven machines - all painted a sickly, pale green and spewing a milky fluid that cooled the metal parts as they were cut, bored, or moulded into shape - I was surprised to see how much manual labor was involved. During one break, while Friedhelm discussed details of the next scene with the factory's production manager, I watched in fascination as a woman in blue overalls, her hair wrapped beneath a colourful bandana, was busy removing metal rods from a box, one at a time, stamping them on a press activated by her foot, and then placing them in neatly arranged rows in a separate case. That transfixing image later spilled over into a kitchen debate with my new "Arbeitgeber"*(employer)* after we had returned from the shoot.

"It's not terribly complicated. They do it because they want to," was Rainer's harsh analysis. "They don't have to think about anything other than their job, their paycheque, the weekend and their yearly vacation... and that's how many of them want it."

"But it looked so incredibly boring. I felt sorry for her."

"I don't doubt that it was, but like I said, many people don't want too much responsibility. Give them a simple task, a decent wage and they're happy."

"But how can you be so sure these people are so 'content,' as you put it?"

"Maybe some aren't, but I bet most are, or at least

they accept that's the way things are. People choose their jobs for a reason."

"But isn't it sometimes the other way around - that the job chooses them? Either because they didn't have the chance to be better-trained or think they're not capable of anything else?"

"It seems I've hired a social worker and a cameraman all in one," Rainer mused aloud, tilting back in his chair. "I think people who accept that kind of work are for the most part just happy to have anything. In English I think it's called a comfortable rut."

The irony of this kitchen discussion was not lost on me when several days later, Friedhelm and I were editing the footage shot at the factory. As I sat there, cooped up in a small, windowless room for fifteen hours, staring at a bank of flickering images on the monitors, it struck me that the woman I'd empathized with at the factory would have never wanted to have such a job as this, and quite possibly would have felt sorry for me.

My "soziales Gewissen"(social conscience) as Rainer called it, would get me into conflict again, when he asked me to film products for a telemarketing client he had recently landed. The primary task was to produce a three-minute film illustrating the features of various products the company wished to market on-air. Although setting up product shots was not my favourite pastime, depending on their complexity, one could usually arrange, light and film at least two products a day. The problem was that many products were of dubious quality, something that would not have been apparent to most viewers. After notching up nearly two dozen items in the span of three weeks, I felt compelled to ask Rainer why he had accepted such a client.

"In German you call it a Stammkunde,"(regular customer), he explained in a mildly irritated tone. "In English I think you would say it is my 'bread and butter' account. It pays the bills when times are slow."

"Slow? I've been here for a few months and I've yet to see anything remotely close to slow."

"Yeah, okay... Churning this stuff out *is* conveyor-belt video, but it frees me up to do more interesting things."

"But some, actually a lot of these products, are virtually useless - the kind of stuff they used to advertise in the back of comic books."

"Some may not be as good as others, but if you want to survive in this business, there are times you have to prostitute yourself. Do things that maybe smell a little. It's just part of the job. That's one reason I have other people doing it for me," he said with a slight smirk.

Feeling the barb, I paused before answering.

"I can see the practical side. For sure you need to bend a bit at times, but still... If commercial television means having to occasionally prostitute yourself, then telemarketing strikes me as the equivalent of getting Aids."

In response to my unsolicited comments, Rainer agreed to remove telemarketing from my responsibilities, provided I would finish shooting the remaining batch of products in stock. Meanwhile, over that first year, the mainstay of my work with Friedhelm continued to be industrial films: covering the manufacture of thread, the installation of industrial dishwashers, the testing of aromas and tastes in food products, the making of futuristic toilets that washed and dried the user, the production of plastic signage logos and even the finals of a national ball room dancing contest to name just a few.

Then, not long after the first anniversary of my return to the world of video, work began to peter out. Now content to dish out exorbitant amounts of money for hardware and software as he pursued his growing interest with computer graphics, Friedhelm was devoting less and less time towards acquiring new clients. Workless days stretched into weeks, eroding my confidence and putting a strain on my relationship with Isabelle, who had moved to the Black Forest with her four year old daughter to be with me. Just as the situation was becoming critical, both emotionally and financially, Isabelle received an offer to purchase a business back in Frankfurt. The time to move on had arrived.

CHAPTER 5

Back in Rhein- Main

Long before social media or the Internet became an integral part of daily life, making a dent as a freelancer in untested waters was considerably more difficult. Short of going door to door like a brush salesman, after our return to the Frankfurt area, I chose to simply pull the names of production firms out of the local and regional phonebooks. Armed with a list of more than a hundred companies, I began making calls to let them know I was out there, asking if it made sense to send in a copy of my résumé. Although ninety per cent of the responses were positive, they almost always came with the codicil, "we already have regular people, but you never know when we might need someone." Encouraging it was not, but experience had taught me a lengthy wait was just part of the process.

Unfortunately, during that initial lull, I didn't have the foresight to familiarize myself with the new generation of cameras that had entered the market, many of which I had never even seen, let alone worked with. Eager to get the first shoot under my belt, I jumped the gun when an assignment finally materialized, assuming I could make myself conversant with the new equipment with a visit to a local rental shop the day before the shoot. Suffice to say, you can't learn much about a camera in half an hour. The next morning, shortly before arriving on location, pre-shoot jitters brought on the loss of my breakfast. Panic continued to simmer just below the surface throughout the rest of the day. Although I did manage to get through it in one piece, feigning "experience" may well have taken months off my life.

By the time my second shoot appeared a week later, it was a relief to discover that the producer, a South Korean woman, knew exactly what she wanted, dictating easy to follow instructions for her interview with a high profile lawyer. Everything seemed to be going just fine until she asked for some cutaway shots of herself to aid in editing.

"Excuse me," she interrupted, as I set up behind the lawyer.

"Won't you be shooting across the axis from there?"

To comprehend what she was referring to, one has to imagine a straight line between the participants of a two-person interview. To keep the audience from becoming disoriented, the camera must stay on one side of this line when shooting either person. If it crosses the "line" (or "axis"), both people will appear to be looking in the same direction rather than at each other when a camera cut is made. People familiar with branch jargon and practices are probably wondering, "How could someone who had spent ten years in television be capable of committing such a basic error?" As improbable as it might sound, it was something that had somehow never come up before.

Momentarily caught with my pants down and my ignorance exposed, I resorted to the number one rule when uncertainty strikes: fake it.

"Oh, sorry… Wasn't thinking," I offered lamely, as I switched to shoot over the lawyer's other shoulder. The look on the her face however, told me the ruse had fooled no one.

*

With only two shoots under my belt, a yawning gap opened up in my workload. It was another month before the third shoot emerged, this one involving travel to a large forging complex in eastern France. Whether it was the "glamorous" prospect of shooting in another country, or merely that I had survived the first two shoots, elements somehow combined to produce a bout of unwarranted cockiness, - that is until we got to the actual location where a huge new forge furnace was under construction. Much to my dismay, unlike the South Korean, this producer walked on to the site, took a brief glance around and said, "Get me fifteen minutes of great stuff. I'll be in the cafeteria." Floundering in the core of a unit that would one day house temperatures capable of vaporizing me, I found myself wondering whether it might have been a good idea to have remained in the sheltered existence of the federal government, a job where it had been considerably less imperative to know anything.

Months passed before I was hired again. When work did finally reappear in the spring of 1991, it was with a firm in the northern German city of Düsseldorf, some 250 kilometres away. This was to mark the beginning of a two-year relationship that would include shooting everything from trade fairs to industrial image films, sports, special events, TV game shows, conferences and trips to Cordoba and Barcelona. Parallel to the adventures emanating from Düsseldorf, jobs were also becoming more prevalent from sources closer to home.

The increasing workload was good for me, producing a corresponding rise in my self-confidence, as well as an expanded view of how some production companies functioned. Rainer's background, for example, had been as a cameraman at a regional network in the Black Forest. In other words, he knew his stuff. Many of the people now hiring me had virtually no prior experience in television production. An ex-cop, a civil engineering graduate, a former salesman who shot weddings; all had discovered there was money to be made in the video business and ventured forth. Working with such neophytes, a category I myself was slowly growing out of, was trying at times but never enough to spawn thoughts of forming my own firm. As someone who had harboured a long-standing aversion to the golden rule of salesmanship, "the customer is king", starting my own company did not strike me as a particularly brilliant idea.

"Hang on, is that really true?" I had asked my college advertising instructor back in 1970. "Let me run this by you one more time so I'm sure I understand. I could spend weeks developing what might be widely acknowledged as one of the best advertising campaigns ever created, but if the client's wife happens to dislike some aspect of it, say the colour of the packaging logo or something, then the whole concept could be tossed out?"

"Crudely put, but basically correct," he had replied. Such statements tend to stick.

But as so often happens in the freelance world, the surge of activity eventually slowed down again. To fill in the gap and replenish my dwindling bank account, I felt inclined to accept shoots in a genre I'd hadn't yet explored. It didn't take long however, to discover that being part of a "hard news" camera team was not my life's calling. Consisting largely of sitting around in a small room at the network's office waiting for a story to "happen," one could easily spend four to five hours a day in said room before suddenly being ordered to race across town to capture a few words from an interview subject, who might or might not emerge from an "important" meeting for another several hours. Unlike many of my colleagues, I did not relish this "soft touch." Fortunately, one month in, relief arrived in the form of an offer to again work as a camera assistant.

※

Another devout follower of the one-man band school of thought, Lothar was a bit of a technical freak whose expressed passion was producing industrial films. As dreary, dull and boring as that might sound and at times was, working under Lothar's tutelage did broaden my horizons. Granted that learning how sausage-making machines function, roof tiles are made, and screws, nuts and bolts are manufactured were not exactly entrancing practices you'd rush to add to your résumé, there were shoots that left an indelible impression. One of the most memorable took place at a former munitions factory an hour's drive north of Frankfurt. Despite having been converted from its wartime functions to the manufacture of engine blocks for the automobile industry, its past was still very much in evidence when we arrived for the shoot. One unique feature was a tall, collapsible smokestack that could be retracted to ground level whenever enemy airplanes were in the vicinity.

Although that was unlikely to happen anytime soon, with some Germans you can never be too sure.

While being guided to our main location within the complex, my attention was drawn to a row of single-story buildings, each with what appeared to be a small forest on its flat roof. Initially assuming the foliage was meant to provide greenery to what otherwise ranked as a dark and gloomy atmosphere, I was surprised to learn its actual purpose had been to camouflage the factory from overhead bombers.

As intriguing as these external aspects of the factory were, they paled in comparison to what awaited us inside the main building. There, in a noisy, cavernous, soot-filled hall, dozens of cast-iron moulds, their insides coated with finely compressed sand, were lined up on lengthy conveyor belts, waiting to be filled with molten iron dispensed from a giant bucket suspended in front of the main blast furnace. With each tilt of the enormous cauldron, blobs of the glowing mass splashed on to the floor, racing out like liquid mercury and dissolving almost everything in their path, including a small section of my shoe and sock, when at one point I got a little too close. In another section of the same hall, the scene called for positioning a powerful 2500-watt back light to separate workers from the blackened walls. In addition to supplying dramatic effect, the lamp inadvertently turned the scene into something straight out of a Dickensian sweat shop. Muscular workers in soiled sleeveless t-shirts, their sweating arms gleaming in the harsh light, moved through billowing clouds of steam and smoke at the foot of a large furnace. Looking like extras from a Village People music video, their silhouettes shattered beams of light amidst air that teemed with black snow as they shifted casings back and forth across the floor. As mesmerizing as the image was in all its beautiful horror, it's doubtful it ever made the final cut.

In addition to exposing me to such scenes, Lothar was also my introduction to the negative side of working with a perfectionist. In contrast to Rainer, who was thorough, demanding and very fast, Lothar could take an excruciating amount of time to set up and light each shot. Granted a certain amount of time was needed to make a sausage machine look interesting, but the extent to which he insisted on putting the final touches on a scene often meant for tedious times for the assistant, namely me. And God forbid if you failed to comply with what were often his obtuse instructions.

Like many perfectionists, Lothar tended to suffer from what I came to call a bad case of "snarkasm." Rather than rationally issuing instructions to resolve a problem, he would attempt to belittle the perpetrator of the infraction, couching each word of advice or instruction in a denigrating tone. The first time this behaviour reared its ugly head in my direction, what might have otherwise been a normal reaction was quashed by the fact that he was technically my boss. When the mini explosions continued to surface on successive outings, ones where there was little or no stress in evidence, it was clear the outbursts were just part of who he was.

Needless to say, as this behaviour continued, my level of tolerance began to diminish. Matters finally came to a head during a three-day shoot at an automative plant in Gyor, Hungary. After what had been an uneventful and productive first day, there was nothing to indicate trouble was brewing. On the second day however, a random tantrum was thrown over something as inconsequential as a wrongly-positioned light. Within seconds, all of my pent-up frustration from previous unanswered taunts came pouring out.

"What exactly is your problem?" opened my barrage, after I'd stopped what I was doing and called Lothar aside. "If you want me to do something different, say so. Stop trying to make it sound like I'm the biggest fool on the planet. I don't need another Lothar lecture - Capiche?"

Lothar didn't answer, choosing instead to busy himself with the camera while I returned to my place to await further instructions. Somehow we both managed to remain civil to each other for the remainder of the day. Later that night, over drinks at a restaurant back in Vienna, he surprised me by apologizing. Oddly enough, even before he was finished speaking, I realized that what he had to say no longer mattered. A line had been crossed, a stand had been taken, and enough was enough. Although he refrained from using his disparaging tone in the few shoots we were still destined to share, contracts from that point on became noticeably less frequent, eventually fading away completely.

CHAPTER 6

Ga Ga land

It was almost as though some greater being was controlling the game board. No sooner had work from Lothar started to decline, the slack was picked up by another production firm I had registered with several years earlier. There had been no contact in the interim, until one day they called up out of the blue to ask me to drop by for a chat the next time I was in the Würzburg area.

Normally, I try not to judge people by first impressions. You can never be sure whether someone has merely been having a bad day or what issues might be plaguing them at that given moment. With my introduction to Siegfried however, a considerable degree of stamina was needed not to make an exception. The first challenge on the day of my visit, was not showing any reaction to a handshake that was comparable to having a dead fish placed in your palm. As it happened, my attention from that moist encounter was diverted by the sight of the few remaining strands of hair plastered across the top of Siegfried's balding pate. It's one thing to observe people with that affliction on television or across a crowded room, but quite something else to be confronted with it in the matted flesh. Seeing as I was ostensibly there for a job interview, thoughts of, *"For the love of God man, what were you thinking?"* remained unspoken.

Shown into an office awash with trophies and

plaques, none of which I cared or dared to inspect, I struggled to remain objective during a round of small talk before quickly agreeing to Siegfried's offer of a guided tour of the studio facilities. Despite my low expectations, I found the layout and equipment quite impressive. I might have been even more impressed were it not for Siegfried's irritating habit of not so much laughing as whinnying at his own jokes, causing tiny bubbles of drool to foam up in the corners of his mouth. But in spite of what many in the world of sales might consider substantial handicaps, the man was for all intents and purposes, an apparent success.

 Back in his office, over weak coffee and stale sandwiches delivered by a frizzy-haired woman he introduced as his wife, Trixie, Siegfried proceeded to inform me of the "tremendous opportunities" trade fairs in Germany offered to those with "the get up and go," a thought that had been hovering since my arrival. Although German regulators tended to frown on "external" firms directly soliciting business during a trade fair, Siegfried had apparently circumvented that obstacle by assuming the role of a journalist. But rather than reporting on events at the fair on opening day, the roving reporter would traipse from stand to stand, enticing prospective clients with the promise of putting them and their products on television. Smaller companies with limited knowledge of marketing were especially attractive targets. The basic ploy was to appeal to a customer's vanity. Following a brief introduction, which undoubtedly included Siegfried's highly unsettling handshake, prospects were buttered up with praise for their display booth or product. Once they were sufficiently lubricated, "the package" would be wheeled out in all its glory. A standard deal included a five minute film on a product of the client's choosing, along with a thirty-second clip to be aired on regional television. What he failed to mention was that said clip would likely be broadcast at three o' clock Sunday morning on a rather obscure private network. All of this was to be had for a sum rumoured to be in the neighbourhood of four thousand Deutsche Marks. Once enough signatures had been collected on opening day, the film team would roll in the next day to fulfill the contractual obligations.

Unfortunately, I never had the privilege of seeing the roving reporter in action, not to mention the responses his 'Spiel' might have invoked. My part in the plot involved jostling with constantly moving crowds, warding off wannabe directors, and avoiding nosey security personnel. The pay was good, but one had to work for it, covering as many as four stands a day. Usually this meant a minimum of ten hours of stress, not including the drive to and from the fair, often as far as 300 kilometres away. Needless to say, it came as a welcome relief when sometime between Siegfried's departure and our arrival, a customer had reflected on the wisdom of their decision and cancelled. Amazingly enough, over all those months I worked for Siegfried, not once were we ever stopped from carrying out our illicit work; not even questioned. Equally bewildering was how many clients seemed to be friendly, intelligent people. Depending on the day's demands, there occasionally would be an opportunity to chat with them, leading me to suspect that some had signed up merely to rid themselves of the guy with the creepy handshake.

It didn't take long for the surplus of work and

subsequent surging bank balance to start feeding fantasies. Based on the assumption I could somehow manage to avoid direct contact with Siegfried, I began harbouring secret visions of lasting long enough to retire at fifty with a boatload of money. Four months later however, that dream came to a crashing end. To understand how it all transpired, it's important to know that an integral part of Siegfried's enticement was to have an attractive female moderator on set. Assigned to help create the atmosphere of a live television show, her job was to introduce the client to an imaginary TV audience and get him to talk effusively about his product and company. Unbeknownst to the client, of course, little of what was said would ever make the final cut. When I came on board, the moderator was a dark-haired woman named Sarah. She left soon afterwards, having grown tired of the stress, not to mention being ogled by a string of clients with overactive imaginations, moving on to bigger and better things, which in this case meant pretty much anything else. Her replacement was drawn from that strain of women Germans often refer to as "Tussies," perhaps the North American equivalent of "floozies." A severe victim of both the fashion and cosmetic industries, Ulrike was a short, curvy bombshell with a mouth like a drill sergeant in a foul mood. Suffice it to say, our first shoot together in Hamburg quickly revealed our differences as to how the "show must go on." Not having received instructions that the general strategy had been altered, I proceeded to follow the format used over the past several months. Ulrike's version, which may or may not have been previewed for Siegfried without my knowledge, called for a distinctly more prominent role for herself.

Added to this combustible mix was a new camera assistant, who happened to bear an uncanny resemblance to Meatloaf, right down to the fancy western-styled shirt, matching cowboy boots and protruding abdomen. Much to my misfortune, Meatloaf and Ulrike hit it off famously, turning the day into little more than a series of on-going arguments. Within minutes of arriving back at the studio that evening, Ulrike disappeared into Siegfried's office. Whatever was discussed, it took him a few days to get up the nerve to actualize her demands. Unable to compete with her apparent persuasive charms, I was out and she was in.

Although the news came as a shock, it was difficult to lament for long. The money would be missed, and early retirement put on hold, but what I would regret the most, would be no longer partaking in the other inane ventures Siegfried had implemented to promote business, the zenith of which was something he had christened "Hole in One." Aimed at those clients who had already taken the bait for a film package, this little extravaganza had encouraged them to bring friends and family to the studio to "make a day of it," and participate in what was billed as a "live television show." It was like shooting fish in a barrel. Capitalizing on techniques lifted from bad TV game shows, Siegfried arranged for each arriving guest to receive a T-shirt with a "company of the month" logo displayed across the front. After being greeted by a giddy, giggling Trixie, and indulging in a round of refreshments in the foyer, patrons would straggle into the studio and take their seats. A constant source of amazement for the assembled crew was that the studio was always packed. Once everyone was seated and the cameras rolling, Siegfried would enter to much applause, and welcome the fifty or so guests to the "program," promising them a day they would not soon forget.

"No matter how much they try," I once whispered into the intercom connecting me to two other cameramen, forgetting that Siegfried's son was listening in at master control. After a brief explanation of the rules was recited into a microphone stuck to Siegfried's lips like a tongue on a cold metal railing; four "teams" were selected, each of which conveniently included at least one pretty, young girl from a pool Siegfried had rounded up with who-knows-what-kind of promises. Contestants were then asked to attempt hitting a golf ball into the open mouth of a cartoonish-looking "Hole in One" mascot painted on a sheet of plywood. Each successful hole-in-one was to be accompanied by a taped organ crescendo, but thanks to the inattentiveness of Siegfried's son at the console, all were invariably a few seconds late in arriving. The competition would drag on for fifteen or twenty minutes, interspersed with Siegfried's attempts at humorous play-by-play narration. Non-competing guests were free to cheer, mingle and take advantage of the snacks and alcoholic beverages that flowed throughout the entire proceedings, further helping to loosen up the prey for the kill. At the end of three rounds, with all guests back in their seats, the winning team was called up and awarded a chintzy-looking trophy, along with several products donated by attending firms, including their own. To close the festivities, Siegfried would inform guests that a video of today's "exciting" program would be sent to them within the week, news that inevitably caused a number of blank stares to make the rounds. But as farcical as the whole event was, there wasn't a single episode of "Hole in One" that didn't generate at least two or three additional contracts for a company image film. Combined with his lucrative trade fair adventures, there can be little doubt about who laughed all the way to the bank.

CHAPTER 7

Oder in der DDR

For those of you who weren't paying attention, the Wall that had separated East Germany from West for twenty-eight years was breached for the final time on the evening of November 9th, 1989. The very next morning, film production firms on the western side of the old dividing line began making plans to invade what they correctly viewed as an untapped market.

Despite registering with several western companies that same month, it wasn't until the summer of 1991 that work started to trickle in. The first company to offer a shoot was located in the city of Kassel. Having snared a "Raum Vertrag"(area contract) with several regional and national television networks, they needed extra staff to help produce a steady flow of daily five minute, magazine-format spots. With interest in the former Deutsche Demokratische Republik,(a.k.a. East Germany, a.k.a. DDR) still running high in 1991, most of the spots centred on people and events in the former Communist enclave.

Although the wall had been down for over a year and a half by the time I ventured across for my first shoot behind the former Iron Curtain, it didn't appear that much had changed since my first visit to "the East" in 1986. In the fall of that year, Gundula and I had driven to the city of Karl-Marx Stadt on the pretext of visiting her extended family. The true purpose of the trip had been to bring back items that her twenty-year-old cousin, Boris, would not be allowed to take with him, now that he'd received official permission to leave the glorious socialist homeland. As I would soon learn, the East German government did not take kindly to citizens requesting to leave its realm, instituting harsh regulations that impacted not only those leaving but also those family members remaining behind.

My first exposure to life under Communist rule came at the border crossing between the German states of Hessen and Thuringen. After joining a long line of cars, the end of which you couldn't see, we sat for at least an hour before being told to drop our passports and visas on to an antiquated conveyor belt running alongside the row of cars. I did so reluctantly, uncertain I would ever see it again. Inching ahead one car length at a time, it took nearly another hour before we finally edged up to a small open window, behind which sat a stern-faced guard in an ill-fitting uniform.

"Purpose of your visit?" he grunted.

"Visiting family," Gundula answered, having previously advised me not to open my mouth.

"Hey, I don't speak German," I'd said to her. "What am I going to say?"

"Say nothing."

"Where does the family live?" the guard asked.

"Karl-Marx Stadt," she said, knowing full well our intended destination was written on the visa in his hands. After several more pointless questions and the compulsory exchange of Western currency into Ost Marks for each day we planned to visit, we were stamped and waved through, threading our way through a channel of heavily armed soldiers whose grim expressions seemed to convey their disappointment at not having a reason to shoot out our tires.

It was startling to see how abruptly the sanitized world of the West was left behind. Within a kilometre of the border, the manicured highway dividers and smooth road surfaces vanished, replaced by a nature left to its own devices, alongside a pot-holed autobahn, empty save for the occasional "Trabi", East Germany's quintessential two-cylinder, plastic-shelled automobile.

Warned at the border that variations from our route would be dealt with "severely," we thought it wise to remain on the transit Autobahn until reaching our designated exit. En route however, we did make a brief pit stop at a "Rastplatz"(rest area) where East and West friends and relatives could engage in semi-illicit meetings under the tolerant but watchful eyes of uniformed soldiers and non-uniformed agents.

My first impression of Karl-Marx Stadt, previously known as Chemnitz, was that it must have been in the running for one of the ugliest places ever seen, and was doing quite well. Before we could embark on a sight-seeing tour of features I suspected were not worth viewing, we first had to take care of the little matter of registering our presence with the local police.

"Good thing they didn't ask us if we had anything to declare,"I told Gundula after we had finished with formalities in triplicate and re-emerged on to the dreary streets of the city centre. "I might have felt compelled to borrow a page from Oscar Wilde and tell them what I thought of their grand metropolis so far."

On the way to the apartment complex where Gundula's relatives lived, we passed an enormous bust of Karl Marx.

"Somebody must have a sense of humour," I

remarked.

"What do you mean?" Gundula asked, dodging a Trabi that seemed to take pride in purposely cutting off the car of a "Wessie."

"That giant bust of Karl is right out front of the employment office. That can't be a coincidence."

"What was that all about?" I asked Gundula, after we'd completed a similar registration procedure with the apartment building's superintendent and finally found ourselves in the privacy of her aunt and uncle's flat.

"It's got to do with the Stasi," she explained in the midst of a round of stiff introductions.

"The who?"

"The Stasi... the secret police. All visitors have to register with the superintendent. He passes information about tenants and guests on to the Stasi."

"You're putting me on. What, we've landed in a spy novel?"

Ushered into a cramped dining room for a midday snack of crackers and salami, my input to table conversation was limited by the fact no one spoke any English other than Gundula and Boris. That wasn't a matter of grave concern; as much like German get-togethers in the West, everyone always seemed to be talking at once, to no one in particular. Unable to participate, I struggled to maintain a lengthy all-purpose smile whenever someone's questioning gaze drifted in my direction. Suddenly everyone's attention was diverted by a phone call announcing that bananas were available in the neighbourhood grocery store.

"That's important enough to call about?" I

whispered to Gundula, after she'd translated. Rather than wait for a second elbow in my ribs, I volunteered to join Boris in his quest to acquire some of the apparently prized fruit.

The first thing noticeable about a grocery store in the East, before the West barrelled in to impose its own standards, was the shop window. Rather than displaying foodstuffs or even posters of foodstuffs, this one was jammed with a hodgepodge of mops, plastic pails and cleaning substances. Inside, there was nothing that looked familiar, with cereals, toothpaste, soft drinks and beer all bearing labels I'd never seen.

"What's that guy up to?" I asked Boris, as he stuffed two batches of rather sickly looking bananas into his basket.

"Testing to see if it is okay," he answered, watching the man in question invert a second bottle of beer up to the light.

"If it looks like it's snowing inside, it's not."

*

The second day of our planned three-day visit saw Boris, and his mother, Stella, Gundula and I, pile into the family Trabi for a trip to Dresden. Sounding very much like a over-revved lawn mower, the Trabi's top speed made you feel you could get out and run alongside. Despite the less than frenetic pace, it took less than an hour to reach Dresden, the outskirts of which definitely left something to be desired. Fortunately, the old city bordering the Western bank of the Elbe river had much more to offer. One of its main features was the Zwinger palace, a quadrangle of museums and art galleries built who-knows-when, but still in remarkably good condition. Add in the Semper Opera House, the Hofkirche, the Fürstenzug, a block-long wall of Meissen porcelain depicting former Saxon rulers, as well as numerous other baroque and rococo-styled buildings lining the cobblestone streets, and you understand why the highly impressive cityscape is listed as a Unesco heritage site.

More disturbing were the ruins of the nearby "Frauenkirche," virtually bombed flat in WWII and left as a reminder of the catastrophe that befell the city in February 1945. On two consecutive days that month, over a thousand heavy bombers from British and American Air Forces carried out raids on the city, dropping almost 4,000 tons of bombs and incendiary devices, turning the entire inner core into a ferocious firestorm. The raids, which resulted in the destruction of the old city and the deaths of as many as 25,000 people, were later seen by many as a war crime, completely unnecessary from a military standpoint, given that the city had been filled largely with refugees fleeing from the Russian Army. Wandering through the charred rubble some thirty-nine years later, I was startled by the sudden image of wading knee-deep in blood. Equally upsetting was learning years later, that my own father had been a navigator on one of the planes that flew on those missions.

The drive to Moritzburg Castle that afternoon was considerably more pleasant. Passing through village after village of quiet, tree-lined, "Allees," bordered by small, unpainted stucco houses, one sensed a lifestyle much more pastoral than its Western neighbour. As neither Boris nor I were interested in visiting the castle museum, we agreed to meet Gundula and Stella in a nearby cafe after a short stroll around the moat encircling the castle.

"How are we going to find the car?" I casually asked as we passed the parking lot filled with at least a hundred identical Trabis.

"Don't worry," Boris chuckled. "Here we are used to that. I have made a note of where we are parked. It is the only way you can tell. It's more difficult at night, especially when you've had something to drink."

Once seated in the crowded cafe, I decided to make use of Boris's excellent English to probe deeper about "life in the East".

"It is shit," he answered, taking a deep pull on his cigarette before tilting his head back to slowly exhale the used smoke. "That is why I leave."

"Gundula told me a friend of yours got put in jail because he said something bad about the government one night when he was a bit drunk."

"Somebody reported what he said to the police."

"What did he say?"

"I don't remember, but it wasn't anything threatening or dangerous… he was just a bit drunk and said what he thought."

"And they put him in jail?"

"For six months."

"Man, it's a good thing I don't live here."

"What do you mean with this?"

"Nothing… it's not so important. I just can't get my head around being given six months for bad-mouthing the government."

As we continued to compare life experiences, Boris nonchalantly mentioned we were likely not doing so unnoticed.

"You mean here, right now?" I asked incredulously, glancing around the room full of patrons.

"Yes, it is quite certain."

"Why would anybody want to watch us?"

"Partly because I have received permission to leave, and partly because you are a foreigner."

"But you live near Karl-Marx Stadt. Who knows you here? Don't these people have anything better to do?"

"Apparently not, just like the people who observe us at our apartment block."

Intrigued by the thought that we were being monitored, the remainder of our conversation was spent trying to determine which of the fellow customers had been "assigned" to us, as well as what I could do that could possibly cause an international incident.

Back in Karl-Marx Stadt just after six, we dropped Stella off at home before heading for the small town where Boris had been living for the past year.

"God, this flat is enormous," I said in awe as we toured the rooms above an old barn a mere fifteen kilometres from downtown Karl-Marx Stadt. Despite having been renovated to relatively modern standards, the place rented for the princely sum of twelve Ost Marks per month, a sum so close to nothing it's not even worth converting. From there it was on to a neighbouring village where twenty to thirty friends had gathered for what was dubbed a "going away" party.

Everybody seemed well oiled by the time we arrived and after a quick round of introductions and handshakes, out came a pair of guitars, bongos and a harmonica. Despite being over fifteen years old, 'Take me Home Country Road' was still a big favourite with the crowd. Smiling benignly as the guests tried to coax me into singing along, I preferred listening to the lyrics being mangled by the heavy German accents. When the musicians finally broke for a smoke and a drink, many guests were eager to try out their English with the visiting "foreigner." For the most part, conversations tended to revolve around what part of Canada I was from, why I had left, and what did I think of the DDR. Noticing their eyes starting to glaze over when I started in on my "fresh buns" saga, I managed to pull myself away long enough to take Boris aside.

"Hey, before we both get too bombed, I have a question. From what I know and have seen of it, the system here really sucks. I suspect I wouldn't last a day before being tossed in jail."

Beer in hand and arms folded across his chest, Boris did not appear terribly interested in partaking in a long conversation.

"All the same," I continued, "When I look around at the camaraderie between you and your friends, I gotta ask, are you sure you know what you're doing?"

"About what," he asked, shifting his eyes from the crowd as he took a sip of his beer.

"About leaving."

"What, are you a crazy man?" he said. "You have seen what life is like here. It is terrible."

"No argument there, but I'm curious what it is you think you are going to. Okay, I haven't lived here and maybe it's not fair to make a judgement after only two days, but when I see the bond that exists between you and your friends, I get the impression that here there's a underlying feeling of 'We're all in this together, so we need to stick together'. In the West, it's more like 'every man for himself,' where the way to get ahead is with your elbows."

Unimpressed with my argument that evening, Boris left his homeland a few days later. His first few years "in the West" were spent in Frankfurt, trying to adapt to a system he found both appealing and disturbing. Six months after the wall came down in 1989, however, he and a number of other friends, who had also sought and received permission to leave, all returned home to the East for good.

*

Returning home was also to become an issue with the production house in Kassel. Contracted for a 10-hour day, portal to portal, the meter had started running the minute I left home in the morning and ceased upon my return that evening. Taking into account it was a 360 kilometre round trip, and that the majority of shoot locations were well into East Germany, sixteen-hour days were not uncommon. It also wasn't out of the ordinary to arrive back at the studio only to discover I was needed again for the following day. Rather than journeying home, which would have entailed even more overtime, the company simply paid for my meals and overnight accommodation.

The workload out of Kassel continued to flourish over the next few months, at one point reaching a high of twenty-five days per month for two months straight. Not surprisingly, visions of grandeur and plans for an early retirement returned anew. But as in all best-laid plans, that figment of my imagination was spoiled when someone in accounting happened to notice the large wire transfers streaming my way.

"How much?" the company director was rumoured to have sputtered when told of the sums. "That's more than I make for Christ's sake. Why are we paying someone from Frankfurt to shoot in the DDR? Don't we have anybody local? He's going to ruin us."

Despite previous expressions of satisfaction with my work and my subsequent offer to lower travel costs, money spoke loudly enough to ensure a parting of the ways. The long days and drives certainly wouldn't be missed, but a part of me was sorry that the cornucopia of themes that had passed before my lens would now end. Assignments such as covering a cherry-pit spitting contest, a wallpaper museum, a medieval shoemaker or East Germany's youngest mayor had been instantly forgettable, but others rated as fascinating and challenging. One that definitely qualified in both categories was a contract to interview a man who had been assisting young East German men to quit the neo-Nazi scene in and around the city of Arnstadt.

The morning we left for the East German city, we had been unaware that a neo-Nazi rally was scheduled to take place there the same afternoon. We arrived in Arnstadt just as the tail-end of a march was dispersing and the attending crowd flocked into the market square to listen to a round of speeches. Pleased by the unexpected opportunity to capture some highly relevant b-roll, the producer asked me to wade into the crowd to gather footage. It didn't take long to realize that most neo-Nazis don't like being filmed. Although I received enough middle fingers to make a necklace during my ten minutes of shooting, it never dawned on me to actually feel threatened, presumably because I naively thought there was no real risk of being pummelled in a public place. The producer however, having noted the increasing number of "We'll take care of you later," gestures aimed in my direction, thought it prudent to call a halt to my endeavours.

Taking refuge near the back of the crowd, we watched as speaker after speaker came to the microphone to bark words of encouragement to the cheering followers. Gazing out on this miniature sea of waving banners, the parallels with the huge annual Nazi Party rallies in Nuremberg in the 1930's were not lost. Even more disturbing than the jack-booted, bullet-headed men churning the air with raised fists, were the little brown-shirted youngsters in their ranks, some no older than four or five. It was chilling to watch them eagerly waving tiny flags adorned with some Nazi-like symbol, obliviously cheering along with the rest of the herd.

"I think I've seen this movie before," I whispered to the producer.

"I think it's about time we got out of here," he answered, glancing at his watch. "We should move on before some of these heroes decide to make an example of the "intruders".

Once back in the relative safety of the parking lot, the producer told me that while filming in the square, two or three individuals in bomber jackets had been filming me. Others had made threatening gestures that suggested an eagerness to alter my facial features, should opportunity knock.

About to leave for our appointment with the youth leader, I was loading the last of the gear into the car when I looked up to see a brown-shirted specimen approaching. Outfitted with a severe haircut and jack boots, he thrust a brochure in my direction, and asked, "Interessieren Sie sich für unser Programm?" (Are you interested in our program?) I didn't bother to read the text as the black and red slogan emblazoned across the front told me all I needed to know.

"Do I look that stupid?" I answered, more out instinct than bravado, as I closed the trunk.

"Sie sind kein Deutscher,"(You are no German) he said with a look of menace, looking around in hopes of spotting some support. When none was forthcoming, he turned briskly and wandered off in search of a mob.

"What did that guy want?" the producer asked as we pulled out of the lot.

"I believe he wanted to leave his bootprints on my forehead."

"I wouldn't take it so lightly if I were you. If there had been a group of them you… or we could have been in real trouble. Half the people here are all revved up just itching for action."

Having avoided what could have been an abrupt end to the shoot, not to mention my career, we headed for the outlying suburb where our rendezvous was set to take place. Ten minutes later, we entered a bleak area of "PlattenBau," a collection of concrete jungle apartment towers so synonymous with DDR skylines.

"This doesn't exactly look like a place I'd want to bring someone on a first date," I said, as we parked near a bar we'd previously been warned not to enter. "And what's the story with this bar? Why aren't we supposed to go in there?"

"Under any circumstances," the producer answered. "That's what our interview partner told me on the phone, so that's what we'll do."

The answer came a few minutes later with the arrival of our interviewee.

"They know me here," he explained, casting a cautious look over his shoulder. "They don't like me, but they know me."

"And?" the producer asked.

"You guys are interlopers and they don't like interlopers…especially ones with cameras."

"So I noticed," I said.

"Some of the same guys who were at the parade or the rally may be in there drinking already. You'd be lucky to get out of there in one piece if they recognized you."

"But that's a public bar," I said. "You're saying it's off limits because of these guys?"

"I'd say it's better to consider it off limits if you value your own safety."

"And the police? Where do they fit into this?"

"You haven't spent much time around here, have you," he asked with a hint of impatience.

Before there was a chance to answer, the producer interrupted to signal me to start setting up for the interview, a clear indication he wanted the subject of the bar dropped.

"We can't do the interview here," our partner interjected.

"Why's that?" the producer asked.

"I don't know how they found out, but I got a tip from a reliable source saying that too many people know about this interview. It would be too dangerous to do it here. Especially once the rally is over and more people start drifting back to the bar. We'd be better offer doing it somewhere up in the woods above town."

"Shit… we should have gotten that on tape," the producer said, flustered by the missed opportunity as well as the sudden change in plans. Caught between the indignation of being denied access to a public street and admiration for someone willing to confront behaviour that made such scenarios possible, we swallowed our objections and drove to a wooded area to complete the assignment.

After the earlier events at the market square, the interview itself turned out to be rather subdued. Perhaps more nervous about being detected than he let on, the youth leader quickly rattled through his answers, while constantly glancing around for unseen enemies. A mere twenty minutes later, we were on our way back to the "West," loaded down with the day's images.

Years later, watching the almost daily news reports of right-wing activities in various parts of Germany, that day in Arnstadt came floating back, and with it, a curiosity over how many of those tiny brown-shirted youngsters had grown up into full- fledged skinheads with offspring of their own already in training.

CHAPTER 8

Shepherd School

Back in the late 1960's, long before a career in television had ever been a serious consideration, I was busy weaving my way through a variety of dead-end jobs, - a short order cook, drywall taper, construction labourer, dry-cleaning warehouse attendant, deliveryman, and gas jockey to list just a few. I'd yet to read anything by the American psychologist Rollo May, but was nevertheless inadvertently following one of his major tenets: "A man often finds out what he wants to do, by finding out what he doesn't want to do." The assumption at the time was that if one tried on as many lives as possible, sooner or later one would fit. But the more my résumé continued to bulge, the clearer it became that I didn't have a clue what I wanted to do.

Growing weary of the persistent queries and taunts from relatives and family friends about my "plans for the future," I got into the habit of answering "soda jerk" or "shepherd" when it came to expressing a preferred career choice. That usually succeeded in bringing the conversation to a swift end. So it was with a degree of irony that twenty years later, I would find myself en route to film at what had been billed as Germany last surviving school for shepherds.

To understand why it was the last of its kind, let alone why there was one at all, one must accept the premise that Germans have a rather peculiar education system. My first collision with it came at a parent-teacher meeting held to discuss Isabelle's daughter's educational future. Having employed a process, details of which were not presented, her teacher had managed to interpret Ida's shyness as "disinterest, and in need of direction," as well as the classic standard when all else fails, "has talent but doesn't apply herself." As a result, he had recommended it would be in her best interests to abandon the track leading to university and enter the less demanding regimen of the middle-level school. What made his comments so unfathomable, if not downright absurd, was that this suggestion, which undoubtedly would have had a profound impact on her future, was being made at the completion of the fourth grade.

"Far be it from me to belittle you or your system, (*you incompetent little worm you*), but don't you feel it a tad more sensible to give her the chance to prove her abilities rather than penalize her for what we feel is an error in judgement on your part?" If only I could have spoken better German. But there I was, sitting across the desk, yearning to ask whether *he* had known what he had wanted to do with his life at age ten. Instead, I settled for merely informing him that we saw things differently and had no intention of accepting his judgement or recommendation. For the record, that same "unmotivated Mädchen," now holds a Masters Degree in Data Management and Computer Science. Despite my enduring pleas, she has yet to agree to send a copy to the teacher who was so prepared to limit her future all those years ago. My point is that the system is rigid, or at least was at that time, and woe to those uncertain of what they want to do.

And so it was, that upon entering the shepherding

classroom that day, I couldn't help but wonder - how the thirty scrubbed-faced teenagers, none of whom were wearing dusty overalls, tattered straw hats or chewing on a long blade of grass, - had come to select such a trade.

After explaining our presence to the class, the instructor proceeded to clarify how all students were required to undertake a three-year course involving both theoretical and practical applications.

"Sorry, but what is there to learn about sheep that could possibly take three years?" I had asked my sound assistant. Not expecting or receiving a reply, I continued to film, as my mind drifted to that old joke, *"Newfoundland, a land where men are men, and sheep run scared."*

Absorbed in a muffled chuckle, I was nevertheless able to pan with the instructor as he moved to a nearby cabinet and removed a life-size plastic model of a sheep. As he set it down on his desk with a loud thump, I couldn't help recalling the Woody Allen film scene where Gene Wilder is in bed with Daisy, an ovine specimen dressed in black lingerie.

As the teacher continued to lecture on whatever there is to lecture on about sheep, he repeatedly referred to the model, turning it around to expose its inner workings complete with removable coloured muscles, organs and blood vessels. Perhaps aware that many viewers were likely to start counting them if there was too much theory on how a sheep becomes and remains a sheep, the lecture was cut short to meet the real thing in a nearby barn.

Prior to our arrival, the instructor had made arrangements for several students to demonstrate the fine art of cutting the sheep's nails. Hoping to get a better angle before proceedings started, I stepped over the low fence of a holding pen within which twenty or more unsuspecting sheep were milling about. Moving toward the animal being attended to, I squatted down for a closer shot. Perhaps it was the distraction of the camera light in the darkened stall, perhaps the unexpected troupe of observers, perhaps merely my aftershave, but something was making the rest of the herd nervous. No sooner had sheep number one's pedicure been completed, it jumped back up on all fours startling its nearby companions. What began as a normal bleating session quickly descended into an appeal for action as a few of the young lambs started to careen around the stall debating their options. Glad to be capturing such lively footage, I failed to notice I was doing so in front of the one and only exit. Confirming the adage "There's one in every crowd," it wasn't long before a lone sheep decided it was time to leave. Watching through the lens as it raced towards me, I looked up just in time to see it arcing over me in what appeared to be slow motion. The rest of the herd wasted no time following suit, some less proficient at leaping than others, not to mention less clean. Once the dust had settled and I was able to free myself from tufts of errant wool and other accoutrements associated with frenzied sheep, we caught up with the flock grazing in a nearby field. Supervising the bucolic scene was a young shepherdess dressed in the requisite long flowing cape with matching floppy hat. Leaning on a curved staff as she surveyed the legion of future pullovers, I was pleased to see she was giving a piece of straw a good run for its money.

CHAPTER 9

Eiskapades

Okay, so it wasn't exactly a hero's welcome with red carpet, brass band and elected officials waiting to grant us the key to the city. All the same, it was with a detectable sense of pride that I stepped off a plane in Thunder Bay in the winter of 1992. The last time this airport had seen the likes of me was nine years earlier, when I'd passed through on what turned out to be a one-way trip to Europe. This time I was back to cover what had been billed as an exciting international ice-climbing festival; my first shoot overseas and my first venture into freelance producing.

A lot of work had gone into getting this far. In addition to making the initial pitch to a German television station, preparing a detailed budget and rounding up support from various sponsors, I'd contacted officials at the local tourist board to see if they were prepared to participate. Once all that was taken care of, it was a minor step to pick up the phone and ask a trusted friend if he was interested in serving as cameraman.

After collecting our considerable baggage and being warmly greeted by the director of regional tourism, we stepped out of the terminal into an astonishing 25 below zero. Barely able to convince Thorsten not to turn around and catch the first flight back home, I glanced out at the familiar surroundings as we drove to our hotel to discuss the facilities the board was putting at our disposal.

"Can you believe this?" I said to Thorsten, once the director had departed. "They've put us up in separate suites. All our meals are being paid. They've given us a van, and possible access to a helicopter… Either they must be really hard up for tourists in this area or we're more important than we think."

"From what I saw on the drive in from the airport, I think it's the former," Thorsten remarked. "Talk about the end of the world… I mean why do people live in such a climate?"

"You're asking someone who left."

"And what the hell was that smell? I could smell it in the van even with the windows closed. It's terrible."

"That my friend, is your Welcome to Thunder Bay greeting from the town's ubiquitous pulp and paper mill. Most unpleasant, but highly memorable."

It was gratifying to see the dividends my preparatory work was looking to provide, although the extent to which the locals were catering to us raised concerns as to whether we could live up to their expectations. Those concerns were driven home with a thud bright and early next morning with our arrival at Festival "headquarters."

"Are you sure we're at the right place?" Thorsten asked as we trudged through knee-deep snow on an unshovelled sidewalk.

A few minutes later, Rick, the event organizer, guided us into his basement to introduce the field of competitors. Trying desperately to not act stunned, I cautiously asked when we could expect to meet, "the rest of the participants."

"This is it… No, hang on a second… Two more will

be arriving tomorrow, so we'll have a grand total of eight… Make that nine," Rick boasted.

"The network is gonna kill me," I whispered to Thorsten. "Uh… Nine?" I said, turning my attention to Rick. "We were sort of expecting something larger in scope. After all, the festival *is* advertised as an international event."

"Well it's true that most of us are from north-western Ontario," Rick admitted, "but Bill here is from the States, - a small town between here and Duluth - and one of the climbers coming tomorrow is originally from Japan, if that counts."

With my heart in my shoes and visions of having to repay all the sponsors, all I could muster in response was a weak nod. Fortunately, with his own head not on the block, Thorsten proved a calming influence, assuring me that the seemingly impending disaster could somehow be turned into a semi-interesting story.

With the actual festival not set to begin for two days, it was concluded we could pad out the program by gathering material on other sport activities Canadians take part in during their long cold winter. That quest was made easier by the fact that the tourist board was keen on promoting the upcoming Nordic Winter World Championships. As a result, over the next two days we were chauffeured around to various locations to film such events ice fishing, skating, hockey, curling, cross country skiing, snow-shoeing, and even ski jumping. The highlight of this tour however, was the arrival of the promised helicopter. Not only were we able to capture aerial footage of all event locations, but also local landmarks and the various ice-climbing venues. Having shot from a helicopter before, and thoroughly accustomed to Canadian winters, I knew how to dress for the occasion. Thorsten on the other hand, while an experienced aerial cameraman, had never shot from one in the depths of the "Great White North". Suffice it to say, skimming across the frozen waters of Lake Superior at 75 miles an hour with the side door removed, was not a treat he was prepared for. All the same, he managed to gather some spectacular material during our hour in the air, in particular a wide angle shot of the ice racing past beneath us before he panned up to reveal a Miami Vice version of Thunder Bay's iconic skyline of cement grain silos. That night at dinner, Thorsten apologized for being late, confessing it had taken him a full hour under a steaming shower before he could feel his extremities again.

*

On the first day of the Festival, we awoke to brilliant sunshine and a thermometer registering a frigid - 27. Over breakfast it was agreed that any notion of trying to make the event look like an "International Festival," should be abandoned. Instead we'd focus on individual climbers in action, together with interviews on how they got interested in the sport. As Rick had explained that first morale shattering night, the sport had developed in Thunder Bay after it was discovered that a series of small waterfalls, which tumbled from an escarpment in summer, would gradually freeze as winter deepened, growing in size until they eventually became thick enough to climb.

"In contrast to rock climbing," Rick had told us, "ice climbers face the additional challenge of an ever changing medium, one that can change daily, sometimes hourly. One has to learn not only how to read the ice from its look, but also from its sound and feel when struck with an ax."

The prospect of filming in -27 weather had not been particularly appealing, so it was a pleasant surprise to arrive at our location deep in the woods to find it not only protected from the wind, but also exposed to the warming rays of the sun. While we unloaded equipment onto a snow-packed parking lot some thirty kilometres east of the city, we could make out a half dozen brightly-coloured figures mulling around the base of an ice-covered cliff fifty to sixty feet high. Outfitted with twin pick-axes, helmets, harnesses, crampons and waterproof clothing, the climbers were inspecting the various surfaces as they discussed ice conditions and plotted the best route to attempt a test climb.

Once having set up near the base of one waterfall, Thorsten began filming one climber as he slowly made his way up the frozen surface, inadvertently providing us a first hand lesson as to why helmets are such an integral part of the gear. Half way up the wall, in preparation for taking another step, the climber had no sooner struck an ax into the ice when it shattered, sending large chunks down on to his protected head and forcing Thorsten to dodge several errant pieces headed his way. Able to maintain his position thanks to his other ax and crampons, the climber simply shook off the loose particles and looked around for a second entry point. Other events over the course of the day were less dramatic but we managed to get great footage of climbers practicing their craft against the backdrop of a faint, late afternoon moon.

After being treated to such clear weather on the first day, it was that much harder to accept conditions the next day, when grey and menacing skies unleashed a flurry of blowing snow. To make matters worse, reaching the site for the day's ascents, - a 100 foot cliff face overlooking a whited-out Lake Superior - required a half mile trek through virgin forest.

"Make sure to walk only where you see the animal tracks," Rick advised as we set off from the parking lot. "That's the hardest part of the trail and you won't sink in the snow."

Moving along single file, the group hadn't advanced more than a hundred yards into the woods when Thorsten was heard to cry out.

"Scheiße!"

Glancing over my shoulder I caught sight of him sprawled on the trail, one leg resting sideways across the path, with the other waist-deep in snow. "Somebody help me… I can't get out."

Able to regain his stature with the aid of two climbers, Thorsten brushed the snow off his dampening pants and rejoined the march. Tipping the scales at considerably more than the average Bambi-like forest creature, it was only a matter of time before the entire process repeated itself, complete with a series of expletives in German and English.

"Thorsten," I said, holding back a chuckle at the sight of him floundering on the path, "if you're gonna insist on playing in the snow every ten feet, it's gonna be dark by the time we get to the location."

"Scheiß snow… Scheiß ice climbing… Scheiß Canada," he grumbled, slowly rising to his feet.

Despite several more submersions en route, upon reaching the cliff Thorsten managed to find a patch of snow hard enough to support himself and the tripod. From there we watched Rick slip over the edge, rappelling himself half way down the cliff face so that he could be filmed arriving back at the summit. Having been previously miked, the plan was to have Rick give a running commentary on the techniques in use during his upward climb. The problem was, we couldn't see him.

"Excuse me for asking," I said, turning away from the portable monitor to address Thorsten. "But all I can see is swirling snow. How are we going to be able to use any of this? He could just as well be sitting in his basement dictating this."

Offering only a glare in response, Thorsten continued to film until Rick's helmet finally bobbed over the crest.

"Das was," he snapped, flicking off the camera and pulling down the rain jacket. "Enough with this Scheiß ice-climbing and enough of this Scheiß Schnee."

Fortunately, during a hastily-called break, the weather cleared, the departing clouds taking any growing animosity with them. What remained of the dwindling daylight was used to film Rick from several different angles, none of which required a detour through the snowy woods to reach.

Back at the parking lot as dusk was setting in, we couldn't help but notice that none of the Festival participants seemed overly perturbed that no actual competition had taken place, nor was any planned. The "International" Festival was, for all intents and purposes, now over.

"Do you suppose we'll ever work in the film branch again?" I asked Thorsten as we each cracked open a much needed beer back in the privacy of my suite.

"I don't *want* to work in this branch again if it means ever coming back here," Thorsten muttered between sips. "What a bunch of dilettantes. International festival my ass…"

With the help of the beer we managed to keep from sliding into panic mode over what we might face back in Germany, assuring one another there was enough material from other sources to make for a decent ten minute film.

"Aw, man… Haven't we had enough shit for one day?" Thorsten groaned as I declined a third beer to remind him of our pending dinner invitation. "I don't know if I can face a meal with people I don't even know. I'd rather just stay here and try to forget about the past couple of days. Tell them I came down with the plague or something."

"And miss out on a genuine German home-cooked meal?"

"That especially."

Earlier that day, upon hearing we were from Germany, a festival volunteer had invited us to join him and his wife, for what he claimed would be "ein echtes Deutsches Abend Essen."(a real German dinner)

"My wife, Gertrude cooks very good." Harald had assured us. "We have Sauerbraten and Sauerkraut, just like back home."

"I hate Sauerkraut," I grumbled that evening, as we climbed out of the cab and walked briskly through the crisp night air to the front door of Harald's modest home. "And what the heck is Sauerbraten - never heard if it." I added, stomping my feet against the cold.

According to the table talk, Harald had emigrated from his native homeland in the 1950's.

"How did you end up in Nipigon?" Thorsten wanted to know. "This place is pretty far off the beaten track."

"I didn't want to live in the city and there weren't a lot of jobs around back then. So when I found work as a fisherman and lumberjack here, I took it. Living way out here can make the winters feel longer but now that I'm retired I don't mind as much."

Rounding out the guest list that evening was an old family friend introduced only as Thomas. Another German ex-pat, Thomas had apparently emigrated to Canada in the late 40's, a time frame that prompted Thorsten and I to exchange glances. Despite several subsequent inquiries, subtly delivered in German, Thomas pointedly avoided elaborating about the timing and circumstances of his departure from "das Vaterland".

"Do you want to check the closets or should I?" I whispered to Thorsten when the two old "Kumpels"(buddies) had gone outside for a smoke and Gertrude was busy in the kitchen.

"Maybe we can somehow fit the story into the film," Thorsten said with raised eyebrows, lifting his beer glass in a secretive toast as Gertrude returned with dessert.

The finished film aired three months later. To my great relief and astonishment, everyone seemed to be happy with it. The clothing sponsor was pleased to see their logo splashed across sweaters, jackets, and helmets. The tourist board was grateful for coverage for the upcoming Games, although I doubt many hotels were swamped with an influx of Germans as a result of the film.

Rick could now strut his stuff around town, boasting of his exposure on international television, and Thorsten… well, despite his complaints, Thorsten came home with a string of fond memories, not to mention a brush with hypothermia and a hatred of snow. Thomas, meanwhile, remains at large.

CHAPTER 10

On tour in the USA

The politest word I can use to describe the sort of jobs I was getting in the spring of 1993 is "mundane." For example, being cooped up in a windowless garage, ten hours a day for two full weeks - filming the installation, removal and re-installation of a car's air conditioning unit - did not make for exciting times. To make matters worse, Michael, the producer on this shoot, was a hyper-perfectionist. Entire glaciers could melt and evaporate in the time it took him to pore over the script and decide what needed to be filmed. One afternoon when he was taking an excessive amount of time to reach a decision, I suggested that such scintillating television risked putting the viewer to sleep.

"Hey, it's your job to make it look interesting," he snapped back.

"Interesting'? Viewers would have to be pumped full of drugs to find this stuff interesting."

"In case you hadn't noticed, we're not talking a prime-time audience," Michael countered. "It's not a Hollywood epic…it's a training film."

"Something the general public can be grateful for, I guess."

It was not that I didn't appreciate having the work; it just all seemed so inefficient and pointless at times. Several other testy exchanges ensued that day, leading me to conclude it best to keep thoughts and comments to myself, primarily because we still had another six days to go - seven if he chose to slip into extra dawdle mode. But when the shoot did finally reach its merciful end, my severely frayed nerves ultimately prompted me to issue a parting query on the drive back to the studio.

"How often do you do these kind of shoots?" I asked, still suspended in a mild state of disbelief.

"Twice, maybe three times a year," Michael answered. "It takes a lot of research and behind-the-scenes preparation, you know."

Longing to tell him it didn't show, I settled for an innocuous "Hmmmmm." The fact we never crossed paths again suggests my question had been interpreted as, "How can you stand doing this kind of stuff," which in all honesty was not far off the mark.

Despite the monotony of that shoot and a conglomeration of other humdrum shoots amassed over the summer, the stamina needed to endure the pervasive boredom saw its reward that fall. Based on a concept similar to the incentive tour in Chateau d'Oex several years earlier, this particular event had been arranged for the year's top salesmen of a large, German automotive company. One hundred and fifty of that breed, along with their significant others, were to be whisked off for a ten-day tour of Washington, DC, White Sulphur Springs, and New Orleans. Our job was to film them enjoying the fruits of their labours.

Judging by the charted jets, motorcycle escorts, five-star hotels, fancy restaurants, and a myriad of activities intended to pamper their favoured employees, money had definitely been low on the agenda of "matters we should be concerned about." One could imagine the enormous amount of planning that went into organizing such an event, yet that did not prevent the shoot from getting off to a rather inauspicious start. No sooner had we landed at Dulles airport in Washington, I was ushered off to a downtown hotel and told to be ready to film the guests arriving for the evening's gala welcoming dinner.

"The arrival bit I understand," I told the man who'd assigned me the task, "but these people just finished a nine-hour plane trip. They're likely whacked and not looking or feeling their best. And besides who wants to watch people eating?"

"Yours is not to question why…" he answered, leaving the sentence dangling before disappearing into the arriving throng.

Fighting off the creeping exhaustion of jet lag, I spent the next thirty minutes wandering through a dark, cavernous restaurant, garnering five minutes of useable footage. I was already looking forward to tumbling into bed when one of the event organizers, the same weasel who'd assigned me to film the meal, tapped me on the shoulder.

"There's been some sort of foul-up with the hotel people," he muttered without the slightest hint of empathy. "There's no room booked for you, so tonight you'll have to bunk up with the other cameraman."

"Does not register," must have flashed across my forehead, as the man with the "Norbert" name tag scowled and repeated the gist of the message.

"No room… bunk with Reinholt tonight."

The poor fellow had no way of knowing I don't deal well with such surprises. Even at the best of times, without the after-effects of a long flight, diplomatic responses to such unexpected scenarios are not part of the equation. Somehow, through a thickening haze of anger, I was reminded I would be working with "these people" over the next three weeks, prompting me to mollify the fiery blast of indignation building in my throat.

"I understand," I began slowly. "But I happen to be a very light sleeper. If I have to share a room with somebody who snores and I can't get to sleep, you don't want to be around me the next day. Nothing against Reinholt, but I need my own space. If it's okay with you I'll just book a room at another hotel nearby and be here at call time tomorrow morning. I'll even pay the difference. Sleep is that important to me, especially after having been in that tin cigar for so long."

But it wasn't okay with him, and he clearly didn't like having his directives questioned. Ignoring my suggestion, he simply turned on his heel and disappeared. Five minutes later, he was back with yet another surprise.

"Here is the card key to room 463. It's the event manager's room. You can use this tonight. It will be free in half an hour," he said sternly. "See you at breakfast."

Before I could offer my profound thanks, he was gone. A good night's sleep was accomplished but only under the suspicion that a black "Prima Donald" mark had been scribbled in next to my name. Nothing like getting in good with the powers that be.

*

Like most major world capitals, Washington, DC is a city of giant post cards. The elegant Washington Monument, the majestic Jefferson and Lincoln Memorials, the sombre Vietnam War Memorial, Union Station, the Supreme Court, FBI headquarters, the Capitol or the

White House, all are there for the gawking. As one might expect, a good portion of our first morning was spent filming people visiting and snapping pix of said venues, purchasing souvenirs and sending home post cards that basically said "I'm here and you're not." One of the highlights of the initial day's festivities was an "exclusive" lunch in the Capitol dining room - exclusive, that is, if you didn't mind sharing your meal with a few hundred lobbyists or big-wigs, who members of Congress like to invite whenever they happen to be in town. How car salesmen from Germany managed to make the guest list was a matter of conjecture. Some felt their status as employees of the daughter company of a powerful American corporation had helped qualify them, while other scuttlebutt simply suggested a large wad of "doneiros" had sealed the deal. Since no one was terribly interested in having us capture the guests stuffing their faces, even in such distinguished company, Reinholt and I were given a few hours off, with orders to report back at six for the evening's planned soiree.

"*This* certainly must have set somebody back a few bucks," I said later that night, as we entered the city's grand Union Station, now decked out in 18th century decor for a sit-down dinner and stage show. Adding to the period piece were two dozen white-wigged waiters and waitresses dressed in Revolutionary era costumes. In addition to the elaborate decorations and costumed staff, organizers had also managed to dig a former well-known German reporter out of mothballs to moderate the proceedings. Evidently still in good form, the emcee managed to fill a good hour with mind-numbing rants about his previous escapades. Once the dishes from the four-course meal had been cleared away, the stage was surrendered to a thirty-piece orchestra that immediately launched into an array of military marches, a style of entertainment that didn't appear to appeal to many in the crowd. It wasn't until enough booze had been consumed and the band eased into something lighter, that a few people ventured out on to the dance floor. Although by then filming had formerly ended for the night, Reinholt and I decided to stick around, if only for the joy of watching people attempt to keep rhythm to a Rolling Stones song played by a band more at home with John Philip Sousa.

Despite having partied into the wee hours, all participants were outside the hotel early next morning to collect their rental vans for the next leg of the adventure. Split into groups of four, each team was handed a detailed road plan and schedule, with instructions simply to "head west." Participants were told the drive to the luxury resort in White Sulphur Springs, West Virginia, would take about four and a half hours. Stopping en route was encouraged, but people were urged to try and arrive at The Greenbrier before sundown. Judging from the limited English language skills of many guests, it was questionable whether some would make it before the end of the year.

Having never ventured to this part of the planet before, I was looking forward to the drive, especially the recommended vistas of Virginia's Shenandoah National Park, the highlight of which was said to be its views of the Blue Ridge mountains. The park lived up to its hype, and for a few hours we were treated to numerous scenic panoramas of guests gazing at scenic panoramas. Since footage of people driving was about as exciting as them eating, Reinholt and I were among the first to arrive at the Greenbrier that afternoon.

What can one say about the Greenbrier except perhaps, "*How much* did you say a room is?" If you have to ask, you've probably never stayed there. While Reinholt went off to confirm our rooms, I slumped into one of the plush chairs dotting the tastefully decorated lobby. Flipping through one of the resort's brochures under the disapproving gaze of several staff, I began to get an inkling of the exclusive territory we had just landed in.

Serving guests since 1778, which was of no real interest to me unless my room happened to be one not yet renovated, the Greenbrier resort sits on 11,000 acres in the midst of the Allegheny Mountains. In addition to its 700 rooms, the complex boasts ninety-six guest and estate houses, three championship golf courses, and over fifty different activities for guests to partake in. A tad overwhelmed by the ambience of the place, I sat there stealing furtive glances as wealthy patrons glided in and out of the lobby. Looking like they were members of the same team, many men were attired in loose-fitting chinos, polo shirts and white loafers, with a pale yellow cashmere cardigan tied casually around each and every neck. Dangling on their arms were women in flowing, floor- length summer dresses crowned with broad flapping hats that brought to mind scenes from *Gone with the Wind*. Many seemed much too "genteel" to participate in such raucous events such as riding, cycling or kayaking, and more in the league of horseshoes, shuffleboard, and falconry. Although none of those latter categories appealed to my own fancy, what would have garnered my attention had it been open to the public at the time, was the emergency Cold War bunker built for the US government. Guests today can book a tour of the underground facilities, but in 1993 it was still very much "off limits," especially for foreigners armed with a camera.

That evening, in a restaurant teeming with white-jacketed waiters catering to your every whim, Reinholt and I felt like a couple of country bumpkins as we pored over the menu and perused tomorrow's shooting schedule. Given that we were expected to cover a dozen of the daily distractions guests could occupy themselves with, it was apparent we had our work cut out for us.

Fortunately, the next day, a good portion of the guests opted to chill, choosing to either sashay around the grounds, imagining how it must feel to be this filthy rich, or take turns being chauffeured from facility to facility in the back seat of a 1959 black Cadillac limousine. After three days of filming various groups at the skeet shooting range, riding stables, tennis courts, golf links, bike trails, and horseshoe pits, or simply acting slightly decadent over drinks at poolside, enough was enough.

On the morning of the fourth day, following one last sumptuous breakfast buffet, guests were asked to congregate in the front lobby, before being loaded on to chartered buses for the short hop to a nearby airport. Waiting on the tarmac was a gleaming silver chartered jet, ready to fly us to the next planet on the agenda... New Orleans.

"What's with all the police?" I wanted to know as we disembarked into brilliant sunshine and a wall of 95-

degree heat.

"We're getting a police escort to the Oilman's Club downtown," an executive of the car company boasted, while donning a goofy-looking hat with the company logo.

"Uh... I don't think so, but thanks anyways," I answered, when offered an identical cap from a bag on his shoulder. "Can't shoot with it," I told him, secretly thinking you'd have to shoot *me* to get me to wear one.

With a separate bus to transport the luggage and amenities lifted from the Greenbrier hotel rooms, all the guests had to worry about was finding a seat on one of the three buses parked alongside the plane. Once all were safely aboard and goofy hats had been counted, a phalanx of a half-dozen motorcycle cops escorted us out of the airport parking lot and directly on to the freeway leading to the city centre.

"Where is everybody?" was the unspoken thought on everyone's mind as we gawked at a four-lane freeway completely devoid of autos.

"They closed the highway for us," the same executive bragged. "It's a good thing we arranged it, too, because we're running a little late for lunch. This way we'll be into the centre a lot faster."

"So not only do we get to pretend to be rich," I mumbled to one of the few guests not wearing a hat, as we both glanced out the back window at the long column of cars held back by the motorcycle cops. "We also can imagine how it feels to be the President."

An exclusive penthouse eatery catering to members and anyone with ten-gallon egos and enough dough to purchase entrance, the Oilman's Club was as ritzy and snobby as one might expect. After a luncheon feast that would have done Henry VIII proud, guests were treated to a ride down the mighty Mississippi aboard a genuine stern-wheeler paddleboat. With little more to see than factories and shipyards along the shoreline, most preferred watching their dough disappear at the on-board casino. On our return to the docks just after three, the rest of the afternoon was set aside for private sightseeing, with the singular request that everyone meet in the lobby by 7:30, dressed for dinner.

"I suppose it's some sort of drawing card," I said to Reinholt as we each sipped a tasteless, colourful welcome cocktail while staring at the signed photo of a former US President on the restaurant wall. Judging from the other celebrities pinned up for posterity, every star since Gloria Swanson had at one time chowed down at this four-star Cajun restaurant on Toulouse Street. Much to the disappointment of gathered guests, no current celebs were in attendance, largely because the entire restaurant had been reserved solely for their dining pleasure. With nothing to film, and food and beverages once again courtesy of the company, Reinholt and I took full advantage of the opportunity to overindulge.

Early next morning, despite a light drizzle, a brief walking tour of the French Quarter went off without a hitch. At its conclusion, the group was hustled aboard several buses for a more expansive excursion through the city, the highlight of which, oddly enough, was a stopover at a local cemetery. Unlike their counterparts in Germany or for that matter Canada, here the deceased were interned in stone vaults above ground, due to the city's high water table. Following a short visit to the gigantic Super Dome, just long enough to induce the "oohs" and "aahs" more commonly associated with fireworks, the entire troupe headed for a cruise across the Lake Pontchartrain Causeway.

"I'm curious," I complained to Reinholt. "Who figured that driving for 38.4 kilometres, where all you can see are endless waves, only to turn around and come back the same route, would somehow make for an exciting time? It doesn't exactly provide breath-taking footage either. Maybe there isn't as much to do in New Orleans as I thought."

That conclusion turned out to be somewhat premature as, unbeknownst to us, the pinnacle of our New Orleans adventure still lay ahead. Confirming the age-old adage that money really can buy anything, that evening guests were regaled with their own private Mardi Gras parade. Led through the streets of the French Quarter by a cavalcade of several Dixieland marching bands and baton-twirling majorettes, guests whooped and hollered themselves hoarse, much to the delight of several drunks heckling them from the sidelines. The exclusive procession ended at the old city hall, where guests were handed feathery masks before being guided into a succession of ballrooms, each decked out in different theme motifs. Free to mingle in any of the rooms, most chose to give the jungle and American revolution motifs a pass, heading instead for the glitzy disco room despite the fact this was 1993.

As the drinks continued to flow and people prepared to dance the night away, my old friend, Norbert was goaded into joining in on a Karaoke number. Accepting the microphone with feigned humility, he immediately slipped into a excruciating version of Moondance.

Frantic finger-waving from the event director indicated he wanted this magnificent event recorded for future generations. After selecting a suitably unflattering angle, I smiled back at him blandly, gave him the requisite thumbs-up, and forced myself to press record, totally convinced some things are just not worth saving. After all, posterity has enough on its hands.

Having been behind the cameras since eight that morning, Reinholt and I were notably wired by the time the event director finally called it a wrap around two-thirty. Aware this was our last night in New Orleans, we declined an invitation to join a small group of guests for an impromptu party back at the hotel and instead took off to explore the city's famed jazz clubs. Hoping to experience first-hand the unique, indefinable coolness that permeates the city, we poked our heads into several establishments before ending up at a suitably seedy location on a side-street off Toulouse. We were in the midst of quaffing a beer and sharing thoughts on the last few days when our conversation was interrupted by an unexpected and uninvited guest.

"Good evening gentlemen," came a husky voice housed in a tall, black woman in a short, black skirt and tight-fitting top.

"Are y'all having a good time here in the Big Easy?"

"The Big Easy?" Reinholt asked.

"New 'awlins, darlin'… New 'awlins… Say, y'all's not from here are yazz."

"No, uh, yes… We have good time," Reinholt answered stiffly.

"Would one of you gentlemen care to buy us all a drink?" she asked, directing the question at me.

"Was? Ich habe Sie nicht verstanden," I answered.

"What'd you say, baby? Say, where y'all from anyhow?"

"Wir kommen aus Deutschland..." I said, signalling Reinholt to join the ruse. "Gerrrrmannnneeee."

Adopting what amounted to a bad imitation of pigeon English, we attempted to get the message across to our guest that her presence was not desired. Not prepared to give up so easily, she switched gears to ask if we cared to sponsor a lap dance.

"Laps? Was sind laps?" Reinholt asked, not having to fake his limited knowledge.

Realizing she was about to start a performance without waiting for consent, I broke into perfect English to convey that we weren't interested in anything but talking... to each other. In the end, it was agreed we'd buy her a drink on condition she'd consume it elsewhere. Several more beers in several more clubs followed, so that it was just after five before we finally stumbled back to the hotel. With a call time set for 8:00, and instructions to film an "awards ceremony" at 9:00, it was one very short and groggy night.

"What are they giving awards for?" Reinholt wanted to know, steadying himself against my tripod as we watched a series of salesmen traipse up to receive a scrolled-up certificate.

"Most likely for surviving Norbert's Karaoke solo, I would think."

Excused from filming the final luncheon, we managed to pack up the equipment soon enough to allow for several hours of last-minute shopping. Around six that evening we bid farewell to the "Big Easy," this time with no police escort. Approximately three hours later, as we were about to leave the North American land mass behind, we were granted one last view of the U.S. of A. And what a view it was. Gazing down on the spectacular nighttime Manhattan skyline bathed in an orangey glow, it felt as though we were aliens on a departing spaceship.

Unable to sleep with the white noise of the droning engines, I had just started skimming through the flight magazine for the third time when two event staffers seated behind me began what they obviously believed was a private conversation. Expressing their deep relief that the whole adventure was now almost over, they casually let it slip that the tour had likely cost somewhere in the neighbourhood of two and a half to three million dollars. Suddenly, everything flashed before me in a downpour of dollar signs - the chartered jets, Capitol luncheon, Union Station, Greenbrier, police escort, Oilman's Club, private Mardi Gras and city hall sendoff. Such overheard news would have likely been filed and forgotten had it not been for a statement released by the company's board of directors a few days after our return. Broadcast on the evening news, the announcement explained that as part of cost-cutting measures deemed necessary by reduced sales, the company was regrettably being forced to introduce a series of lay-offs. With the figure of $3 million still fresh in my mind, I briefly considered the potential repercussions of having a copy of the finished film end up in the hands of the union rep. After all, what harm could there be in having two black marks against my name?

CHAPTER 11

Bunte Mischung

Langkofel

They wanted something different, something dynamic, something that represented rising to the occasion, showing the stamina needed to push through to success etc.etc. The slogan ultimately selected to express that sentiment was, "Reaching for the summit of your potential"; and the location, a thirty-two hundred meter peak in the Dolomite mountains of northern Italy. According to the preliminary script, three experienced mountain climbers would be dropped just below the summit of the Langkofel, allowing their final ascent through the virgin snow to be filmed by a crew already stationed at the top.

Scheduled for late October, the two day shoot was a welcome change from the dull routine of the past months that had left me feeling as though I'd filmed inside every factory this side of the Milky Way. Two full teams made the journey from Frankfurt to the Grödner Valley in Southern Tyrol, stopping off in the town of St. Ulrich to meet up with our guide and team of expert climbers. It was already late in the afternoon by the time of our arrival and we had fully expected to carry on to our hotel after briefly greeting our mountaineering colleagues. Instead we learned our guide wished to test our endurance and climbing abilities …"right now."

"This guy must be joking," I said to Conrad, the

producer, as we stared up at a tiny bell near the top of a fifteen metre climbing wall attached to the side of a building in the centre of town. But he wasn't, and one by one we were each harnessed into a safety rope and requested to "ring the bell." Left pretty much to our own devices, when my turn came I started my scramble towards the summit - unaware of the common error of concentrating too much weight on my fingertips. Needless to say, halfway up, the strength in my digits gave way, forcing me to endure an embarrassing descent at the hands of the snickering guide.

The next morning, our planned ascent to the summit of the Langkofel, had to be postponed due to the onset of inclement weather. While waiting for it to break, time was passed over a prolonged breakfast, listening to our helicopter pilot explain our flight path and the fact we wouldn't actually be landing on the mountain.

"Oh," I said, the unease in my voice clearly detectable. "Why is that?"

"Eees too smalla place," he answered in a thick Italian accent. "But ees beeg enough for you tree. Eees lika tennis court. No problemo."

"A tennis court eh?" I mulled, my concerns somewhat calmed by the image of traipsing around on an expansive snow-covered plateau. The break in the weather came just after lunch and within half an hour, Conrad, an assistant guide and myself were moving up the side of the mountain. Flying close enough to the rock face that we could see clumps of frozen grass protruding from the tiny crevasses, it felt as though we were looking out from a glass elevator. Just as we rose over a ridge to begin the final approach, I caught sight of the fabled "tennis court"

"When was the last time this guy played tennis?" I yelled above the roar of the rotor blades as Conrad and I jumped out into a cloud of swirling snow.

"We must be insane," I intoned as the helicopter slowly arced away leaving us on a platform not much larger than a table-tennis court.

"Not quite, but I'm working on it," Conrad answered, casting a nervous glance at the eight-hundred meter drop surrounding us on all sides but one. "In the meantime it's probably a good idea to not make any sudden movements. And thank God there's no wind up here."

Once the disturbed snow had resettled, the first task was to figure out where to plant the tripod. Much like the lunar module landing so many years ago, I extended one leg into the snow to probe where there was solid rock and where only 800 meters of air. Once ready to roll, Conrad walkie-talked the actors, who'd been dropped off on a lower slope fifteen minutes earlier, to begin their final climb. With my eye glued to the viewfinder, I followed the trio of bouncing heads as they emerged from behind a ridge of snow. At that same instant, I was suddenly aware of the sensation of falling backwards. Realizing that any rapid counter reaction could send me tumbling off in the other direction, I managed to remain stationary, hoping it would pass. Having noticed I was no longer panning with the main protagonists, Conrad called a halt to the filming.

"Hey, are you okay?" he asked, placing a hand on my shoulder.

"Yeah, yeah... Just a slight dizzy spell. I'll be alright."

"Not the best place in the world to get dizzy, I'd say."

But I really wasn't okay, and used the brief pause to

put a question to our guide.

"This line you attached to me," I said, holding up a portion in my hand. "What's it for? If I fall, it just means you're coming with me. Or?"

"If you fall," the man with the weathered face began. "I jump the other way."

"Other way? Where are you going to jump? This ledge is two and a half meters wide…tops."

"I jump to other side to keep you from falling further."

Fixated by the image of the two of us tethered together while dangling on opposite sides of the summit, I pressed on.

"And how do we get out of such a predicament, if you don't mind me asking?"

"As fascinating as this conversation is, can we finish it some other time?" Conrad interrupted, waving to the actors to get ready to resume their climb.

With no further spells or questions forthcoming, it wasn't long before Conrad gave a thumbs-up, signalling his satisfaction with what had been captured. But before there was a chance to step back, figuratively, to take in the breathtaking view, the pilot's voice crackled over the two-way radio.

"Eeesa cloud frawnnnt coming in," he warned. "I must peeck you up soon as posseeebull."

Without even enough time to snap a souvenir photo before the whirr of the rotors drifted back into earshot, we watched as the tiny speck grew larger and larger. If we'd thought our arrival had been precarious, it was nothing compared to the departure. As the 'copter approached and hovered nearby, blowing snow began to swirl around us.

"I can't see the door can you?" I shouted to Conrad.

"Door? I can't even see the *chopper*."

"*Jump*," a voice onboard commanded.

"Jump? Jump where?" I yelled. "Where's the friggin' *door*?"

Immobilized by the blinding snow and deafening chatter of the blades, I was about to slip into panic mode when an arm suddenly poked through the blur and dragged me on board. Reassured to feel something besides eight hundred metres of nothing beneath me, I collapsed in a heap on the rear seat.

Several months later, long after the trauma of those treacherous moments had passed, I was to learn that my "spell" on the summit may have been caused by the rapid change in elevation. As a belated treat, I was also given a copy of the footage shot from the helicopter by the second crew. Although it offers a excellent perspective of just how high we had been, because of the distance, viewers will have to take my word for it that one of the tiny flecks visible against a panoramic ridge of Dolomite peaks was indeed me, out of my tiny little mind.

※

Empty Spaces

For those of you who've never had the pleasure, there's nothing quite like riding in a helicopter. That fleeting instant of suspended animation as the chopper jostles free of the earth's grasp, hovering for a second before tipping forward and sweeping up into the sky, is incomparable, especially if you lucky enough to be sitting up front next to the pilot. One might think that after having experienced the dizzying heights of the Langkofel, I'd had enough of "rising to the occasion" for awhile. Yet several months later, there I was climbing back aboard a chopper, albeit this time hundreds of kilometres away from the nearest mountain.

It was a cloudless, spring morning that we took off for what would turn out to be a nine-hour endurance test, to gather aerial footage of a large furniture store's newly opened outlets in the former East Germany. Within seconds of being aloft in the four-seater bird, Germany was transformed into a fairy-tale landscape, its red-roofed towns and villages framed by fields, forests and roadways dotted with miniature autos. As we headed east, leaving the more populated areas behind, the pilot dropped lower, skimming over grassy fields and hilly contours in what felt like a slow-motion roller coaster. With no need to film any of the scenery, it was possible to just sit back and enjoy the ride, that is until catching sight of a tiny row of electrical towers stretching across the horizon up ahead.

"This guy seems to be taking his time acknowledging those obstacles," I thought to myself as the towers continued to loom closer. A quick glance at the tachometer indicated we were approaching said towers at an airspeed of 150 kph, which seemed to not leave a huge margin for error. Just as I was about to let him know in no uncertain terms what I thought of his aerial acrobatics, the pilot pulled back on the stick, sending my stomach up into my throat as we flashed across the top of the grid, clearing the wires by what I was certain was no more than a few inches. A short while later, as my

breakfast was easing its way back down my esophagus, we entered a narrow valley, cruising along just below the tree tops as the pilot performed a series of smooth, gradual arcs as if schussing down a steep ski slope.

Similar vistas of the countryside continued to dazzle all the way to our first pit stop at a small airport just outside of the city of Gera. Strolling to the airport cafe for lunch, dressed head to toe in a bright purple and yellow, mountain-climbing outfit to protect against the wind, I undoubtedly resembled the clown they shoot out of a cannon when the circus is in town. Once tanked up and serviced, we proceeded to fly to Dresden, Leipzig, Halle, Magdeburg and Berlin, all of which lay under perfect azure blue skies. Given all the panoramas we'd witnessed to this point, the actual task of filming the large, flat-roofed complexes surrounded by sprawling parking lots, struck me as being somewhat immaterial. By the time we'd captured all of the new outlets, we'd been in the air for almost six hours, which helps explain why the producer and I fell asleep for a good portion of the return journey.

To *this* day, images from *that* day remain deeply embedded, with each and every swerve and dip of the German countryside recalled in the blink of an eye. As if those memories weren't already occupying considerable mental shelf space, three weeks after that glorious flight, word came down that the client was unhappy with the footage because of the limited number of cars in the parking lots that day. Asked to do it all again, several weeks later, that we did.

❖

The Golden Car

For the two people on Earth not aware of it, Germany is, and has long been, a nation of car-loving fanatics; ones who treasure the right to drive at insane speeds on their beloved Autobahns. I know of no other country where you can legally cruise along at 190 kph, only to have someone zoom up behind you at 250 kph., flashing their headlights as a warning to get out of "their way." On the rare occasion I was presented with such an opportunity, the temptation was to respond by staying in the same lane and driving at 251 kph. Such an act of defiance however, was guaranteed to produce more flashing, a blast of the horn and the muttering, "Männer!"(Men!) if my partner, Isabelle, happened to be sitting next to me.

Given such speeds and the fact there are over 43 million registered cars in a land smaller than the state of Montana, it's amazing that traffic deaths and injuries are as low as they are in Germany. One of the reasons for those statistics is that for the most part, Germans tend to be good drivers. They get that way because it's not so easy to attain a driver's license. Unless one of your parents, siblings or family friends happens to be a licensed driving instructor, forget about going out to a deserted parking lot on a Sunday morning to learn the do's and don'ts of the road. Instead you can expect to spend 'X' amount of time at an official driving school, where you'll be required to complete an eye test, eight-hour first-aid course and both theory and practical exams. Class and road time varies depending on a learner's skill, but you can safely assume this little adventure will set you back a tidy sum. Once they have their "Führerschein" (license) in their eager little mitts, many feel like kings of the road, granting themselves free rein to do as they please in the driver's seat. Having foreseen the anarchic chaos that could result from such lax limits, German traffic officials instituted a comprehensive list of rules and regulations to be followed. A half dozen years before the Euro came into circulation, I happened to come across a catalogue titled *"Bussgeldkatalog, Punkte im Strassenverkehr"* (Catalogue for Street Traffic Fines). As painfully dry as that title may sound, perusing it was actually quite humorous, not to mention enlightening. As only German "bureaucretins" can, officials of the State Department for Economy, Traffic and State Development not only offered a staid explanation of the rules of the road, but also documented the penalties for infringing on said rules. As in most countries, if you exceeded the posted speed limit or ran a red light, you were obligated to pay a hefty fine. Depending on the severity of the offence, points were charged against you in the central registry. Gather up enough points within a given span and you could say "Aufwiedersehen" to your license for a specified period of time. To make it clearer to potential offenders, German officials broke the information down into additional categories. My all-time favourite was the graph showing "Insult, Insulted and fine in German Marks." As dour or absent as the German sense of humour can be at times, this section came across as a work of comedic genius. For example, if in the heat of the moment you happened to call a policewoman an "old cow," you'd be liable for a fine of 600 DM. If you used the same expression with the female driver of another car, it could set you back 150 DM, although it wasn't spelled out how that fee could be collected. Referring to a female meter reader as a "bloody woman" would cost you 1200 DM, while displaying your middle finger to a policeman would see you dinged for 2000 DM. Highly intrigued, I skimmed through the list to determine what the most expensive outburst would be on a day you had it in for the world. I discovered that telling a policeman "the sun has burned his brain and he belongs in a mental institution," would deplete your bank account to the tune of 3000 DM. In case you were feeling extra generous, calling the same policeman an "idiot in uniform" would cost another 3000 DM. Just for fun, I added up the entire list and came to the conclusion that a bad hair day could cost you 24,300 DM. The lesson to be learned here is that before slipping behind the wheel in Germany, one must think about how courteous you can afford not to be.

To cater to the interests of this vast fleet of nice and nasty drivers, an array of car magazines have sprung up over the years. One of the most prominent is Auto Bild, which in addition to its weekly edition, attracts attention each year by awarding a prize to the vehicle deemed to be the "Car of the Year". Despite its being primarily a print medium, someone at Auto Bild decided it would be a good idea to hire a film crew to document just how the winner of the "Golden Lenkrad" (Golden Steering Wheel) award was determined.

It was early October when we headed off to a luxury resort in the Schwäbische Alb section of Germany to film various "Promis" (celebrities) as they participated in two days of test-driving various new model autos. Invited guests that year included Formula One driver Michael

Schumacher, former Bayer Munich soccer star, Karl-Heinz Rummenigge, television personality, Wolfgang Lippert, and a host of other names most people outside of Germany have never heard of.

Using the hotel as their home base, participants were asked to complete a series of tests on comfort, design, style, performance and handling on each of the cars. Filming aspects such as design and style proved relatively harmless, whereas handling and performance, done from the back seat of a car, was the equivalent of being thrown into a mix-master. Granted that racing up and down small country lanes, scaring the bejeezus out of locals enjoying a quiet stroll was not particularly conducive to small talk, some "stars" nevertheless made an effort to communicate. Others, however, were rather snooty individuals, not uttering a single word during the entire twenty-minute test drive. Back in the comfort of the hotel lounge, drivers compiled their findings on to form sheets before climbing into the next test vehicle. After two days of testing, the assessments were collected and tabulated. That evening, guests were invited to wine and dine at an awards dinner where the prestigious Car of the Year plaque was presented to a representative of the winning car's manufacturer. I have no recollection of which car won that year. The only memories that remain, aside from having taken advantage of the free, fully- stocked watering hole, were that all participants undoubtedly received a fat honorarium for their efforts; Michael Schumacher is much shorter in real life than he appeared on television; and that Karl-Heinz was a testy little dude who wouldn't have received my vote for Mr. Congeniality.

Hot off the Presses

There are certain accomplishments in life that might appear rather insignificant when viewed in isolation, but that one can still look back on with a degree of pride. Having never purchased a record by Madonna, or even as much as listened to one by Justin Bieber, are just two examples that come to mind. Another notable feat, attained during my first eighteen years in Germany, was never having doled out a single "Pfennig" for a copy of the Bild Zeitung. That record ended on September 12th, 2001, when I broke down and bought the issue with coverage of the 9/11 disaster, a moment of weakness that can perhaps be blamed as genetic, rooted in the same instincts that had possessed my father to hoard a May 9th, 1945 edition of the Winnipeg Free Press with a full-page headline and caricature declaring "Nazis Quit," that he no doubt thought would be a collector's item someday.

For those unacquainted with the Bild Zeitung, it can pretty much be described as a purveyor of "boulevard journalism," sort of Germany's answer to England's The Sun, or a subdued distant cousin of America's National Enquirer. Known for its provocative, sometimes insulting, often inane, and repeatedly ridiculous, banner headlines, in the 1990's it boasted a circulation of over four million, making it by far the country's most-read newspaper. Considering its similarity to another more odorous item often found on grassy boulevards, perhaps it's more accurate to say the most-purchased, as I doubt anyone takes the time to pore over its entire contents. Despite the fact that everyone is entitled to their own tastes, every time I'd been in a supermarket checkout line and happened to notice a copy of the BZ amongst the articles of the person in front of me, there was always a passing urge to ask, "What's wrong with you?"

Given my take on the paper, I was not entirely thrilled to learn we'd been contracted to film *behind the scenes* at the Bild's Hamburg headquarters. Intended as part of an image campaign for the paper, we were to document how a daily edition moved from a tiny spark in someone's warped mind to lining the bottom of a garbage can the following day. Our first stop on the tour was a large, glass-walled conference room atop one of Hamburg's tallest buildings. Holding court there was the then editor-in-chief, a man in his early 40s with gelled hair and thick horn-rimmed glasses perched above his forehead. Numerous journalists stood silently as he stalked alongside a table of photographs, picking up images at random and setting aside those he considered important enough for a second round. Throughout this inspection, thick curls of cigar smoke wafted up from a fat stogie, which he occasionally removed when he wished to make a point. While all this was going on, the collection of journalists and editors strewn about the room continued to remain closemouthed, speaking only when spoken to. Once the preliminary circuit was completed, the editor-in-chief returned to the pile of four or five photos deemed worthy enough to compete for next morning's cover.

Over the next few minutes, questions and standpoints were batted back and forth across the table by those competing for a potential headlining story.

Hoping to convey the action without disrupting the ceremony in process, I trailed the chief editor back to the head of the table, settling down behind to capture a wide shot of him seated before his domain of expectant employees. Clearly enjoying the suspense, he continued to listen to pitches and deliberate in silence, all the while sending more plumes of smoke up through the framed shot. Once the decision was taken, the winning photo and headline were swept off to be entered digitally into tomorrow's developing edition, all part of a ritual repeated each and every morning.

Now among the few outsiders to know what the future would bring, at least on tomorrow's front page, we left for Berlin that afternoon, planning to follow the headline through the steps it would take to reach its millions of readers. Next stop was a layout and production centre in the German capital where the data sent from Hamburg was arranged and set into a final layout before being transferred to "the yellow room." According to our guide, the reason the entire room was bathed in yellow light had to do with the etching process, which entailed electronically transferring the completed digitized information to curved chrome-plated panels that would later be used on the actual printing presses. While it's theoretically possible there's at least one human being on earth who doesn't look goofy in a hairnet, he or she wasn't amongst the ten or twelve people working in the sterile, glassed-in cubicle that day.

Just for the record, the phrase "the yellow press," which from time to time had been applied to the BZ, was coined in the 1890's as competition heated up between two US newspaper magnates. Attempting to out-do each other in the circulation wars, Joseph Pulitzer and William Randolph Hearst had increasingly resorted to using "sensationalism" in their journalistic style, even going so far as to print in yellow ink.

As luck would have it, technical difficulties at the neighbouring printing plant prevented us from following this edition through its final paces. Instead, that procedure was filmed three evenings later at a huge new printing plant located near Heidelberg, one of several facilities in Germany where the millions of daily Bild see the light of day. Ultra-modern, ultra clean and insanely fast, this monstrous press ran at a speed that defied imagination. Only by setting the camera's shutter speed to 1/2000th of a second could you hope to catch a glimpse of what was being printed. Despite the efficiency of the massive machines, every once in awhile a section of the speeding paper would snag, sending several metres of undulating news out on to the floor. Within seconds, however, red and orange lights started flashing and the presses automatically came to a halt. One or two blue-smocked workers quickly appeared, tearing off the offending portions before resetting the roll of blank newsprint. Once the all-clear signal was given to a nearby control booth, the behemoth surged back into action. Printed, collated, folded and stacked, the papers ended up on pallets before being loaded on to waiting trucks that soon peeled off into the night.

As impressive as it was to see how it all came together, I still won't buy a copy. But the next time I'm in a checkout line, about to witness another imminent purchase, I can now say , "Excuse me. I happen to know how that was made… What's wrong with you?"

CHAPTER 12

Toilet Paper

I've always believed salesmen to be a breed apart. What other way to explain the manner in which they can deliver a convincing performance of their devotion to a product or service one day, only to switch allegiance the next if a competitor happens to offer them a better salary? Such thoughts were drifting through my head as I prepared to change tapes for the third salesman in a row tasked with extolling the undeniable benefits of his company's brand of toilet paper.

The saving grace was that they were doing so onboard a ship slowly plowing its way through the cold, grey waters of the Ostsee, headed for Oslo, Norway. I'd come to find myself on board thanks to company officials, who in their quest to try something different, had arranged for their annual sales meeting to take place during a two-day cruise to and from the Norwegian capital. As it happened, passage had been booked months in advance, making it impossible for officials to have foreseen the tragedy that would strike less than twenty-four hours before their salesmen from across Germany were scheduled to gather in the northern port city of Kiel. The night before our departure, the ferry Estonia, traveling from Tallin to Stockholm, had gone down in heavy seas with the loss of over 850 lives. The disaster had made international headlines by the time employees from the paper products company arrived at the harbour only to learn that their conference was to be held aboard the Estonia's sister ship. The trepidation on peoples' faces at dockside clearly reflected their concerns. But life aboard a large eight-deck ship is designed to help you forget almost everything, Aided by the logic that tragedy was unlikely to strike twice in such a short period of time, once the twinkling lights of Kiel harbour were left behind, passengers flocked to the ship's numerous bars to strengthen their resolve.

The next morning, participants crowded into the main conference room to get down to business. Prepared to document their testimony on the wonders of everything from kitchen rolls to toilet paper, I was relieved when the producer made a slicing motion across his neck, indicating that footage of the lengthy opening statements was not required. With over an hour until individual presentations were to commence, I decided to take a break up on deck. Staring out at a dull, flat sea barely distinguishable from the overcast sky, any thoughts of extending my stroll around the ship were quickly discouraged by a stiff, cold breeze. Not wishing to return to the conference room sooner than necessary, I took shelter beside the bulkhead near one of the ship's many restaurants, from where, it was possible to observe what I assumed was the sparsely inhabited Danish coast crawling past

Unless you happen to have an excessive interest in the features of various paper products, the day's speeches and presentations did not provide much of interest to elaborate on. Salesmen who didn't occasionally nod off, sat stoically through the scheduled itinerary, downing litres of coffee or mineral water in anticipation of the evening's planned parties. Planners had not left anything to chance within that arena, arranging for live entertainment in all four shipboard nightclubs, each with its own theme and playlist. The producer demanded that we focus on the disco room, mainly because it had attracted the largest crowd. Organizers, however, seemed to have overlooked one small item. Out of two hundred sales people attending the conference, a hundred and eighty were men, leaving those women wishing to dance with the pick of the litter, and most men seeking the encouragement provided by a bellyful of booze, before venturing out on the floor.

After a day of being inundated by sales reports, future objectives, and saccharine pep talks, not to mention the after-effects of a night on a rolling ship, participants were allowed to sleep in to a late breakfast before the boat docked in Oslo. Stunned to hear there was no need to film during our scheduled five-hour stopover, I immediately abandoned ship to head for one of the city's touted highlights. Home to over two hundred bronze and granite sculptures created by one of the country's most popular and prolific sculptors, Vigeland Park ranks as one of Oslo's must-see destinations. The genesis of the park stemmed from Gustav Vigeland's offer to donate the majority of his life's work, on condition that city fathers establish a space to display his sculptures to the world. Wandering through the park's well-kept walkways, dozens of interesting statues quickly attach themselves to your memory. That said, it is hard to imagine any more striking than the Monolith. Situated on a raised plateau near the centre of the park, the fifteen-metre obelisk defies comprehension, especially considering that this work was carved from a single slab of granite. Reputed to depict the cycle of life, it manages to capture a variety of human emotions while conveying man's eternal struggle and yearning. Humbled by its extraordinary beauty, it felt odd to realize I ultimately owed a debt of gratitude to the lowly roll of toilet paper for the chance to experience this amazing work of art.

After roaming the grounds for almost three hours, there was still enough time to make it over to the Holmenkollen Ski Tower. At a height of forty-two meters, the observation deck provided a grand panorama of Oslo and surrounding countryside, including a familiar looking ship docked in the distant harbour. The highlight, however, was the ski ramp itself. With no visible staff there to dissuade me, or signs forbidding it in a language I could understand, I eased myself out on to the bench jumpers use as their starting perch. Confronted by an incline so steep it nearly took my breath away, I realized I would have to be drugged before ever shooting down the slope into what looked appropriately enough like a toilet bowl with cantilevered bleachers.

After having viewed such features as Vigeland Park and Holmenkollen tower, the return trip to Kiel turned out to be painfully uneventful. What was to remain unforgettable on that final night aboard ship and in the weeks to come, was the realization that laying in my cabin was not unlike being sealed inside a can of luncheon meat, making the idea of escape in the event of an emergency all but a distant fantasy. As the rhythmic slapping of waves and muffled thud of the ship's engines lulled me towards sleep that night, I couldn't help wondering if any of those aboard the Estonia had experienced similar premonitions.

CHAPTER 13

The saga begins

It was a loud metallic thump that jarred me from my sleep. With one foot still in the twilight zone, I glanced around to get my bearings before being shunted back to the here and now by the look of panic on my companion's face.

"Pull over first chance you get," I shouted, leaning forward to determine the source of the clanging. "The bloody thing sounds like it's gonna explode."

Six weeks before this incident began to unfold, I had been searching for a way out of what had become an unexpected and unappreciated slump in work. Hoping to drum up more business, I decided to send out a newsletter trumpeting my abilities to as many production companies as possible. Hours were spent combing through my archive in search of a suitable photo, until finally deciding on a black and white print that showed me filming a rural landscape in the French Alps. What with being new to the game of photo software, it took awhile to fumble through the labyrinth of options to create a layout for what I hoped would be an effective marketing tool. After first distorting the image with a fish-eye effect, I inserted my contact information on the roof of a barn at the right of the frame. Overlaid on the grass below my feet, was the message, "*Greetings from the World's Best Cameraman*****" - with the key to the asterisks placed at the bottom of the photo revealing; "**... *is something he's no doubt too busy to send. Besides, he's probably too expensive. But if you happen to be in the market for a good and reasonably priced cameraman, feel free to give me a call.*"

Given that irony, sarcasm and above all, humour are not traits closely associated with Germans, it was a risky strategy to pursue. Not that any further proof of that thesis was needed; out of a hundred and fifty letters sent, there was only one response. My introduction to what would eventually evolve into "Buddy's World," came in the form of a shoot in the German town of Winterburg. Ten years my junior and the absolute antithesis of a perfectionist, Buddy had found his way into the business much like an erratic projectile in a pinball machine gone berserk. A native American, he'd landed in Germany after a short stint in Bulgaria, and in just three years had already worked his way through a lengthy list of cameramen. Sitting in the car that day, there was no way of knowing that I was embarking on what would ultimately become a fourteen-year working relationship.

"There's an exit five hundred metres up ahead," I said. "You gotta take it."

In the first of what would be many uncanny coincidences within the realm of "Buddy's World," a large revolving sign at the end of the Autobahn exit indicated the presence of a nearby garage. As if caught in an outtake from The Wizard of Oz, we rolled to a stop within feet of the mechanic's bay just as the engine gave a final gasp and shuddered into silence. Attracted by the clattering, the mechanic on duty walked out of the bay and lifted the hood. Without bothering to ask or wait for an explanation, he simply picked up a warm spark plug laying on top of the cylinder head and held it in front of Buddy.

"You no tighten Zundkerzen, (Spark plugs)" he admonished with a grin.

"I cleaned them all yesterday," Buddy admitted sheepishly, looking like a kid caught with his hand in the proverbial cookie jar. "I thought I tightened them all again."

Evidently tightened enough for the car to start and run, the vibrations on the Autobahn had loosened a single plug until internal pressure blew it out into the underside of the hood.

"Crazy Amerikaner," the mechanic mumbled to himself as he ratcheted the plug back into place, accepted a small fee, and let us be on our way.

With no further obstacles to overcome, we arrived in Winterburg just before dark, and booked into the same hotel as the US Olympic bobsled team we'd come to interview. Life was made considerably easier that evening when Janet, the producer, suggested we shoot the interviews in the hotel restaurant.

"We're practically the only ones staying here," she explained, "so we won't have to worry about disturbing anyone or anyone bothering us."

In town to practice for an upcoming competition, six members of the team and their coach, lumbered into the restaurant just after eight. Purportedly celebrities in their discipline, half of them turned out to be overbearing jocks whose primary objective seemed to be to kibbutz before the camera.

"Are all sports guys such Nervensäger?" I asked Janet, after the dreary interview was over and the stars had trundled off to bed, leaving us to close down the bar.

"What, pray tell, is a Nervensäger?"

"A Nervensäger is someone who really grates on your nerves."

"Not all... but these guys would certainly pass that litmus test," she answered, accepting a glass of Chianti with a friendly nod to the waiter.

"Are you going to be able to use any of this stuff? I mean they didn't exactly have a lot of interesting things to say."

"I wouldn't worry about it too much," Janet assured me with a seasoned smile. "This whole thing was more of a PR junket. The sponsor wanted us to put in an appearance. I doubt we'll use any of it," she concluded, hoisting her glass for a toast. "Anyway, here's to wasting your time but getting paid for it."

Fortunately for us, the sponsor also didn't consider it necessary to gather footage of its goslings on the course. Still, having never actually been on a bob sled course before, the next morning Buddy and I took advantage of the opportunity to check out the facilities.

"Any chance of taking a test run guys?" Buddy asked a couple of Spandex-clothed racers as they sharpened the blades of their sled.

"Sorry, mate, but it's not allowed," one replied in what sounded like an Australian accent.

Encouraged by the passable common language, Buddy asked what it felt like to go hurtling down an ice channel at what often seemed close to the speed of light. "Doesn't it scare the hell out of you?"

"Maybe at first, but you get used to it pretty quick," the other racer said in a slow drawl. "Besides, you don't start off going full throttle. You gotta build up to it slowly."

"Oh yeah? But what's it feel like? Buddy persisted.

"You ever leaned back on two legs of a kitchen chair and tried to hold your balance between tipping forward or falling back on your arse?"

"For sure."

"Well imagine holding the point where you're wavering... Suspended animation for 60 to 70 seconds. That's what it's like. Except that you're movin'... Fast."

With no other teams in sight and our Aussie friends seemingly content to merely sharpen their edges, there was no chance to witness competitors enjoying this unique sensation.

Later that afternoon, as we departed the snow-covered hills of Sauerland to return to the brown, winter landscape of middle Hessen, I asked Buddy, "Are all your shoots so productive?"

"What's to complain? We get paid whether they use it or not."

In what was either a stroke of remarkably good timing or merely another example of how things happen in "Buddy's World," the next day's newspaper carried a story on how a former coach and advisor to the US team had been the victim of a terrible accident at the Winterburg course, just a few hours after our departure. According to the story, despite years of experience, the coach had inexplicably tried crossing the lower part of the course at precisely the wrong moment. Clipped by a two-man unit on a practice run, he had survived the collision but was injured badly enough that doctors had to amputate one of his legs below the knee.

Snared in the vision of that split second before impact, it was difficult to dismiss the troubling thought

- that if caught in a similar spell of non-cognitive limbo, could the person responsible for the spark plug fiasco have also easily made the same terrible mistake.

CHAPTER 14

Elmer Fudd Live

Prior to 1997, I had yet to meet a single soul who owned a white dinner jacket. The reason for that was that I tended not to associate with such individuals, having assumed they were cut from the same cloth as those who felt compelled to wear white bucks or leisure suits. Thus it came as no small surprise to walk through the front door of the Munich hotel to see Buddy standing in the lobby attired in said white garment.

"Are you planning on earning some extra money as a waiter tonight or do you simply sideline as a gigolo?" I asked as we sauntered over into the ballroom foyer.

"You never know when opportunity might knock," Buddy answered, casting a glance at the costumed throng gathered there.

"If opportunity gets a look of that jacket, it's more likely to make a dash for the exit."

Joining the collection of top carpet salesmen and their significant others, there to celebrate their annual awards gala, we helped drain flutes of welcoming champagne until the call came to enter the main ballroom. Once the guests had taken their seats and settled in, a short, balding man bounded on to the makeshift stage. Introducing himself amidst requisite squeals of feedback, Edward welcomed the crowd before announcing the names of several top executives scheduled to deliver remarks. Ignoring the muffled groans that statement elicited, he attempted to ease the restless crowd by launching into a series of stale jokes that judging from the ensuing silence, many had evidently heard before. A vivid reminder of the slings and arrows random fate can hurl at a single person, in addition to his casket of bad jokes, Edward not only had the misfortune of bearing a striking resemblance to the cartoon figure, Elmer Fudd, he also sounded like him.

Despite those questionable traits, Edward plodded on through his routine, seemingly aloof to the lack of laughter and clearing of throats in the crowd.

"We've got a great show planned for you tonight folks. After a fantastic meal, a few short speeches from our top guests - at least we hope they'll be short," he added with a snicker, - "We'll get right to this year's awards. After all folks, that's why we're here."

"I weally hope there's no wascally wabbit on the menu," Buddy garbled over the camera intercom, just as a lull in conversation rolled through the crowd. Despite Buddy's attempt to hunker down behind a row of monitors on his table, a stern glance in his direction suggested the comment had been registered. But rather than rebuke him publicly, Edward simply shifted gears, pointing to two lamps on either side of the stage, set there to bolster the dimmed house lights.

"Say, Buddy, can we do something about these lights?" he barked.

"I'm afraid we need them for the cameras, Mr. Johnson," Buddy politely informed him over the house PA.

"No we don't," Edward snapped back, a less than subtle reminder about who was in charge. "Lose them… Now! "

With the lights extinguished, Edward appeared

unconcerned that he'd been transformed into little more than a silhouette as he bore down on his closing remarks.

"Not interested, are we Rick?" he grumbled, now taking aim at an embarrassed member of the audience he felt was not paying enough attention. His authority re-established, Edward finished up by thanking those about to be honoured for their hard work, discipline, etc., etc., before wishing everybody a "wonderful evening." Watching him leave the stage to lukewarm applause, I asked Buddy how the picture looked on the monitor.

"My shot is totally worthless," I pointed out. "Without lights you can't even make out who's who on stage."

"Same for me," echoed Stefan, the second cameraman, a German already stricken with a pronounced dislike of anything American before this evening's proceedings.

"Don't worry guys," Buddy replied, his voice starting to betray the number of welcoming drinks consumed in the lobby. "Just do the best you can. Flick on the gain if you have to. Eddie's the boss. If he wants no lights, then no lights it is... Just kick back and enjoy the party. As long as you keep rolling, we'll be fine. That's what they're paying us for."

Following the dinner and speeches, a parade of indistinguishable presenters and recipients made their way to the stage to collect their awards, each accompanied by the identical recorded fanfare and smattering of applause from a not-always attentive crowd. In between awards it was possible to indulge in a little people-watching under the guise of collecting crowd cutaways. Equipped with a fourteen-to-one zoom lens, candid shots of crowd dynamics could be snared with little or no detection. Panning across the sea of grainy faces in a ballroom awash with alcohol, it was interesting to observe blind ambition rearing its head, as newcomers toadied up to those inhabiting the higher rungs. Many company elders, basking in the glow of acknowledged position, appeared to enjoy doling out random tidbits of wisdom to the up and coming.

As the evening rolled on, awards, awards, and more awards brought proceedings to the point where it seemed a category had been created for every kind of carpet ever made.

"Next thing you know they're going to award us something as well," I told Buddy in a moment of boredom. "I mean, who *hasn't* won something yet?"

No sooner had I made my point, when one of the executives jumped on stage to announce what he claimed were the night's final top winners.

"Great, another two hours of acceptance speeches," I groaned moving the camera back to cover yet another dimly-lit speaker. Clearly relishing his moment in the non-existent spotlight, the exec began to describe the next prize category in a style that made him sound like the host of a bad TV game show.

"Ladeeez and gents… I wanna ask you… How many carpets do you think our next sales wizard managed to sell last year?"

When the question was answered by a lone cough, the executive wisely chose not to wait for a more definitive response.

"No, it was not a measly hundred," he told the silent audience, before consulting a sheet in his hand. "Not two hundred, not even three hundred... but three hundred and fifty carpets. That's almost one a day, ladeeez and gentlemen. I want you to put your hands together for Mr. Ray Donovan."

With no idea where Mr. Donovan was seated or even awake to hear his name called, it was a scramble to locate him before he actually reached the stage. Following a hearty handshake, slap on the shoulder, and a stiff pose with trophy held aloft, Ray was allowed to return to his table.

"Old Ray-baby didn't seem terribly thrilled about all that," I opined into the camera intercom.

"Would you want to put that chintzy cup in your home where anyone could see it?" Stefan added.

Tedium reigned supreme in most of the audience as the next few winners repeated Ray's act to forced applause.

"Man, this guy nerves big time," I complained as the presenter proceeded to roll out yet another winner in his loud, staccato "not two... not three..." routine.

"But four hundred and ten carpets. That's a new record, ladeeez and gentlemen... so let's give it up for..." etc.etc.

Already running an hour over schedule, Edward finally saw fit to interrupt matters, suggesting that the remaining recipients refrain from lengthy acceptance speeches, of which there hadn't been any. Nonetheless, it was another twenty minutes before the ceremony finally ground to a halt. Despite the near comatose state of the crowd, news that tables would be cleared so the partying could begin brought a roaring round of applause and a stampede for the bar.

As drinks were dispersed and people prepared to trip

the light fandango, a wave of mild dismay swept across the room as an elder executive took to the stage and launched into a rehearsed pep talk. Unfortunately for him and the rest of us, by this time everyone was well past needing or wanting any encouragement about topping records.

"Are you sure this guy is at the right ceremony?" I asked my colleagues. "He sounds like an evangelist."

"Serves him right," said Stefan as we watched the speaker endure a sparse round of applause at the conclusion of his speech.

With the official festivities now at an end, couples wasted little time gyrating, groping or draping over each other out on the dance floor. Observing the action from behind the camera, I asked Buddy whether it made sense to capture any of *this* unless of course for purposes of blackmail.

"Just get me five or ten minutes of people having fun and go for it yourself," he advised, taking another sip of whatever was in his plastic cup.

Despite the instructions to "chill and enjoy," a part of me still fretted about delivering what I felt was an inferior product. Hoping to grab at least a few entertaining shots, I wandered out into the melee with the camera, occasionally glancing back to see if Buddy had anything to offer in the way of guidance. I needn't have bothered. Having apparently helped himself to considerable refreshments at the bar during the course of the evening, he was now far too busy doing a credible imitation of Michael Jackson, dancing up a storm behind the row of monitors he should have been watching. With both hands flailing high in the air, and his infamous white jacket flapping from side to side, Buddy's cavorting was the signal to give myself the rest of the night off. Joining Stefan at a ringside table, I sat down for a well deserved drink and the chance to ponder the continuing revelry, only remotely aware that Buddy might have a problem.

CHAPTER 15

The Yukon Quest

Under normal circumstances most men wouldn't mind being confronted with such a dilemma at least once in their lives. You've just checked into your hotel and are on the way up to your room. As the elevator doors glide open at your floor, you're met with a bevy of costumed dance-hall girls who at that precise moment turn their backs on you, bend forward in unison, and flip up their frilly skirts to reveal a line of lace covered bottoms. Caught completely off guard, all I could manage was, "Wow! Do you greet all your guests like this?" which given the situation wasn't too bad a repartee.

"Oh, I'm terribly sorry," said an older woman on the end of the row, moving to shut off a boom box as the rest of the team struggled to suppress a burst of giggles. "I knew it wasn't a good idea to practice here."

"Hey, you won't see me complaining to the manager."

Several hours before being greeted with this unique display of hospitality, an enticing slogan had jumped out at me from the pages of an in-flight magazine somewhere over northern Canada.

"Come see the world in its original form."

Intrigued with the message, I had jammed the booklet back in its overfilled pocket and sat there thinking, *"I'll be there in a few hours... yet what do I really know about this place?...Even more important, if that guy behind me punches his touch tone screen one more time I'm going to order a coke and pour it over his head."*

It was just after five that evening when the plane landed in the place where people reportedly run off to, a place that for some reason had yet to gain the status of province, a place as much a philosophy as a habitat... a place called, the Yukon.

Once sufficiently recovered from my hallway welcome and unpacked, I decided to check out what the city of Whitehorse had to offer. It had been awhile since I'd done anything at -25, and I'd forgotten just how bracing that can be, even with a down-filled parka, fleece sweater, pants, boots, toque and gloves the sponsoring company had supplied me with before we left Germany. Shivering as I hustled along the street in the early dusk of a northern winter, I turned a corner on to the main drag only to be engulfed in plumes of thick exhaust billowing from a row of diagonally-parked pick-up trucks. Faced with either asphyxiating or renewing my acquaintance with Canadian beer, I chose the latter and slipped into a nearby crowded bar.

"I'd like a Moosehead," I asked the middle-aged waiter, as I slumped down at one of the few empty tables while trying to clear my fogged-up glasses.

"Wouldn't we all."

"Pardon?"

"Not satisfied with your own are we?" the waiter added. "Sorry, we don't carry it," he relented. "Blue, Canadian, Alexander Keith's, and a couple of BC beers, that's the lot up here."

After years of German beer it was an effort to keep the first few sips down. I was just in the process of adjusting to the back bite when two baseball-capped men approached, asking if the other seats at my table were taken.

"Help yourself."

After ordering a round of draft for themselves, one reached across the void to ask if I was in town for "The Quest".

"I'm here to film for German television."

"Didn't think you looked like a musher," he quipped. "The Germans interested in dog sled races?"

"They better be, or the sponsor that sent me and thirty-five other journalists is going to be plenty pissed. Guess I'll find out when I get back."

"Say... Your English is pretty good for a German."

"I suppose it is... too bad I'm Canadian."

"Canadian? Hey, my man," the other one cut in with a smile. "Whereabouts you from?"

"Manitoba... Winnipeg to be exact."

"Allllright man... Name's Ron," he said, extending a hand.

"Swift Current is where I call home, and my friend here, Rick, is originally from Torronna."

Declining a handshake, Rick settled for a perfunctory nod and toast with his newly arrived draft. Now officially native spirit brothers, the three of us spent the next half-hour comparing life in Germany and Canada, filling in the inevitable gaps in conversation with details on the Quest.

"Longest dog sled race in the world," Ron boasted. "Sixteen hundred kilometres from Whitehorse to Fairbanks one year, and Fairbanks to Whitehorse the next. Takes just under two weeks if you include the layover in Dawson."

"How you gonna film a race that's mostly in the bush?" Rick wanted to know. "Runs through the night as well you know."

"To tell you the truth, I've no idea. All they've told me was that local people are co-ordinating it and we're supposed to have access to ski-doos, four-wheel drives and a helicopter."

While ski-doos and four-wheel drives were a given, the look of their shared glance made it apparent they thought the helicopter claim a trifle far-fetched.

"I read someplace there's a German team this year," Ron said, changing the subject. "He's been here practising since the fall."

Acknowledging his remarks with a shrug as I finished off the last of my beer, I was about to take my leave when a question came to mind.

"Got an early start gents, but before I call it a night… What's the story with all those trucks outside?"

"How so?"

"Why are they all idling? I've been in here for at least half an hour and haven't seen anyone come or go. What is it, Whitehorse's version of Le Mans?"

"They're all likely in here having a few suds," Ron explained, clearly having no idea of the reference to Le Mans. "Everybody leaves their trucks running. 'Course they're locked. That's why everyone has two sets of keys. Hard to sit and enjoy a beer if you know you gotta go back to a freezin' cab. This way we both stays warm."

Given his tone, there seemed little point mentioning how such an environmentally unfriendly habit would be viewed in Germany. Bidding them farewell, I stepped back out into the night air, the first breath sluicing down my throat like a sharpened sword. To increase the odds of making it back to the hotel alive, I shielded my mouth and nose with a scarf, scrunching up against the cold, grateful it was only two blocks away.

Although it came as no surprise, it was nevertheless a let-down when the elevator doors parted to reveal nothing more than a mediocre painting hanging off-kilter on the opposing wall.

※

Next morning at breakfast, we were told part of the day would be spent traveling to a remote cabin to film a "musher" preparing for the race. The first fat snowflakes were beginning to fall as we left Whitehorse. By the time we reached the shores of a frozen lake, twenty kilometres outside of town, flakes had become a flurry, putting the entire trip in jeopardy.

"Not to worry," our guide assured us as he flipped down the tailgate of the trailer carrying four ski-doos. "We're used to this weather. To be honest, we don't get that much snow. Believe it or not, the Yukon's what you might call a winter desert. The wet air from the Pacific gets trapped in the mountains so our level of precipitation is pretty low. We actually kind of like when it snows this hard."

With the last machine unloaded, we set off across the frozen surface, disappearing into a greyish cloud of blowing snow. Visibility was far from great but it was possible to stay on track by keeping in single file with an eye on the person in front of you. Fortunately, the snow had let up when we arrived at the far end of the lake some twenty minutes later. Following the guide's hand signals, we pulled up on to a gradual slope streaked with tracks from ski-doos and what I assumed were dog sleds. After the last of the ski-doos shuddered to a stop, a wave of dead air came roaring off the lake to smother us in absolute silence.

"You hear that guys?" our guide asked, waiting for us to acknowledge the complete absence of anything audible. "That's the sound of nothing… Enjoy it while you can. You won't hear anything like it back home."

Half an hour later, the silence was still lingering as I squatted in a snow bank in the middle of the forest, waiting for the musher and his team of harnessed huskies to breach the crest of a nearby hill. A light snow had started up again, but there in the windless woods, the silence was so pervasive it seemed one could almost hear the odd snowflake hitting the ground.

Just after eight the next morning, I stood perched on a hotel rooftop overlooking the race's official starting line. Here it was the beginning of February, but the general lack of snow had forced organizers to bring in truckloads to groom the first 300 metres of the course. From this vantage point I could look down on dozens of heavily-dressed on-lookers lined up on each side of the improvised track, shivering in the cold as they sent out regulated breath signals. With an hour to go before the opening gun, I decided to move to ground level to get some footage of the mushers preparing their teams. It was subdued pandemonium in the stand-by area with a cacophony of yelps, yowls and yaps providing the soundtrack. Expectant furry heads protruded from small cubbyholes cut into wooden campers mounted on six or seven parked pick-ups, making their home-made quarters look like a wall of barking trophies. Those dogs already removed from their makeshift lairs were being harnessed up, one by one. Pumped with adrenaline and raring to get on with it, some of the dogs leapt a metre or more in the air before being yanked back to earth by gravity and the shortness of their individual lines. Filming up close, I couldn't help noticing how weird and skittish the eyes of some huskies appeared, almost as though they were embarrassed about something.

Once I'd resumed my rooftop vigil, I watched as the first team was guided towards the starting line, its musher struggling to keep his dogs under control. High-strung by nature, the dogs went ballistic the second the start signal was given. The crowd erupted into a chorus of hoops and hollers as the sled tore down the prepared surface, weaving precariously from side to side on the elevated track before cutting off into a field of virgin snow to begin twelve days on the trail.

"Bloody hell it's cold on this thing," I mumbled the next morning, the words crystallizing in my breath as I tightened the strings on my hood, leaving only nose and eyes exposed. Despite adequate clothing, which today also included a chemical warmer case stuffed inside my parka, I was chilled to the bone. The only thing keeping me alive in this 70km. piercing wind was the broad body mass of the driver who'd been guiding the ski-doo along the edge of a snow-packed highway somewhere between Carmacks and Pelly Crossing. In the midst of what I felt certain would be my last breath, the lowered whine of the ski-doo's engine indicated we were slowing down. A quick glance revealed that we'd turned off the highway on to a narrow unmarked trail. Two hundred yards in, I was dropped off in the middle of the bush to await the arrival and departure of the first of the top teams. Grateful to be sheltered from the wind, under a sun that had turned the fresh snow into a carpet of diamonds, I was suddenly aware I was being left to my own devices, as the ski-doo's motor slowly faded. Quietly reminding myself that bears hibernate, and wolves are shy creatures, a part of me nevertheless wondered what other animals might be out there contemplating revenge for my having trespassed on their territory.

At that very instant a faint noise broke the silence. Quickly firing up the camera in the hope it was a team and not some crazed moose, my efforts were soon rewarded as I saw a lead dog bound around the corner of the trail just seconds after the final tape loop had threaded. Zooming out from the first dog to reveal the full team hauling a sleek, fully-packed sled; the only audible sounds were the boot-padded paws of twelve dogs hitting the compacted snow. Abandoning the task at hand long enough to offer a wave, the musher shouted orders only his dogs could comprehend, before he and the team disappeared into the trees. Although they'd come and gone in less than fifteen seconds, the image of teamwork out here in the elements was a lasting one.

A series of similar forest encounters occurred over the next few days as the racers closed in on Dawson City. Made famous by the Klondike Gold Rush in the late 19th century, it was in Dawson that mushers and dogs were forced to spend a day's layover, undergoing thorough medical check-ups and recouping their strength. Up to this point all teams had been required to stop at designated stations along the route, not only to feed and rest their dogs, but also to have them examined by qualified veterinarians. Although the vets had the authority to pull dogs out of the race they felt were suffering or had been abused in any way, given the respect mushers had for their dogs in such an unforgiving climate, such infractions tended to be rare. Only once the dogs had been examined, fed and bedded down at the stations did mushers head for the shelters to take care of themselves. Inside the station shack, it was interesting to observe the subtle strategies at work. There primarily to eat and catch a bit of much needed shuteye, the men slumped over table tops were not necessarily sleeping, but rather grabbing as much rest as they could while still keeping an eye on what their competitors were doing. One of the tactics mushers often used to keep challengers second guessing, was to depart as soon as they'd eaten and been given the go-ahead from vets, only to park a few miles down the trail to catch some needed sleep. Dawson however, was compulsory R & R for all concerned.

With nothing to film on our first evening in town, we headed to the nearest watering hole right after dinner. Seated amongst a group of German-based journalists whose red fleece sweaters branded them as "Quest hangers-on," it was with fond memories that I watched a troupe of costumed dance-hall girls take the stage.

"Good evening gentlemen," a waitress suddenly asked. "What's your pleasure this evening?" Glancing briefly at the matching logos on the sweaters, she stopped jotting down orders long enough to ask if we were part of "that German team" in town for the Quest.

Nods, smiles and a few grunts, offered the answer to a question half the group hadn't understood.

"And what's with you?" she asked, directing her attention at me. "How come you're not wearing a Quest sweater and why aren't you as boisterous as all these other guys?"

"I'm the token Canadian in the crowd," I replied. "You know, the quiet, self-deprecating type."

Not particularly humorous, the remark nevertheless brought a laugh

"It wasn't *that* funny," I said. "Or is it that Dawsonites, or whatever you call yourselves, just don't have much to laugh about?"

"Oh, I can tell this is going to be a fun table tonight," she replied with a friendly, mock sneer. "Be right back with your drinks, gents."

Whether it was a fun evening, depended on how much entertainment value you put on listening to Germans share bad German jokes.

Despite the late night, the alarm still went off at six a.m. Even more alarming was the temperature outside; minus thirty-four. Breakfast in the hotel passed quietly as we all pondered ways to contract an illness that would somehow prevent having to go outside until it warmed up, preferably in mid-May. Out in the early morning light, headed for the race coordinator's office, evenly spaced puffs of breath literally hung in the air behind me, as my boots made a familiar, crunchy squeak on the packed snow, reviving memories of walks to school in the depths of Winnipeg winters.

A few shivering minutes later, I was blindly feeling my way around a crowded table in the small improvised conference room as my glasses slowly defogged. The first order of the day, I learned, would involve travelling

up the Yukon river to visit a musher's outpost, ten miles north of town. Instructions for the afternoon's agenda were to be handed out back here at noon.

Awaiting us at the dormant ferry docks were four ski-doos. Now that the temperature had risen to a balmy minus twenty-five, I was once again eager to enjoy the thrill of racing across frozen tundra and river. That wish was dealt a setback, however, as I followed the leader out on to the river and turned north on to a packed trail.

"God, I can *run* faster than this," I growled to myself, hoping he would sense my displeasure and get things moving. But he didn't, and for the next few minutes we continued up the frozen waterway at a speed more amenable to a Sunday afternoon drive with the grandparents. Tiring of the boring pace and hoping to test the power of my machine, I repeatedly dropped to the back of the pack, only to crank open the throttle and close the emerging gap. About to risk both wrath and limb by zooming ahead the next time the narrow trail opened up wide enough to pass, I suddenly realized, "*Hang on... If I'm driving this ski-doo alone... and the other two have the producer and the musher's assistant, who's got the bloody camera?*"

Those who've worked in the business, know that producers come in all shapes, sizes and temperaments. Some can be "Prima Donalds," others "Spielberg wannabees." Most tend to be decent, tolerant people but few would be prepared to forgive you for arriving at the shoot location without the camera. Despite the frigid temperature, I could feel a tiny drop of sweat run down my back, unleashed by the image of the camera still belted to rear seat of the van that had taken us to the docks. With the roar of the engines eliminating any chance of calling a stop to our caravan, the only way to attract the leader's attention, short of throwing a tomahawk at him, was to careen off into the deep snow and race ahead to pull up alongside him. Hoping the virgin surface was not hiding a frozen tree trunk that could bring the ski-doo and me to an abrupt and unpleasant halt, I slipped off the trail, plunging ahead through drifts, the motor straining and whining as I hit patches of various density. After finally managing to catch the leader's attention, I briefly explained the situation and got him to agree to wait until I returned.

Despite being able to open up the ski-doo on the trip back, it was impossible to fully enjoy the thrill, consumed as I was by the thought of how I was going to retrieve the camera unnoticed. Moving through Dawson's snow-covered streets at a reasonable facsimile of a safe speed, I pulled up out front of the office only to discover the camera was no longer in the van. Sweating from exertion and nervousness, I gamely entered the conference room only to spot it sitting at the far end of the table, directly in front of the sponsor's lead executive. Although he was in a discussion with several local officials, all eyes turned to me as I reached across the table.

"Thought this might come in handy," I said with as much nonchalance as I could muster.

"Do tell," he said as I headed for the door. "No doubt it will make the job easier."

With the camera strapped into a knapsack, I made good time getting back to the waiting posse. With our destination still ten minutes away, we continued up the river, warily passing several patches of open water before driving up a steep embankment and on to an almost invisible trail. Despite the din of the ski-doos echoing in the forest, the yelping of dogs was audible before we actually caught sight of the camp.

"Did you see that open water back there on the river?" I asked the producer, as a musher emerged from a small hut to greet us. "What was that all about? It's twenty-five below."

"Forget about the water," the producer said tersely. "Just be glad you were able to get the camera without causing us further delay."

Somehow, filming a pack of leaping, ravenous dogs being fed chopped-up slabs of frozen fish did not compensate for having risked life and limb, not to mention sullying my reputation as a reliable cameraman.

Back in town just after one, I was excited to learn the afternoon schedule was to include both a helicopter trip to the nearby Tombstone mountains and a tour of Dawson's famous sites. Unfortunately, both were to be carried out simultaneously, making it necessary to draw straws. Unfortunately, I came up short, convinced the process had somehow been rigged by the still-miffed producer. As a result, my colleague got to fly off to film breathtaking panoramas of the haunting Tombstone peaks, while I got to cover such highlights as Jack London's house, which happened to be closed for the season.

*

With the compulsory layover having ended at midnight and the majority of mushers already back out on the course, the next morning saw the rest of us headed for the land of the free and home of the brave. As Dawson had been the end of the trail for the print journalists, largely because of the difficulty and cost of transporting them to the next leg of the race, "we" were now down to eight. With no road passable at this time of year, river traffic closed by ice, and the distance to the next station too great to cover by ski-doo, the only method of travel left was by small plane. With eight of us jammed in amidst the gear and personal luggage, and loud droning engines eliminating thinking, let alone talking, it was anything but a pleasant trip. Fortunately, in little over an hour we were circling in for a landing.

"Welcome to the Yewnited States of Amerrrika boys," a white-haired man drawled in an accent that sounded like it belonged much further south. He appeared to be the only employee of Eagle's tiny airport terminal which consisted of two rickety desks in a tiny wooden shed. He also appeared to have just woken up.

"Where you boys all headed?" he asked with a yawn.

"Likely, nowhere at this rate," someone in line behind me grumbled. Once our passports were checked and stamped, a process that took almost as long as the flight itself, we cleared Customs by walking past an empty desk marked Customs. As the town of Eagle was not large enough to warrant a hotel, we'd been billeted into an enormous two-storey log cabin overlooking a section of the Yukon as it curled around a high peak on its western shore. With no filming scheduled until well after midnight, the rest of the day was spent hanging out, charging batteries, and getting bored.

"What do you suppose people actually do here?" I asked Thomas, the second cameraman, during a leisurely after-dinner stroll through the town.

"Not a lot," he answered.

Although I managed to get to bed early and enjoyed a fairly sound sleep, it was nonetheless a struggle to force myself up at 2:00 am. Still half asleep as our SUV jostled along a snow-rutted road through the forest, I was roused back to clarity when the headlights suddenly fell upon a channel of trees and bushes that looked as though they'd been sprayed with a coating of white paint. Used to hoar frost from Manitoba winters, I'd never seen anything like this. Thick enough to have blotted out any semblance of colour, the frost was still thin enough to maintain the delicate patterns on the branches. As if this hypnotic vista wasn't spectacular enough, a short distance later, we emerged from the forest to a phenomenal display of the Aurora Borealis. For the next twenty minutes the producer and I were held spellbound by the constantly changing patterns of greenish light that at times looked like a genie let out of the proverbial bottle.

"Man, we could have easily slept till four," I groaned, making no attempt to disguise my displeasure that my watch had just inched past five with still no sign of our first musher. "If I'd known I was just gonna have to stand around and do nothing, I could have stayed with the Feds... At least there I would have been warm."

No sooner had these words been spoken, a dozen sets of eyes on the edge of darkness, could be seen reflecting in the station's flood lights. Fortunately, the camera at that moment was on standby, making it possible to capture the first team as it came bounding into the light-drenched feeding area with such energy that it almost looked as though it wasn't going to stop. Dropping anchor and whooping his dogs to a halt, the musher wasted no time freeing them from the main harness and attaching them to lines that still gave them access to their food. Melting snow in a pot taken from the sled, the musher dumped a load of dry dog food into the bubbling water and stirred it to an even mix before portioning out meals to his expectant teammates. Focused entirely on gorging themselves, the dogs only occasionally glanced up from their bowls, their reddish eyes beaming like beings from *Invasion of the Body Snatchers*. Meanwhile the musher was busy pulling out bundles of straw from stacks lodged alongside the station's shack. After laying out a series of makeshift beds, he made certain all the dogs had eaten and were bedded down before wandering into the shack and flopping down in front of a bowl of steaming goulash.

It was still steaming the next evening, only this time the vapour was coming from a hot, spring-fed pool in Circle, the last scheduled stop before Fairbanks. Told of the town's sole highlight at dinner, a group of us had walked the short distance to the outdoor pool to check it out for ourselves. I'd been paddling around in the heated water for fifteen minutes, enjoying the spectacle of staring up into a -30 degree starry night whenever a light breeze poked a hole in the clouds billowing up from the surface. Having spent the last ten days in and out of the wilderness, there was an unspoken apprehension amongst the crew that night about our impending return to the "real world." Perhaps that explains why everyone seemed to be ignoring the recommended twenty-minute stay in the pool. Then again, the overindulgence might have simply been due to the fact no one had been brave

enough to attempt venturing from the warm water to the change rooms. It didn't help that previous patrons had dripped water on to the walkway, turning the entire patio into a virtual skating rink. Convinced the soles of our feet would stick to the icy surface, much like the youthful folly of putting one's tongue on a cold, metal lamppost, all of us lingered. Finally, it took one of the locals to show us how it was done. Hoisting himself up in one quick movement, the steaming hulk reached the heated cabin in a matter of seconds, a radiant glow of heat protecting him from the cold as he endeavoured to keep his balance. Despite that apparent rescue strategy, I was content to remain in the pool even longer, reflecting on the events of the past two and a half weeks and recalling a chance conversation I'd had on my first day in Whitehorse.

"Is this your first time in the Yukon?" a friendly salesclerk had asked as I thumbed through several jackets to see if they had my size.

"It is... We're here for the Quest..."

"It started off for me like that too," she admitted. "Came here on vacation for two weeks... Loved it so much I went home, packed my bags and moved back. That was sixteen years ago... You either hate it or love it. There's no in between."

I was startled out of my warm tranquility when another face loomed out of the mist, nodded hello and glided silently past. Despite a host of other images lined up to traipse down memory lane, shrivelling fingertips and icicles in my hair forced me to cut the journey short. Back in the changing room, surprised at how immune I'd been to the cold air dash, I was again lost in thought; this time about how much the wilderness had enamoured me with its isolation, severity and serenity. For a moment back in Dawson, I had mulled over the idea of purchasing a lot and building a log cabin in the middle of nowhere. Things had even gone as far as getting an agent to take me across the river from Dawson to view a potential site. Already somewhat dented by the vision of forty million mosquitos and long dark winter days, the dream was dealt a death blow at the realization of possibly becoming an ax murderer in response to a neighbour's loud, constantly running generator. I settled for a post card.

On our last day "on the trail," the first on a paved road in ten, the first item on the agenda was to film teams crossing one of the most difficult stretches of the course - a long, snow-packed incline that required mushers to literally get out and help push the heavily-laden sled up the slope. After slogging it half way up the hill with the camera and heavy tripod, I set up just in time to capture unique footage of the first team's struggle to conquerer the Quest's last big obstacle. Unlike the contestants who were still racing against the clock, I could take the time to reward myself for my endurance, with a lunch of genuine "moose burgers," delivered to us in the middle of nowhere via snowmobile. Although it was stringy and virtually tasteless, I was hungry enough to down it all.

From there it was a short haul into Fairbanks, which after two weeks of witnessing "the Earth in its original form," appeared painfully nondescript. Then again, in all fairness, set against the pristine nature of the Yukon, what place wouldn't?

Despite the large, cheering crowd assembled at the

finish line, watching the winner and his team cross turned out to be rather anti-climactic. After all, how can you top an act like the Aurora Borealis?

Bright and early next morning, the flight path to Whitehorse took us over Mt. McKinley, or Denali as the natives call it, North America's tallest peak, barely visible through the light clouds and whited-out landscape. That night, back at the same bar I'd visited my first evening in town, I spotted a familiar face in the crowd.

"Excuse me… Haven't we met somewhere?" I said with a mischievous grin. "I rarely forget… uuhhh… a face."

Still dressed in her dance-hall costume, it took her a second to place me, but when she did, it was with a smile and laugh.

"Oh God. I hoped we'd never run into you again. That was so embarrassing."

"Hey, I didn't tell anybody… Except for that pesky reporter from the Enquirer."

With ten minutes until showtime, there was just enough time to trade a few anecdotes on what we'd been up to since our last "meeting."

"How long are you staying?" she asked abruptly, glancing at a group of her colleagues gathered at the edge of the stage.

"What tonight? I'm not sure. I guess I…"

"No, no, I mean in town…" she interrupted. "I have to work now, but later maybe we could…"

"We fly back to Germany tomorrow."

"Oh," she replied, clearly disappointed. "That's too bad…Sorry, gotta run. It's showtime."

The next morning, adrift somewhere over the Rockies en route to Vancouver and a connecting flight to Frankfurt, I sat gazing out at the peaks of my home and native land, wondering, sporadic cad that I am, what the penalty was for perjury in the Yukon.

CHAPTER 16

The Jet Car

It remains a mystery to this day, what could have possibly prompted someone to come up with the idea of welding a jet engine to a car frame. But whoever the perpetrator, he or she must have been as much of a marketing whizz as an innovator. How else to convince a well-known car radio manufacturer that having a jet car blast down a runway would make for a great advertising spot? But convince them they did, and in the spring of 1997, we were headed to an abandoned Russian air-base near the former East German town of Luckau to actualize those wishes. In accordance with the script, which called for making the spot as dynamic as possible, we came loaded down with a crane, a dolly and a top-of-the-line camera. Unfortunately, what wasn't included was enough money to hire extra crew for those devices, leaving it to me and my long-term assistant, Alex, a colleague since "the smarmy days of Siegfried," to set up and operate them on our own.

After arriving at the desolate wind-swept plain, the first order of business for the day was to lay down and level twenty feet of dolly track, running out from the test tarmac at a 90-degree angle. The crane was then mounted on the dolly and counterbalanced so that Alex could adjust its vertical movement with the mere touch of his hand with the camera and me aboard. The opening shot was to feature the jet car's sleek carbon body in a frame-filling profile. Accompanied by music similar to the haunting "Jaws" theme, the plan was to have the dolly slowly creep forward, as the camera focused on the client's company logo on the rear-side panel. Once the dolly was within several yards of the car, the jet engine would be ignited and the crane would swing upwards as the camera panned right, shifting focus to capture the car as it hurtled off down the track. That at least was the plan. As all the complicated moves needed to be done in one smooth sequence, timing was crucial, especially given it cost four hundred Euros in fuel each time the jet car shot down the runway. With less than subtle pressure to stay within budget, we practiced dry runs for over an hour, while technicians continued preparing the car for its launch.

"You guys figure you're about ready?" our producer Conrad, asked in a tone that didn't exactly exude confidence.

"Hey, it's only jet fuel," I answered, dubious as to whether we *could* pull off what looked to be one of the toughest shots we'd ever been asked to do. "Give us one last run and then we'll go for it. If we blow it, you can take it out of Alex's salary."

"If you blow it, we'll tie you to the end of the car for a *really* special shot," Conrad fired back.

With the live run set to go, all peripheral work on the set came to a halt; the only sound being the rustling grass in the field opposite. On Conrad's nod, Alex slowly eased the dolly forward. Positioned to initiate the rapid pan as soon as the crane began its rise, I could feel my heart pounding as the narrow margin of error approached. It was literally all over in a flash.

"What the hell was *that*?" I yelled, half expecting to

see a mound of burnt clothing and bones where Alex had been standing.

"What?" Alex shouted, stumbling away from the track as he desperately slapped his right ear. "Scheisse!... I can't *hear* anything... What did you say?"

It's difficult to say which was worse, the thundering roar or the scorching blast of heat. In any case the gust from the engine had been powerful enough to shake the crane and dolly on its moorings. Left with only three senses still functioning, I could smell the pervasive odour of spent kerosene, see the look of astonishment on Alex's face, and taste the revenge I wanted to wreak on whoever was responsible for putting us in harm's way.

Glancing around, I could see that preparations were already underway for a second run, making it apparent that nobody on set was overly perturbed at the turn of events. Astounded that no one had had the foresight to warn us of the potential consequences of filming behind a jet engine, Alex and I struggled to contain our anger as an argument broke out between the sponsor and the owner of the jet car. Rather than complaining or expressing concern about our safety and well-being, the gist of their discussion was simply over whether a second run was really necessary.

"Tell him not to forget to include the lawyer's fees and the millions we'll sue him for in the extra charges," I said to Conrad.

Despite the apparent fierceness of the debate between the two men, it didn't take them long to reach an agreement. Resuming our positions, we repeated the whole procedure, this time with the protection of noise-reducing headphones, baseball caps and safety glasses, all of which had been available, but not offered, for the first run.

In hindsight, I can say with some authority that there's nothing quite like finding yourself behind a jet engine as it takes off. Unlike hundreds of birds, ducks, geese and other flying objects that had the misfortune to be in the wrong spot at the wrong time, we survived. Ironically, I happen to have one of the sponsor's radios installed in my own car. To this day, I'm constantly being asked by passengers to turn it down, to which I merely replied, "What?... Did you say something?"

CHAPTER 17

Hunting Höttl

By the fall of 1997, the Second World War had been over for more than fifty-two years. Despite the shrinking number of first-hand witnesses, both perpetrators and survivors, during those years, everyday images in the German and Austrian countryside continued to provide haunting reminders to anyone with an overactive imagination trying to comprehend the past.

Take for example finding oneself at a railway crossing, mindlessly counting the cars of a freight train as it rumbled past. Without fail, questions would arise as to whether bystanders at this crossing over a half century ago would not have seen arms protruding from the sealed cattle cars, or heard cries above the screeching wheels. Neither could one enter the central Markplatz (market square) of a large German or Austrian city without recalling scenes of it awash in a sea of Swastika flags, held aloft by thousands of Nazi supporters as they listened to their Führer speak from the balcony of city hall. In what often felt like a scene from a war movie, it was difficult to stroll through a forest on a misty fall morning without imagining what it must have felt like to hear a shot ring out or to encounter a passing SS patrol. Waiting alone on an empty railway platform bathed in yellow light as a nighttime fog wafted across the glistening tracks, one half expected a sinister figure with SS insignia to emerge from the shadows.

Although such reminders and the inherent

indignation they induced, began to subside after my first few years in Germany, diminished for the most part by the obligations of daily life, what failed to disperse so quickly were the discreet glances on a crowded subway carriage. Directed at those clearly old enough to have been there, they were usually accompanied by the unspoken questions "What did they do?... What did they know?"

The man opening the door that October morning in 1997 looked every inch his eight-two years. Shunning the customary welcome of an extended hand, he merely nodded us in, a pinched half-smile unable to disguise his irritation at our having arrived a half-hour earlier than planned. After ordering that our shoes be left in the lower hallway, he ushered us up a wooden staircase into a cramped but comfortable second-floor living room. Almost immediately, our whey-faced host excused himself to attend to other matters, leaving us to set up for the interview. Glancing around the cluttered room, the only lifetime mementos to offer a clue to its occupants' past were a slew of framed photos on a table behind the sofa. Closer inspection of the smiling and pained faces of friends and relatives did little to distinguish them from thousands of other familial collections.

Our host returned twenty minutes later, attired in a grey, loden sweater with a small unidentifiable medallion pinned to its upper left quadrant. Standing slightly hunched over at one end of the sofa, he slowly arched back on to a cushion, exhaling deeply as he brought both hands to rest on the cane in front of him. Master of this secluded domain, he could have easily passed for any of a thousand other docile, aging grandfathers had it not been for the look in his eyes. Lost in an absent gaze at the mountain vista looming outside the picture window, they seemed far too clear for someone his age, infused with the look of someone who had witnessed power as well as its decline.

The man we'd come to see was Wilhelm Höttl, a former high-ranking Austrian SS officer and member of the Nazi intelligence service. The interview with the former Nazi operative had been arranged to take place in the small, picturesque hamlet of Alt Aussee, located on a small lake in the Salzkammergut region of the Austrian Alps, and Höttl's refuge for the last half century. Driving into town the previous evening, it had struck both Buddy and myself that the sleepy locale seemed an incongruous setting to be discussing aspects of WWII and its aftermath.

As we'd only been given twenty-four hours' notice prior to leaving for Austria, there had been no time to conduct any research into Höttl's past. The sole chance we had to learn anything about the man, emerged from an unexpected encounter with the owner of the restaurant we had dined at the night of our arrival. Having overheard portions of our table discussion, Herr Glatt had introduced himself, claiming to be a bit of an amateur historian. After patiently listening to him dabble in the local scuttlebutt so common to small villages, things took an interesting twist when he excused himself and returned a few minutes later with a brochure in hand.

"This was written by an American soldier stationed here at the end of the war," he explained, placing it in front of me. "I think you might find it interesting because it concerns the activities in and around Alt Aussee in the dying days of the war. Your friend Höttl is mentioned in it."

Later that night, huddled beneath a cone of yellow light in my hotel room, I was able to catch brief glimpses of the figure we were about to meet.

"Man oh man… " I said to Buddy over breakfast the next morning. "From what I read last night, this guy had so many aces up his sleeve, it's a wonder he could get his uniform on."

"Don't get carried away," Buddy warned. "Remember we only have him for three hours,"

"Three hours and not a minute longer," I repeated. "And don't, under any circumstances deviate from the list of questions. I know, I know… I read the fax too."

Up to this point, our brief discourse with Höttl had been conducted in limited German. Having fully expected to switch to English to conduct the interview, it came as a shock when Höttl claimed he could neither speak nor understand that language. With no way of proving or challenging his assertion, I was forced to add the role of translator to my dual performance as interviewer and cameraman.

"This should be fun," I whispered to Buddy, as I finished framing Höttl in the shot and sat down across from him. Having set the control monitor at an angle where I could keep an eye on it, I glanced at the list of questions on my lap, took a deep breath and told Buddy to start the camera.

Having to wear the three hats and under strict orders to adhere to the scheduled time limit, there was little opportunity to take advantage of sitting across from a suspected war criminal who had known and worked with so many top-rung Nazis. Other than a few misunderstandings caused by my rough translations, Höttl breezed through most of the questions with ease. It was only when queries veered to such subjects as his friendship with Adolf Eichmann, or events that threatened to imply criminal activity on his part, that he began to obfuscate, casting aside any contradictions of his own previous statements as creations of the press or envisioned opponents. The fact that segments of Höttl's fractured version of history differed greatly from even a layman's knowledge of events, made it clear he had spent the intervening years diligently polishing his past to salvage a future.

Despite efforts to stick to the schedule, the interview ended up running a half-hour over the allotted time. Höttl's reaction to this minor imposition was telling. Initially, he pretended to dismiss it, saying, "Machen Sie sich keine Sorgen darüber" (Don't worry about it). But as we would later learn, as soon as we left his house, he placed a call to the production company in the States to demand payment for the "overtime."

"Talk about disingenuous pap," I said to Buddy once the payment to Höttl had been settled and we prepared to leave Alt Aussee. "How much did this guy get paid for this anyway?"

"You don't wanna know," he answered, putting the signed receipt in his folder and tossing it on the back seat.

"No really, tell me. I want to know."

"Twelve thousand Schilling," Buddy admitted reluctantly.

"Schilling?... How much is that in dollars?"

"Give or take a few... I think it's about a thousand

dollars."

"For three hours? You've got to be kidding."

But he wasn't. Incensed by the injustice of paying such an amount to such a man, I returned to Germany determined to conduct my own research on how and why an educated man, (Höttl had obtained his Doctorate of History at 22) became and remained a Nazi.

My first port of call was the Bundesarchiv (National Archives)in Berlin, where I was told that access to both Höttl's SS and NSDAP files could only be obtained with his written permission. Fortunately, I recalled having read that before pulling up stakes in Berlin in the 1950s, American military officials had microfilmed all the documents captured after the war and taken them back to be deposited in the National Archives in Washington. What followed was a straining series of phone calls in which I was diverted from department to department within that institution. After several days of this run-around I was on the verge of giving up when I finally reached the proper archivist. Three weeks later, notice arrived that hundreds and hundreds of pages of Höttl's past would be provided to me on microfilm, through a program known as the Inter Library Loans. Faced with a veritable mountain of documents, a good portion of which were barely-legible photocopies in German, I swallowed hard and arranged to view the material at the University of Frankfurt, unaware I was entering a labyrinth it would take me almost twenty years to escape.

CHAPTER 18

The Ugly Stepsisters

What's the first thing that comes to mind when you hear the word Luxembourg? That was the burning question since hearing we'd been booked for a three-day shoot in the tiny Grand Duchy. Having yet to venture there myself, I decided to take other people's word for it by conducting a small local survey. Polled at random were a supermarket butcher, postal clerk, dental receptionist and bank teller to name just a few.

"Tax haven... Money laundering... Castles... Cheap cigarettes... Great roads for motorcycles." And my all-time favourite... "Nothing."

At the time I couldn't say how accurate these assessments were, but they did leave me wondering how a small country in the heart of Europe, considered by some to be as dull as toast, had come to create such impressions? But a comprehensive explanation would have to take a back seat to the primary task at hand, that being, to film a "behind-the-scenes" segment for a made-for-TV movie titled *Tales of The Ugly Stepsisters*. Meant to be a darker version of Cinderella's exploits as seen through the eyes of her jealous and vindictive step sisters, the film was being shot in a sound studio on the outskirts of Luxembourg City. Although the original story of Cinderella is thought to have originated in China and was later transported to Europe via Italy, the producers of this epic version decided to set it in 17th century Holland.

Anyone driving to Luxembourg's capital from the east, has to pass through a rather dreary, landscape before reaching the city limits. It's at this point however, that the topography suddenly shifts, transformed by clusters of slick glass and steel edifices that border both sides of the Autobahn. Looking as though they were constructed the previous week and are yet to be inhabited, the buildings evoke the eerie spectacle of a shiny but sterile Potemkin Silicon Valley. Given Luxembourg's status as a favoured tax oasis, one can't help but wonder whether the whole setting is nothing more than an elaborate high-tech front for off-shore, postal-box companies.

Following the directions droned out by our rental car's synthetic, nasal-voiced "navi," we made our way to an industrial park on the southern edge of the city. According to the address, our destination was a large, windowless warehouse with a grey concrete facade and no identifying logo whatsoever. Anonymity sought was anonymity found, as no passerby would ever have had the slightest inkling that behind these blank walls lay a 17th century Dutch palace.

Inside was the inverse scenario as actors, set helpers, script assistants and others scurried through a narrow foyer crammed with set decorations, lights, wardrobe and boxes of who-knows-what-else. Amid the tumult, a young production assistant was waiting to greet us. Following a round of hand-shakes and introductions, we were guided down a set of long corridors and through a steel door whose overhead red light had just stopped flashing. Entering a darkened cavernous warehouse, we moved along the back walls of 17th century Holland, held intact by numerous two-by-fours and cables. Brought to a halt at the edge of a sound stage, we stood there gawking like hillbillies seeing New York for the first time, as cast and crew prepared for the next scene. Following what appeared to be a strict regimen, the main actors not required in the scene retired to their dressing rooms to rehearse or cool their heels. Lesser mortals were sentenced to kill time in make-up or wardrobe while the crew moved sets, re-lit, and plotted camera angles with the director. Within a relatively short span, an assistant director shouted for everyone to find their marks. Distances to the camera were measured and noted, light readings taken, and sound checks run. The director exchanged a few last words with the script assistant as the last extras moved to their designated spots.

"*Quiet on the set*" echoed through the immense hall before several dry run-throughs were carried out. Only when the director was satisfied everything was in order, did he utter "roll camera" once, twice, perhaps three times, barring a major faux pas. Once a successful take was "in the can," organized pandemonium resumed with the crew repeating the entire process for the following scene.

Mesmerized at how this conglomeration of talent, energy and equipment managed to function, we continued to watch in silent awe as the director conferred with actors and the director of photography, while a nervous-looking script assistant, clipboard and walkie-talkie in hand, stood by, waiting for an opportunity to diplomatically butt in. Off to one side sat the stern-faced producer, recognizable by his tweed jacket, penny loafers, loose scarf knotted at the neck, and unpronounceable name on the back of his chair. Just as I was about to comment to Buddy on the controlled chaos we were witnessing, I was schussed into silence by a frazzled-looking assistant seconds before a loud buzzer sounded and another tribal yell of "*quiet on the set*" was bellowed across the room.

※

Day Two started on the set at the ungodly hour of 6:00a.m., only to learn that our scheduled interview with Ms. Stockard Channing had been delayed until 11:00. There was no point in returning to the hotel, so we accepted an invitation to take up temporary lodging on a set some distance from the morning's planned action. Joining us in a pseudo-17th-century salon largely devoid of furniture or decorations, were several white-wigged footmen in brocaded costumes. Gathered around the only table in the room, the group was busy scanning local journals in a futile attempt to relieve their obvious boredom.

"Hopefully this delay is not going to prevent us from grabbing interviews with the other stars," our producer Roger complained. "It's always good to have footage of them fawning over the perceived attributes of their co-stars and how wonderful it is to work with *this* director."

"Do I detect a tinge of jadedness in thine remarks?" I asked.

"When you've done as many of these as I have, it's hard to take anything seriously," he answered. "And in case I forget, we also need copious amounts of B-roll to help show how this blur of activity actually has a purpose."

The Ugly Stepsisters | 149

As the minutes slowly crawled by, a glimmer of hope arose around 9:30 when it was announced that Ms. Channing might be available in twenty minutes. We scrambled to set up in an adjacent room, only to hear a short while later thag she'd in fact decided to return to her hotel. Again facing the prospect of hanging around like death on standby, Buddy and I started bouncing ideas off one another as to how we might sabotage the interview, if and when it ever took place. The longer the wait, the more off-the-wall the remarks became. Shortly before noon, bored out of my skull, I wandered back to the main set to discover the much anticipated Ms. Channing in discussion with the director. In all fairness, she may have had other commitments that were a higher priority than talking with us, but all I could think of at the moment was, *"Where the hell have you been?"* But instead of voicing such a thought, I chose to remain silent, hidden amongst a forest of dormant lights. It may have been just wishful thinking, but it appeared from his gestures that the director was speaking to her in less than warm, comforting tones. But before I could be certain, my "Schadenfreude"(malicious joy) was interrupted when a script assistant tapped me on the shoulder to inform that Ms. Channing would be ready for the interview in ten minutes.

Much to everyone's surprise, this time she actually showed, outfitted in a sleeveless costume that pushed her cleavage up to the point where she could almost rest her chin on it. As I finished tweaking lights and adjusting the tripod for the rather diminutive actress, Roger ran through the questions he intended to ask, all the while effusing about how huge a fan he was. A bit of comic relief was added watching Buddy search for a way to attach a clip-on mike without puncturing her. As if on cue, the instant the signal was given to roll, a chorus of power drill and table saws revved up from somewhere in the hall. The script assistant was quickly dispatched to locate the source, but it took several minutes before relative quiet returned.

"Okay, that's better...Sorry about that," Roger said, settling back in his chair. "So let me just start off by saying it's nice to meet you, Ms. Channing. Thank you for taking time out of your busy schedule to sit down with us."

"My pleasure... Roger, is it?"

"That's right... By the way, I'd just like to say I loved you in *The Lion in Winter*. I found your performance superb."

"Why, thank you, Roger. That's very kind of you."

"I thought you were perfect for that role. Put old Kate Hepburn in the shadows, if you don't mind me saying so, Stockard... Oh, I'm sorry. I hope you don't mind my calling you Stockard... It's just that I feel I almost know you."

Forced to endure this wave of smarmy goo, I found myself drifting back to the imaginary interview we'd concocted while waiting for "Stockard" to put in an appearance.

"Nice to meet you, Ms. Channing."

"Likewise."

"I won't keep you too long today, just half a dozen questions or so."

"That's perfect. I'm due in make-up in half an hour."

"Great. I'm sure we'll have you out of here by then. So, ready to roll guys?... Alright then, my first question is... actually...before we get started... I like to keep my interviews

informal so if it's okay with you, would you mind if I address you by something other than Ms. Channing?"

"Certainly, that would be fine."

"Great, that's really great... and much appreciated... So, Stocky... Would you mind telling our viewers how long your comeback has been underway? We haven't seen much of you lately and, truth be told, I actually thought you were dead."

Brought back to reality by a burst of Stocky's shrill laughter, I struggled to remain alert for the remainder of the real interview, convinced our subversive creation would have made for much more entertaining television.

CHAPTER 19

Quite the Night at the Opera

Go ahead, call me a soulless boor... an uncultured buffoon... a lumbering ignoramus. Point is, it won't change the fact I've never been much drawn to opera. Granted, the voices are exceptional and stage settings often spectacular... It's just that there are too many other events I'd rather attend than one that treats me to lyrics I can't understand, for periods I can't endure. Hence, it was with muted enthusiasm that I received word we were booked to travel to the Vienna State Opera House to film the Canadian opera star, Ben Heppner, in his starring role in Wagner's four hour epic, *Lohengrin*.

Coming directly on the heels of a week-long shoot in the Austrian Alps, where we'd been filming yet another behind-the-scenes segment, this one for a TV movie called *Death on Everest*, the Vienna shoot promised to be a welcome escape from the swarm of B-list actors whose antics made *Death to Everyone Who Thought it a Good Idea to Make this Movie,* a more appropriate title.

Following a final day in the snow and a late-night drive across Austria, the next morning we were introduced to Ben in the lobby of the hotel he resides in every time the world of opera brings him to Vienna. As we were about to learn, opera stars are creatures of habit. Being on the road for much of the year, when in Vienna it's standard practice for Ben to lodge in the same room, in the same hotel, taking his meals at the same nearby restaurant, going for walks in the same

Quite the Night at the Opera | 153

park, and practicing in the same private apartment located behind the Opera House.

"Simply routine," he explained as we strolled along one of the city's grand avenues on our way to the Stadt Park. "When I don't have to think about where I'll be staying, eating, etc., it helps me concentrate on the business at hand. I don't want, need or like surprises."

"Boy, have you hired the wrong crew," I thought to myself, glancing back at Buddy who'd stopped to toss bread crumbs to a flock of fluttering pigeons while the rest of us passed through ornate wrought-iron gates into the city's central park.

On a scale of parks, Vienna's Stadt Park tends to be on the small side, with a poor excuse for a river coursing through a concrete channel along its eastern border, and a large, duck-filled pond at its centre. Its long, treed alleyways and islands of flowerbeds however, do manage to provide sanctuary from the noisy traffic of the nearby Ring Road. Scattered throughout its cloistered spaces, statues of various famous composers keep watch. Before reading the identifying plaque, one is tempted to hazard a guess as to whose likeness is being portrayed, but unlike the multitude of pigeons relieving themselves in the park, one is usually wide of the mark.

Ben seemed a trifle nerved that morning, when asked to fake a walk along a leave-covered path. "I'm not a big fan of this stuff, you know," he complained.

"I promise it will be painless. I'm going to position myself here," I told him, pointing to a long row of benches bordering one side of the treed pathway. "I want you to start maybe twenty yards up the path, walk towards me, pass by on my right but don't look at the camera. I will pan with you. Just follow the path to the edge of the pond until I say Cut. Is that alright?"

Nodding somewhat impatiently, he sauntered off to his starting point.

"One last thing," I called after him. "See that old lady feeding the ducks at the edge of the pond?" He nodded. "Well as you pass by, I want you to casually shove her into the water."

"Nah..." he answered without missing a beat. "I think it would be better if I just tossed her hat in and kept walking."

"Your call."

A half hour later, we had our "walk" without the lady in question having to sue the Canadian Opera Association. Abandoning the pond for a quiet spot near the river, we set up for a brief interview to ask Ben how it felt to be on the road so much.

"I'm booked solid for the next year and a half in major opera houses around the world. Obviously I miss my family and I try to get home as often as possible. But I have to take advantage of the gift I have been given while it's still intact."

That afternoon we had the pleasure of witnessing just how intact that gift truly was. Right after lunch at an Italian restaurant near his hotel, a half-hour was spent gathering footage of Ben leisurely strolling through Vienna's main pedestrian mall, admiring St. Stephen's Church and the many baroque buildings nearby. From there it was a short walk to the studio apartment owned by fellow tenor Placido Domingo, where many fellow opera stars rehearse when in Vienna. It was a sparsely furnished flat, with the main room containing little more than a grand piano and several chairs. Resting his hefty frame on the piano bench, Ben began to tickle the ivories, explaining how he often finds normal practice somewhat boring.

"Doing the scales helps to limber up your vocal cords but I prefer a little boogie-woogie," he said, offering a quick run up and down the keyboard before breaking into a raunchy number to accompany himself. "Makes for a lot more fun."

With the piano taking up almost the entire room, I was forced to jam myself between the end of the keyboard and the wall to capture the moment. Squatting down level with Ben's beefy hands, I had just enough space to manage an occasional tilt up to his ruddy face.

"Ready any time you are," he signalled with a smile, before launching into the first verse of *Amazing Grace*. Listening to the sheer power and range of his voice singing one of the most moving songs of all time, I could feel my forearms starting to sprout goosebumps. So moving was this private concert, it almost turned me into an opera fan… But almost, as we all know, doesn't really count. And besides, *Amazing Grace* is not part of any opera I've ever heard of.

❋

That evening saw us all dressed to the nines, although few patrons could appreciate it given that we were perched in our own private box on the third level of the Opera House. Once we were set up to record the action, there was time to observe the glittering members of Viennese society making sure they were seen taking their places. With the exception of boogie-boarding in the waters off Biarritz, schussing down the slopes of Swiss, German or Austrian Alps, or hiking along trails in the Dolomites of southern Tyrol, there are not many things I can tolerate for four hours without a break. So it came as no surprise that *Lohengrin,* even with its two intermissions, was well beyond my comfort zone. The audience on the other hand was spellbound throughout the performance, granting Ben and the troupe six or seven curtain calls, even though the last two seemed to have a sense of obligation to them.

Outside at the stage door, we briefly filmed Ben being mobbed by a gaggle of squealing autograph hunters, before following him as he walked off into the rainy Vienna night. A half-hour later, we were back at the same restaurant where we'd dined for lunch. But this time, instead of mixing with the locals, we were escorted upstairs to a private dining room that looked like it had been laid out for a royal banquet. Taking our seats directly across from Ben and his leading soprano, Buddy and I nursed our aperitifs as other members of the cast slowly trickled in. If the food and drink at other post-performance locations are as exquisite as they were here, I suspect I know why opera stars tend to be on the large size. The casual, intimate atmosphere was made even more enjoyable when the producer told us that no filming would be necessary, leaving us free to knock off and relax. By the time the dinner party broke up just after one-thirty, both Buddy and I were considerably "relaxed." Following the exchange of goodbyes with Ben and his guests, we wandered down a cobble stone street to the subway station, the yellowish lamplight reflecting off the wet bricks making it seem as though music from the Third Man theme should be playing in the background.

Quite the Night at the Opera | 157

*

"I'm very sorry gentlemen, butI'm afraid the bar closed at midnight," was not exactly what we wanted to hear from the balding, be-spectacled clerk at the hotel reception desk. "If you'd like, I can sell you a couple of beers to take to your rooms," he added.

A quick glance between us confirmed this idea appealed to no one.

"Isn't there any place around here that stays open later?" I asked.

The red neon sign above the doorway and the glowing hearts in the windows made it pretty obvious what kind of establishment we were about to enter, but just to be on the safe side, I stopped Buddy before we ventured in.

"We limit ourselves to one beer okay? Two tops… And only if they don't want ten bucks a pop for the bloody thing. Got it?"

I could tell his nod was insincere, but thirst overruled any further objection.

"What's forty-eight Schilling in real money?" I asked, handing Buddy the drink menu. "I think that works out to about four bucks a beer. Not exactly cheap, but doable."

Less than a minute after our drinks were placed in front of us on the long bar, two women slithered out of a darkened booth to join us. Hoping pure English would grant us some peace, I made no attempt to understand when one of the perfumed ladies requested a drink in German.

"Sorry, but you're barking up the wrong tree," I said, belatedly aware of the potential connotation of my remark. "He's the guy with the dough tonight," I told her, gesturing towards Buddy with my half-drained glass. Despite the previous warning, Buddy's response was to wave for the bartender. A bad feeling washed over me when a moment later, two small bottles of Champagne known as "Piccolos," were plunked down on the counter.

"It might not be a bad idea to find out what these things cost you know," I suggested. "Better to ask now before ending up with a huge bill."

Nodding in agreement but refusing to take any action, Buddy made it clear it was ultimately his call. As it was, I had other matters to contend with, namely fending off the feigned interest my new would -be partner was trying to bestow upon me.

"Excuse me for a second," I interrupted. "I know you're just working the crowd... and it's part of the... job to chat with clients. It's just that I'm not terribly interested. We've just come off a long night and only want to..."

"I am just talking to you," she interjected, acting as if affronted by the suggestion it was anything more.

Not wishing to cause a scene, I turned to look at her for the first time and simply nodded.

"Okay, fair enough... So let's just say I'm not much in the mood for talking tonight. We just came in for a beer and that's all. Can we just leave it at that?"

Had it been left at that, the evening would likely have taken a different course. But as it happened it was a slow night and she had no intention of letting me off the hook so easily. For awhile she was content to simply drain the contents of her flute, starting anew only when Buddy agreed to order a second round.

"Don't you want to talk to me?" she cooed, leaning on my shoulder and sending a whiff of her potent perfume. "Don't you like me?"

"Yeah, sure I do... Why don't we run off and get married? Lady, I don't even know you, so what possible reason do I have to like or dislike you?"

Accustomed to dealing with reluctant customers, she switched tactics.

"Why are you here in Vienna?"

"We came to film at the opera," I answered, immediately sensing my mistake in giving her an opening to extend the discussion.

"Ahhhh... The opera," she sighed. "I have lived in Vienna for nearly ten years and have never been to the opera."

There was an urge to tell her she hadn't missed much, especially if it was for a four-hour endurance test, but instead I just cast a glance over at Buddy. Somewhat in horror, I watched as he interrupted the discussion with his own new acquaintance to signal the hovering bartender to deliver yet another round.

"Buddy," I called out over the in-house music. "What are you doing? Did you just order another new round for them? It's almost three-thirty. We've got a long drive home tomorrow. Don't you think we should call it a night?"

Judging from his glassy-eyed response, the idea was not a top priority. Keenly aware I couldn't handle another drop, I took the initiative to press the bartender for the bill once the next round had been delivered. Undoubtedly sensing what was to come, my heretofore talkative partner suddenly decided it time to bid me adieu and returned to her table with her latest acquisition.

Several minutes later, with bill in hand, the bartender gestured to Buddy for a signature.

"I'll take it," I told him.

Despite the fact it was dark and the charges in Austrian Schilling, it didn't take long to figure out something was drastically wrong.

"Buddy," I said drolly.

"What's up?" he slurred, pulling himself free from an embrace.

"I'm not a hundred percent sure I've added this up right, but I have a feeling the bill is $600.00"

"What?" he shrieked, jerking himself upright and almost sending his partner to the floor. "Are you friggin' kidding me? Let me see that," he demanded, grabbing the bill out of my hand.

"Look… It's in Schilling," I repeated. "But at twelve Schilling to the dollar, it's just under $600.00."

"That's impossible," he fumed, demanding I re-calculate. But after several attempts, the assessment remained painfully accurate.

"What did the bartender tell you these Piccolos cost?"

"He said they were the same as the beer," Buddy offered meekly.

"On what planet does champagne cost the same as a beer? Didn't you think that a bit odd? How many of them did you order? We only had three beers each, so that's still only about…"

"I had five beers," Buddy admitted.

"Okay, five, then my three is eight… Times four or five bucks is still only $40.00. How many champagnes did you order?"

"I can't remember. Maybe six? Three for each."

"Oh Jeez," I moaned, handing him back the bill.

In the meantime, the bartender had remained at a safe distance, letting us absorb the shock.

"How you like to pay?" he said, sensing we'd reached a plateau.

For the next fifteen minutes things did not go well, as our demands for an explanation on the exorbitant bill were stonewalled with claims of having informed Buddy of the true cost of the Piccolos, now revealed to be $40.00 a bottle.

"That still only adds up to around $300.00," I said with thinly disguised venom.

"The conversation with the ladies is also part of bill."

"But we didn't ask for that."

"But you buy them drinks."

"And?"

"That means you interested."

"Interested in what? Getting stiffed for boring conversation? I think not, lad. We came in here for a lousy beer. And now you hand us a bill for $600.00. There's no way we're paying that."

"I call police when you not pay."

"Call the friggin' police, then," Buddy snarled. "And while you're at it, call the tourism board so we can let them know how businesses in Vienna treat foreign customers."

With the gauntlet thrown and battle lines drawn, we withdrew to a back booth to discuss further strategy. What with Buddy's having freely agreed to keep the drinks flowing, it was clear we didn't have much of a defense. All the same, I sensed it was a bluff. The bill had been padded in the belief neither of us would notice until sobering up the next morning. It was simply a question of who would back down first.

"Just between you and me, I think you're screwed," I said to Buddy, casting a sneer at the two ladies who'd been "entertaining" us. "It's his word against yours that you weren't told the right price, but maybe we can bluff this dink into at least reducing it. He said he's called the cops but I'd be willing to push it. Shit, let's go to jail for the night just to bring this out into the open. I get the feeling it's not the first time something like this has happened. It's too slick."

Shortly before the boys in blue arrived, I returned to the bar, hoping to reach a compromise. It turned out to be a bad idea. Having smelled victory, the bartender rejected any claim of a misunderstanding and reiterated his demand for payment in full. It was not an encouraging development when two policemen and a policewoman entered the bar and were warmly greeted by the bartender and other patrons. As the more sober of the pair, I took on the task of trying to explain the evening's events to the policewoman. She listened somewhat sympathetically, but before moving over to hear what the bartender was telling her partners, she admonished me with the remark, "Please do not try to tell me that you didn't know what kind of place this is."

Once armed with both sides of the story she attempted to negotiate a settlement but the bartender stood firm. Returning with a glum face, she kept it simple. "I am sorry. You must pay. If you do not you must come with us."

"What do we have to lose?" I said to Buddy privately, reiterating my willingness to be locked up, which had now evolved to an outright eagerness. "It will be more of an embarrassment to them than to us. I still think they're bluffing."

While Buddy was contemplating his options, an older man, who'd been enjoying the proceedings from the far end of the bar, decided to enter the fray. But before he could get out more than a few words, I quickly cut him off, accusing him of being nothing more than a drunken "El Pimpo" which was a little misplaced seeing we were in Vienna. This little display of temperament however, used up the last of the policewoman's patience. Realizing Buddy's wallet held the key to resolving the situation, she issued an ultimatum.

"Don't buy it, Buddy," I urged.

But Buddy was wavering. Citing the need to return to Frankfurt early, he finally folded, pulling out his credit card and reluctantly handing it to the policewoman.

"Ahh man," I said with genuine disappointment. "They're hosing you. This whole thing reeks of complicity."

Handing Buddy his receipt with a pained expression, the policewoman excused herself and followed her partners out the door. Before our own departure, we made sure to leave the bartender, the ladies, and the silenced drunk with a few choice English phrases to contemplate. Obviously able to understand words not usually heard in polite company, the bartender chose not to risk his victory by escalating the situation, simply telling us to "get out while you still can."

Although it wasn't my finances that had taken a beating, on the way back to the hotel I felt the need to share in licking our wounds by offering up a series of should-haves, would-haves, could-haves. A few minutes later, pausing to watch Buddy wobble down the hallway as I attempted to find the slot for my own card key, all that came to mind was "I told you I didn't like opera."

CHAPTER 20

Women and children first?

It was on the afternoon of January 30th, 1945, that the luxury liner, Wilhelm Gustloff, sailed out of the Baltic port of Gotenhafen with over 10,000 people on board. The Nazis' pride of the seas, the Gustloff had previously seen service as a cruise liner, hospital ship, troop transport and Marine residence before being commissioned to help evacuate refugees fleeing from the advancing Red Army. Having started its mission in East Prussia on January 21st, as part of Operation Hannibal, the ship was in Gotenhafen to pick up more civilian refugees, military personnel and wounded soldiers, with the intention of ferrying them on to what was thought to be safe haven in the distant port of Kiel.

Having made the decision to travel the fastest route, the crew of the Gustloff set a course further out to sea, rather than staying close to shore to avoid submarine activity. As it happened, its departure from Gotenhafen had fallen on what happened to be the twelfth anniversary of Hitler's rise to power, and many of the crew that night had been listening to "the Führer" deliver a radio broadcast to his "Volk"(People). At 9:15, in the middle of Hitler's speech, three of four torpedoes fired from a Soviet submarine struck the Gustloff approximately twenty-three sea miles off shore. Although twelve hundred people were rescued, the stricken vessel sank in less than an hour, condemning an estimated 9000 lives to a watery grave. It was the worst loss of life in a maritime catastrophe in history.

On board the Wilhelm Gustloff that night was an eighteen-year-old, ship's purser's assistant by the name of Heinz Schön. Fifty-five years after the event, Schön sat down in his living room in Bad Salzuflen to once again relate details of that terrible night. Framed by a model of the lost ship and an array of books he'd written on the subject over the years, Schön began his saga by describing how he had been in his bunk listening to Hitler's speech when the first torpedo hit. Thrown to the floor by its impact, he somehow managed to make it to the main deck where panic and chaos had broken out. With the damaged ship listing badly, many passengers struggling to reach the lifeboats were sliding off the ice-coated deck into the frigid water. Knocked overboard by an errant wave, Schön was lucky enough to be rescued by a nearby lifeboat. One less fortunate casualty of the catastrophe seems to have been the credo of "women and children first." When all was said and done, it turned out that all four captains of the Gustloff, including co-captain Friedrich Petersen, were among those rescued, having somehow clambered aboard one of the first lifeboats launched.

Although deeply affected by his experiences aboard the Wilhelm Gustloff, Schön had gone on to become an archivist, publicist, theatre director and author, professions that were all somehow linked to that fateful night on the Ostsee. Listening to him describe events, one couldn't help wondering how he had reconciled the fact that a considerable number of the crew had survived while so many people had perished.

"*At some point, did it simply become a scenario of 'every man for himself'*" - was a question that begged asking and would have been posed had the producer not warned me about interfering.

"No extraneous questions," he said when Herr Schön was out of the room. "I don't want to derail the interview by asking something he might view as accusatory."

"But isn't that part of the story too?"

"Certainly it has a bearing on the whole event, but I haven't read all he's written on the subject, so I can't speculate on how he's dealt with that aspect, or what degree of guilt or remorse he feels… if any. Leave it alone."

Despite my strongly disagreeing with her strategy of not wanting to "upset" Herr Schön, the question remained unanswered, suspended in a fog of speculation as to how any of us might have reacted on such a night.

CHAPTER 21

Healing Waters

The entrepreneurial venture we were on our way to visit, first opened its doors to the public in the mid 1980's. The "wonder" it promulgated at the time was the alleged mending powers of an underground spring in a disused slate mine, the entrance to which just happened to be located directly under a hotel and restaurant complex owned by the man who had discovered it. In order to help his fellow man, a procedure was developed, whereby for a nominal fee one could enter the premises, breathe the mist, drink the water, and go forth to spread the word about a recovery, a renaissance of spirit, or whatever other improvements happened to occur. Promotional material was careful never to describe the experience as a miracle; that assessment was left to zealous patrons. Instead it was the word of mouth that quickly made the spa popular, so much so that management was soon forced to start running "treatments" in shifts.

On the morning of our arrival, a generous portion of clientele was already lined up in the reception area. Many appeared to be pensioners, with some either in wheelchairs, on crutches or pushing "rollers." One couldn't help noticing a few scowls present in the crowd, suggesting that some individuals had been dragged there by a well-meaning but insistent spouse. For guests like ourselves who were there on their inaugural visit, it came as a bit of a shock when a sonorous voice crackled to life on the sound system. Wafting reassuringly throughout the waiting area, it stressed the sensibility of not expecting too much the first time, informing patrons that the "powers" of the waters were limited and not everyone might benefit in the same way. "Some pray tell," the soothing voice went on, "may not notice any improvement in their condition whatsoever, but not to worry for that percentage was extremely low and could easily be resolved through repeat visits." The announcement was reinforced as several of those waiting could be overheard boasting about a third, fifth or even tenth visit to the "wonder" cave.

Far from being restless, the current crowd simply waited patiently for its turn to enter. As soon as one group exited, - suitably far enough away to discourage unwanted queries from those in line - the next was marched in through a heavy metal door and trotted down a long neon-lit tunnel carved into the mountain. A short time later, a uniformed guide pulled Buddy, the producer, and myself out of the line-up, explaining that she was there to lead us separately into the cave. As there was no need for extra sound or direction, it had previously been agreed that I would be the only one taken in, pun intended. Once outfitted with a hardhat to protect me from the jagged rocks in the narrow tunnel, I bid my colleagues adieu and followed the guide into the passageway.

The cave turned out to be a lot smaller than I expected, perhaps forty feet across and fifteen to twenty feet high. A sign off to one side indicated a temperature of eight degrees Celsius but I didn't need any visual confirmation to realize I was not dressed for the occasion. Damp and cool enough to see one's breath, the underground amphitheatre was the perfect location for the warm fleece jacket I had neglected to bring.

After a quick survey to determine the best place to capture the action, I selected a rocky outcrop overlooking what appeared to be some sort of shrine. No sooner had I scrambled to the top of a stone-strewn slope, the guide announced she was leaving to fetch the next group. Although the bulk of my attention was focused on setting up before their arrival, I couldn't ignore how strange it felt to suddenly be there alone. Things turned even stranger when seconds later, the lights were suddenly extinguished, pitching me into total darkness.

"Thanks… just what I needed," I said aloud, hoping there might be a hidden in-house microphone that would relay my thoughts to the technical wizard responsible for the blackout. Holding my mini-flashlight in my mouth, I was making final adjustments to the camera just as the lights fluttered back to life and a squeaky door announced the group's arrival. Quickly panning to catch the first of the twenty bewildered-looking cure seekers filing into the cavern, I watched as the guide had them form a semi-circle around the little shrine directly below the source of the water.

From my perch in the upper reaches of the rocky temple, I listened as the guide began her introductory speech, with the enthusiasm one might expect from someone who had probably delivered it a thousand times. The parishioners were then instructed to take hold of the hand of the person on either side of them and close their eyes. This last request seemed rather pointless as seconds later, the guide decreed that the spooky, yellow lights be turned off, plunging us back into darkness. Except for the occasional nervous cough, sneeze or whisper, - "Johnny, was that you?... Cut it out!" - the only perceptible sound was the gurgling of the underground stream.

While still cloaked in darkness, which was making for stunning television, the guide began to chant softly, urging everyone to join in. Although the initial response was not overwhelming, the group soon found its confidence. But just as they seemed to be hitting their stride, the guide interrupted to propose that all participants now begin several minutes of utter silence, to concentrate on the healing powers of the cave. Well on the way to my own oblivion by this time, I had to stifle the urge to shout out, "Hey, what's wrong with you people?" Despite the fact the darkness would have concealed my identity, I held my tongue for fear of instigating a volley of answers. - *It's my asthma... I have a bum leg... Psoriasis is hell.* -

Suddenly the silence was broken with the request to, "Please collect your thoughts and keep your eyes closed until the lights are turned back on. We shall be leaving the cave soon as overexposure to the radiation from the rocks surrounding the healing water can be unhealthy."

"*Awfully nice of them to let me know,*" I grumbled, as the lights came up, and the troupe was transported back to reality, a destination that just happened to require passing through the hotel dining room, where hot coffee and an expensive menu awaited those with the need for nourishment while pondering the benefits of the healing mist.

Left to my own devices to pack up, I traipsed back through the tunnel alone, still grappling with the fact that nobody had deemed it necessary to warn that my reproductive capabilities might be endangered by remaining in the temple. Half way back I ran into an incoming group. Nodding hello to the guide, I wondered why none of the staff seemed overly perturbed about their own repeated exposure, suggesting it was perhaps simply a convenient way of limiting the stay and cramming more people through on a given day.

Back in the crowded restaurant, I was eager to eavesdrop on those clients in the process of sharing their impressions. That quest was delayed however, by the producer's order to prepare for an interview he had arranged with the complex's owner. As the man in question took his seat in the shade of a large tree in the hotel's courtyard, his confident demeanour made it clear he had done this before. Adept at countering questions aimed at debunking the cave's healing powers before they were even asked, he began by telling the producer, "Skeptics are everywhere. I cannot offer you a scientific, foolproof explanation why the place has the effect it has on some people. You must ask the customers themselves. You have seen how many people have traveled here. That is largely a result of recommendations from previous visitors. That in itself should silence critics."

Convinced that he was likely to hear more of the same tune, the producer artfully brought the interview to an early end. Once the manager had excused himself to attend to other business, we decided to follow his advice and cajoled several elderly couples into voicing their thoughts.

"I heard a story where one woman recovered her sight after rinsing her eye in the healing water," one guest stated earnestly.

"I heard of a man throwing away his crutch after being in the cave," said another.

"My blood pressure dropped dramatically," explained a third. "I no longer had pain in my neck."

"My rash cleared up."

"I no longer have headaches"

"I used to be insane." Well not quite, but from the comments emitted, it was clear that misery did indeed love company. Add to that the human trait of not wanting to be seen as one of the "incurable losers," and it was no surprise that none of those approached had anything negative to say about their experience.

In retrospect, I can't say the visit was a total waste of time. Close... but not total. After all, the mere opportunity to document man's capacity for helping his fellow man has to count for something. I prefer to think of it as having done my part to provide evidence to future generations that intelligent, caring beings once walked the face of the earth, but somehow never quite managed to find their way to this sleepy little town in southern Germany.

CHAPTER 22

Through the Mill

I can't put my finger on it precisely, but there's definitely something inspiring about standing on a catwalk fifty feet above a factory floor, looking down at the main section of a paper mill in full operation. Perhaps it had something to do with the sheer enormity of the place, which gave new meaning to the word immense and made you feel as though you were staring into the engine room of the Titanic.

The panorama witnessed that morning was part of an introductory tour designed to demonstrate how trees are turned into paper. Even though the bulk of the production process took place inside a machine the length of a football field, it was still interesting to watch the preliminary phase where trees were stripped of their branches and bark, and fed into the colossus to be ground up, boiled, stirred, and mixed with a variety of chemicals. Combined with the high volume of noise present, the grand scale of the operation made it all quite overwhelming. Despite having details shouted to us by our guide, the procedure that ultimately resulted in huge rolls of paper emerging from the far end, each the size of a small trailer, remained beyond comprehension. One thing that *was* retained from the hour-long tour was a renewed value of being more cognizant about the use of paper in general.

But beyond the fact the process was loud, hot, smelly and enormously impressive, there's not much more to say about the three days spent at the plant in the northern Germany.

Seeing that it was my first time in that part of the country, and the shoot was split up by the weekend, I decided to spend part of my free time exploring the lay of the land. Initially, I'd intended to do so on Saturday, but those plans changed at the last minute when Jerome, the camera assistant, asked whether I'd be interested in traveling to the Dutch city of Gröningen. Being able to experience another culture within a few hours drive from wherever you might happen to be in Europe, had long been one of my favourite past times, so it didn't take much to get me to agree.

We set off early, looking forward to taking in some of the Dutch architecture and countryside en route. Shortly after crossing the German-Dutch border however, Jerome let it be known that rather than lazily gawking at the passing scenery, he preferred our getting to Gröningen as soon as possible, in order to visit one of Holland's infamous coffee shops. Despite not having partaken in the "evil weed" since the early 80's, I had nothing against dropping in to check out one of the legal dens of iniquity.

Once in the city centre, there was a wide selection of shops to choose from. The one we ended up inflicting with our presence gave you the feeling of having just stumbled into a friend's shabby living room. Sprawled out on worn-out sofas and chairs, other guests were in various stages of euphoria as they listened to sixties-era music. But with no timetable to adhere to and a previous agreement we would not risk transporting any "stuff" back across the border, I could sit back and watch Jerome enjoy the fruits of his labour, as he began to morph in the comfort of a cushiony bean bag chair.

Following a brief tour of the city, which included grabbing some "munchies" at a Turkish Kebab Shop, we departed just after three. Taking full advantage of the country's lenient drug laws, Jerome finished the last few hits of his remaining joint just as we were approaching the German border. From the time we had left the coffee shop in Gröningen, Jerome's voice had started to sound like a 45rpm record being played at 33, with someone occasionally leaning on the turntable to distort it. Once we crossed back into Germany, just for the fun of it, I began responding to his continuing litany of comments in a similar manner. It took a bit of practice to slow down my own tempo but by the time we arrived back at our hotel an hour or so later, the power of suggestion had left me feeling stoned out my own gourd.

*

Sunday morning brought a solo flight into countryside about as flat as you can possibly get. The further west I drove, the more the terrain yielded to a series of small villages, with each street lined with identical stone houses, identical manicured lawns and identical Mercedes parked in the driveways. What made up for this rather tacky display of modern civilization were the many canals, thatched-roof cottages, and treed-arched alleyways threading through the intervening landscape.

Later that afternoon, having looped back eastward, I was cruising along a narrow country lane when my attention was caught by an elevated structure that at first glance resembled some sort of high-tech aqueduct. In the midst of speculating how and why such an object had been erected in the middle of a vast, seemingly endless vegetable field, my thoughts were interrupted when a sleek, bullet train streaked in one side of my peripheral vision and out the other. I'd heard about Germany's magnetic levitation train before, but never actually seen it. Given the speed with which the Trans Rapid had just come and gone, one could say that status hadn't ended.

The next morning I awoke to learn that our schedule had been altered. Rather than continuing to film at the mill as expected, we were now scheduled to travel to the nearby town of Lathen to visit the headquarters of the same train I'd seen the day before. What the Trans Rapid had to do with the production of paper was not explained, and I didn't ask, not wanting to jeopardize the chance to see the unit up close by quibbling about minor details.

Much to my delight, within an hour of our arrival we were on board said unit, speeding along the test track at close to 300 kilometres an hour. Sitting there, marvelling at the technical perfection that allowed the world to flash by without so much as rippling my complimentary glass of mineral water, it was easy to be lulled into a false sense of security, with any thoughts of impending disaster the furthest thing from my mind. That disaster would arrive seven years later. Thanks to what was determined to have been a series of catastrophic errors in judgement, the Trans Rapid slammed into a maintenance wagon that was parked on the single track. Despite the fact the collision occurred nowhere near the train's top speed, it was enough to take twenty-three passengers to an early grave. There but for the grace…

CHAPTER 23

Medicinal Magic

Some have cited the origin as low blood pressure, while others simply viewed it as psychosomatic. My partner, Isabelle, has repeatedly referred to it as "sissiness," until I bluffed her into believing there was no such word in English. The actual blame probably lays with a variety of factors, but whatever the root cause, the fact is for as long as I can remember I've always felt queasy at the sight of blood, especially my own. Even the routine task of having a blood test can quickly devolve into a spell of light-headedness, dizziness and in some cases near blackout.

Up to that point, I'd been fortunate in never being confronted with the prospect of a medical shoot. That all changed in the late 90's when Buddy called to inform me about a job offer to film what he claimed would be a "minor" operation in Hamburg.

Other than as a patient, this was my first encounter with an operating theatre, and I was grateful that my initiation was going to involve what I assumed would be one of those "non-invasive" endeavours. Whereas a smarter person might have inquired beforehand, I didn't bother to ask for details. As a result, it wasn't until we were scrubbing up in the surgeons' changing rooms, well past the point of no return, that I learned we were about to film the removal of the cancerous portion of someone's esophagus and see it replaced with a section taken from their large intestine.

As with any hospital operating room, one of the top priorities is assuring the highest possible standard of cleanliness. One of the facets of maintaining that level is to make sure all participants are covered from head to toe in green surgical gowns, supplemented by gauze face masks and plastic shoe covers. As we stood waiting to enter the theatre dressed in that garb, it struck me as a contradiction that no prior inspection or cleansing of the camera, tripod or monitor had been requested.

"How do they know we didn't just come from a bat cave?" I asked Buddy.

"What are you talking about?" he answered, momentarily distracted by one of the nurses.

"Our equipment. Nobody checked to see if it was… I don't know… contaminated."

"Contaminated with what?"

"Bat shit… Who knows? Nobody asked us anything about the gear. Don't you find that a bit weird?"

"What's weird is what made you think of bat shit."

"I don't know. Everything else is so spotless and thoroughly checked, why not the tripod and monitor?"

"Maybe bacteria can't survive on a piece of equipment long enough to be dangerous."

"Okay, maybe you're right. Let's just hope there are no clumps of you know what wedged into the feet of the tripod."

Once inside the operating theatre, we were told to stand off to one side with strict instructions not to touch anything. From this vantage point we watched as a gurney with the patient was rolled in and the doctors and their assistants followed an efficient procedure for their final preparations. Having expected to be briefed on what I could and couldn't do, it came as a bit of a shock when the operation got underway without so much as a word in my direction.

"Hey," I whispered to Buddy. "This is it? Are they expecting us to film from here? All I can see is a row of backs."

"Do what you can for now," he shrugged. "We can't interrupt the operation. You should have cleared this up before we got in here."

Holding back my rebuttal as to whose responsibility that was, I waited for a natural break in the procedure before catching an assistant nurse's attention. After a brief discussion, one of the assistant surgeons nodded his permission, and the nurse guided me to a small, three-step ladder she'd placed directly behind the chief surgeon, gesturing that I could stand on it to shoot down over his shoulder. From here I peered down into a conglomeration of tubes, clamps and instruments protruding from a glistening mass of black and white entrails. The "minor" operation that Buddy had so inadequately described had involved opening the patient up from just above the groin to her upper chest. But as luck would have it, Shakespeare had been right, "Future imaginings were worse than present dangers" and the sight of blood did not seem to bother me.

For the next half hour I kept busy following various aspects of the operation and the people performing it. At one point, I happened to glance down into the core of the patient with my naked eye. Rather than fainting, I was transfixed by the sight, wishing I'd majored in anatomy so I'd have some idea what all these brightly coloured objects actually were. Utterly awed by the chance to see inside a life, it took a purposeful throat clearing from one of the nurses to snap me back to the task at hand.

Just into the third hour of the scheduled five-hour operation, Buddy indicated we had enough material. With a simple "Danke" and "Aufwiedersehen" to the staff, we packed up and quietly made our exit. Still dressed in our scrubs, we retreated to a small room down the hall, where two physicians who'd been assisting in the OR were now having coffee.

"I hope you were able to get what you needed," the older of the two said.

"More than enough, thank you," Buddy answered. "We've got some great stuff. We really appreciate your allowing us into your theatre. It was really fascinating to watch."

"Oh, you're more than welcome. It's not everyday we get to be TV stars," he chuckled before shifting his chair to discuss something with his colleague. As we quietly finished our drinks, I couldn't resist the temptation to ask Buddy if he'd like to see me "raise some eyebrows".

"You're not gonna start with that bat shit stuff again are you?" he said with a frown.

"No, no… Although I am still curious about that."

Rising to the challenge, I stood up with one hand clasped to my chest, patting around my empty pockets, before leaning over to address one of the assistant doctors.

"Excuse me, you wouldn't happen to have seen my pen around here anywhere would you? I know I had it in the operating room."

CHAPTER 24

Bad Beer & Bologna

One of the most enjoyable benefits of living and working in Europe is the tremendous variety of culinary treats you are exposed to. One needn't be a gourmet to appreciate the diversity and one of the best places to take advantage of it is when you're on the road. That is especially true if that road happens to lead to Italy. Having had the good fortune to visit that country on numerous occasions, our expectations were understandably tweaked upon hearing we'd been booked for a shoot in the city of Bologna.

To avoid the hassles as well as the costs of flying with a load of equipment, Buddy and I decided to cover the nine hundred kilometres by car, thereby providing both time and opportunity to brush up on my non-existent knowledge of the city. Home to over 385,000 residents, a considerable number of whom are students at what is purported to be the oldest university in the world, Bologna was at one time the fifth largest city in Europe; after Cordoba, Paris, Venice and Florence. As the capital of the Emilia-Romagna region of northern Italy, it was widely known as a trading centre during the time of the Medicis and other wealthy families. Many of the city's towers and lengthy colonnades built during that "golden age" still exist today, creating an impressive panorama of what life must have been like back then; that is if one can ignore the annoying clatter of mopeds echoing down the narrow cobblestone streets.

Our first night in the city found us strolling along one of the city's many elegant avenues in search of a decent place to dine.

"Man oh man… Check those guys out," I said to Buddy, pointing to two swarthy-looking characters parked beneath a red neon sign marking the entrance to 'Ravina's.' "If you ever get tired of life in Videoville, I know where you can get a job."

"What are you talking about?"

"The jackets… Those guys look identical to what you wore to the carpet salesmen party. You can dig it out of mothballs and apply for a job there. The moths probably haven't gone anywhere near it."

Despite our reservations, we decided to give the place a try, ignoring the denigrating glances from the two waiter/guards as we entered.

"Do you suppose they're dressed in white cause you have to be somewhat disturbed to eat here?" I asked, as we accepted two leather bound menus and ordered a bottle of Chianti.

"With thirty marks for a salad, I'd say we're heading in the right direction," Buddy replied, perusing the list of dishes with a frown.

Despite the fact we could count at least six jacketed waiters floating around the scarcely-populated room, it took forever and a day for someone to bring our wine.

"Forget the salad," I told Buddy under the gaze of a grim-faced wine steward. "I'm going for the Schnitzel with donkey spit."

"The what?"

"Page two, near the bottom… 'burro salvia.' I suspect it's a typo but I'm gonna play dumb and see what I get."

"I'm too hungry for guessing games, so I'm gonna go

for the meat platter," Buddy announced, snapping shut his menu.

"Don't quote me on this, but I think that's just an assortment of meat. I don't think it comes with anything else."

"At 36 Marks it better," he said, taking a second look.

Twenty minutes later, both meals arrived on silver platters with matching domes. Following a pretentious ceremonial lifting of the lids, Buddy's was revealed to contain three slabs of grey-coloured meat garnished by a blob or two of tartar sauce.

"What do they expect me to do with this?" he sneered, poking at it suspiciously with his fork. "I'm not gonna eat this."

"You better do something with it. The guy who just brought it wasn't impressed with your reaction. He's probably on the phone right now calling his cousin, Luigi to come take care of you."

To my own eternal disappointment, the "burro salvia" turned out to be sage-laced butter atop a schnitzel the size and texture of a gym mat. Despite our unfortunate selections, both of us managed to endure the cuisine, not to mention the snotty looks and choice Italian commentary offered by the waiters as we left the premises.

※

The next morning, as we were setting up in a small, nondescript conference room at the client's office, a secretary who'd been watching me adjust a light for the sixth or seventh time, remarked, "I guess you must really love your work." Already plugged into automatic pilot for the set-up phase, the comment barely registered and for a moment I had to struggle for an answer.

"To be honest, I've never really thought about it before," I stammered. "I guess it's just ingrained in me to try and make the shot look the best it can."

As it was, any further conversation was cut short by the arrival of the company's CEO, a well-dressed Italian, who appeared to be anything but a button-down businessman. Given his laid-back attitude and considerable expertise, the interview went off without a hitch. That afternoon we were back in the city centre hoping to capture some local colour that could be edited into the interview.

First stop was one of the city's tallest towers, an impressive brick structure with a wooden stairway that ran up the inside of all four of its walls. Hoping to grab a shot of the city's skyline from the tower's observation deck, we started the long climb up the creaking steps. A long time sufferer from a fear of stairs, Buddy was less than thrilled to accompany me, especially given that I'd asked him to carry the tripod. To make matters worse, the higher we ascended, the more the steps tended to slant inwards, creating the precarious sensation that one could easily tumble into the inner court at any inattentive moment. Able to scale faster than my tremulous partner, I soon had gained enough distance to watch Buddy on the opposite side, grunting and groaning his way upwards; a process made more difficult by the fact he couldn't hold on to the railing and tripod at the same time.

"I'll never forgive you for this," Buddy growled as he emerged on to the windy platform only to find that the gangway running around its outer edge was too narrow to set up the tripod. "Never. *You* can haul the bloody thing back down. Either that or it goes down on its own."

Fortunately, for Buddy's sake, visits to other sites that afternoon proved to be much less cumbersome. As a reward for his perseverance at the tower, that evening I offered to treat him to a well-earned drink at one of the small kiosks that dotted the ornate stone colonnades. Seated at an outside table, watching the world of Bologna pass us by, I ordered two of what the menu said were "light local birras."

In retrospect, one should have known better than to order a beer in a country renowned for its Chianti, Barolo, Valpolicella and Montepulciano reds, not to mention an equally great assortment of whites.

"Bloody hell, what is in this?" I gasped, spitting out my first mouthful into a nearby gutter, just as a group of moped drivers made a feeble attempt at roaring past. "This can't be beer. You can't even see through it," I noted, holding up the murky liquid to the light.

"Tastes fine to me," Buddy said, wiping away a smudge of foam with the back of his hand.

The disappointing taste should not have come as a surprise. After all, fish and chips go well together, as do spaghetti and meatballs… just not beer and Bologna.

CHAPTER 25

Dracula

I never learned to speak Romanian. There hadn't exactly been much of a call for it back in Winnipeg, but now, peering down at intermittent tracts of civilization in rural Romania, set to land as part of a team to cover the exploits of one Vlad Tepes, I couldn't help wondering whether overcoming that North American aversion to learning a second language might not have been a bad idea. What harm could there be in possessing a few emergency phrases such as, "Where is the nearest hospital? What time does the next train leave?" or "How much is a large beer?"

"What do I really know about Romanians anyways?" I asked myself, as we slowly taxied past a row of rusting maintenance sheds gracing the dull, lifeless landscape of the Bucharest airport. I'd yet to meet a live specimen but general knowledge suggested that the Romanian legacy of being a fair and morally inspiring folk contained a few gaps, - case in point, their having chosen to be on Hitler's side during World War II. Then again, Romanians did deserve credit for having given short shrift to their former despot, Nicholas Ceausescu. Rejecting the norm of letting a tyrant abscond with half the National Treasury and a life of luxury on some distant Riviera, the people of Romania saw to it that events unfolded somewhat differently in December 1989.

"Hey Nick… Yeah… yeah, great to see you too… Say,

can we talk to you for a minute? Over here… Just take a minute. Yeah sure, bring the wife along too." Bang, bang, bang.

Come to think of it, Romania seems to have had its fair share of evil characters over the centuries, a prime example being Vlad Tepes, - or Vlad the Impaler, as he was more affectionately known. A legendary figure from the 15th century, who's believed to have been the model for Bram Stoker's fabled Dracula, over time Tepes has been viewed as both hero and villain by his fellow countrymen. The hero label apparently stemmed from his on-again, off-again role in halting the Ottoman advance into Europe, a feat I assumed had saved me from learning yet another language. The villainy aspect of his legend had grown out of his unique "modus operandi." Unlike your average run-of-the-mill villains who were largely content to use dismemberment, boiling, decapitation or skinning alive to dispense with those who didn't agree with them, Vlad's preferred method had been impalement, depositing the heads of his hapless victims on stakes at the entrance to a city to serve as a decorative warning to any foreign interlopers who dared challenge his reign.

Fortunately times had changed and the only figures waiting to greet me inside the airport terminal that day, were a group of uniformed officials, none of whom appeared to have any intention of doing whatever it was they were supposed to be doing. Searching for something to hold my attention during the long wait in one of the inanimate lines at passport control, my gaze happened to fall to a sign advising that all visitors, excluding Americans, were liable for a $70 visa fee upon entry. A wisp of mild panic brushed past at the realization that I had no funds of any kind at my immediate disposal. Hurriedly scanning the hall, I caught sight of Buddy just as his bald pate disappeared into the crowd on the other side of the control booth.

"Why only Americans?" I asked the rotund immigration officer grimacing at me from within his glass cubicle. Momentarily distracted by patches of hairy skin peeking out between the buttons of his over-stretched shirt, I briefly debated the value of falsely arguing that Americans and Canadians were "basically one and the same." Judging by the fat jerking thumb directing me towards an open doorway, it's a good thing I didn't bother for he was definitely not interested in anything I might have to say, let alone cultural comparisons.

"You pay there," he slurred, before lazily waving the next traveler to advance.

Stopped by another sullen guard at the entrance to a cluttered office that had the ambiance of an auto-wrecking bureau, I was guided to the second of six wooden desks aligned along one wall. I took a seat across from a grey-faced clerk in a matching uniform, hoping I could somehow bluff my way through the predicament. Attempts at light banter were quickly acknowledged as unappreciated and futile, and following a ten minute discussion in fractured English on both sides, I conceded that the case was lost, and gained passage into the country with the aid of a credit card.

Out into "Arrivals," the masses parted like some lost biblical horde as I pushed my heavily-laden cart through the hall and out into a heat as fierce as a bad case of halitosis. Shielding my eyes from the harsh sunlight, I spotted Buddy waving frantically from amidst a small group congregated around what looked to be a battered old VW bus. Closer inspection revealed it to be a battered old Peugeot, crammed to the roof with an assortment of suitcases trunks, and plastic bags.

"Thanks for waiting for me," I said, giving the vehicle a once over. "Is this what we're going to be travelling in the whole week? Where the hell is all our stuff gonna fit?"

"What happened to you?" Buddy wanted to know.

"You owe me $70 'cause I'm not American."

Buddy was about to respond, when he was interrupted by a short, dark-haired man stepping forward out of the group.

"Hi," the man said, extending his hand. "I *am* an American. Name's Rob. I was just telling Buddy here how glad I am to meet another person who speaks English."

"The producer... right?" I replied.

"No sloucher this guy," Rob said, directing me to a couple who'd taken shelter in the shade of a nearby tree.

"Got some people for you to meet... This is Magdalena," Rob said, introducing a short, sixty something woman with coke-bottle glasses and a coiffeur straight out of the 1940's. "She's going to be our translator for the week."

Decked out in a floral-patterned dress that descended to mid-calf, Magdalena was loaded down with a bulge of folders in one arm and a beat-up purse in the other, looking for all the world like a flustered librarian.

"Nice meet you," she said, offering her bejewelled hand and a broad grin that revealed several shiny gold crowns. Before there was a chance to reciprocate, Rob cut in to announce with just a slight hint of hesitation,

"And this gentleman will be our driver, Dimitri."

"It's nice to meet you," I said, my words partially drowned out by a passing jet. "So you speak English?"

"Yes… I am."

Balding and somewhat paunchy, Dimitri's sartorial ensemble consisted of a short-sleeved checkered shirt and a pair of wrinkled slacks that stopped two inches above his ankles. Somewhat younger than Magdalena, he greeted me with a firm handshake and a somewhat friendlier demeanour. None of these attributes however, was sufficient to distract from his most prominent feature; a grisly, deep indentation on the left side of his forehead that suggested a recent encounter with a wayward steel girder.

"Who's the guy hitting on Magdalena?" I asked, as Buddy and I began the task of finding room in the van for our cases.

"Oh, him," Buddy mumbled. "That's our production assistant."

"Our what?" I sputtered, my back muscles straining as I lifted up one end of a heavy case. "The guy looks ancient. What kind of help is he gonna be when it comes to schlepping this stuff around? I mean, the lad is not exactly busting his butt to help right now. And how come we weren't introduced?"

"Rob probably didn't want to scare you," Buddy smirked as he swung his end up and pushed the case into someone's personal luggage.

Tall and thin, the lazy, mystery man harboured a sallow complexion embellished with a permanent frown. There was definitely something odd about him, but I couldn't quite figure out what it was. My first guess was his eyes, which were set far enough apart that one could imagine his being able to look east and west at the same time.

"Hey… love the hat," I told Buddy.

"What hat?"

Unconcerned about the pile of equipment still waiting to be loaded, our prospective production assistant was busy donning a varnished-straw hat several sizes too small, using the side window of the van as his mirror. Somewhat stupefied, I watched as he fastened the headwear under his chin with a blue-beaded, draw string. Suddenly, it came to me that the last time I had seen such a piece of apparel was on the Howdy Doody Show in the mid 1950's.

While Buddy and I continued to load, Rob moved off to engage a fourth person who'd just joined us. Somewhat more official looking, despite a bad-fitting suit and hideous tie, the newcomer appeared to be making demands I was too far away to hear.

"Sorry about this," Rob apologized a short while later, throwing a glance in Howdy's direction. "I know Heinz should be helping you guys out, but I had to settle some final arrangements with the organizer. The office in L.A. set things up with some officials from the local tourist bureau, but I get the feeling this guy…" Rob said, pointing to the figure now talking to Magdalena, "This guy has gone and hired a bunch of his old cronies. Don't worry though. For what I'm having to pay this troupe, I'll make sure they earn their keep."

Howdy's wages, I would later learn, would amount to $100 US a day, a princely sum in Romania in 2000, especially if all you were doing for it was standing around in a goofy hat. Dimitri on the other hand was at least going through the motions, trying to supervise the on-going struggle to find room for our remaining belongings.

"So you *do* speak a little English eh?" I asked him, hoping small talk would diffuse my growing anger towards Howdy.

"I am... I am," Dimitri assured me, as I tried in vain to keep my eyes from wandering to his misfortune.

※

Pulling rank, Rob commandeered the front seat to serve as self-anointed navigator, leaving the rest of us to battle it out for a place in the back rows. Buddy, the weasel, managed to slither into the lone seat at the rear, stranding me between Magdalena and Howdy, who had finally gotten round to introducing himself. As we got underway, I could sense a growing desire to tell him how impressed I was with his work ethics, not to mention his chapeau, but was held back by the rationalization we were going to be spending an entire week jammed together in this van.

"Actually, it's not Brasov we're heading for," Rob informed us once we'd hit the highway. "Well, eventually it is, I guess... but first we'll be stopping at a place called Snagov."

"I know that place," I piped up, leaning forward to gain a little elbow room. "Isn't that where Boris and Natasha Badenov are from?"

Magdalena smiled blithely, while Heinz merely tilted his hat forward in preparation for sleep. The only two capable of understanding the joke from Rocky and Bullwinkle days simply chose to ignore it.

"Snagov is only 40 kilometres from Bucharest,"

Magdalena noted aloud, her nose buried in a folder. "In an area that served as a weekend getaway for Nicolai Ceausescu."

Snagov turned out to be a small village plunked down alongside a lake bearing its name. Much like Romania's former dictator, it was the lake we were interested in, - to be more precise, an abandoned monastery on the lake's sole island. Taking his cue from Magdalena's brief performance, Rob consulted his guidebook and began reciting the tale of how Vlad came to find himself on the island. On the losing side of a battle with Ottoman troops near Bucharest in 1476, Vlad was reportedly betrayed by his brother and rival Rad. Thanks to his treacherous sibling, Vlad was captured, presumably tortured and eventually beheaded by the enemy. After abandoning the body in the woods, the victors returned to Constantinople to parade Vlad's head before the Sultan and citizens of the city. Meanwhile back in Romania, local monks stumbled across Vlad's headless corpse. Thinking it the proper thing to do, they took the body and buried it near their monastery at Snagov.

"How did they know it was him if he had no head?" I wanted to know, as we pulled into a dusty parking lot on the shore of the lake.

"This is it," Rob announced, ignoring my question and shutting the guidebook with a loud snap.

"Who believes in this kind of stuff?" I asked Rob once we'd pried ourselves loose from the van.

"That's why we're here son. That's why we're here," he answered, glancing around the empty lot. "There's supposed to be a boat waiting for us around here somewhere."

Presumptuously concluding there'd be nothing for them to do on the island, Howdy, Dimitri and Magdalena remained sedentary, their silhouettes still visible in the van as a small aluminum boat ferried us the few hundred meters to the island.

"Judging from the scenery," I said, as we glided to a stop alongside a slanted dock that had seen better days, "Romania must have been short of places to go on the weekend if the leader of the country chose this place as a retreat."

With the island not much larger than several soccer fields, it didn't take long before we'd located the plaque denoting Vlad's reputed whereabouts.

"I know there's not much to shoot," Rob explained, "but I only need a minute or so of footage. Do what you can and I'll take a look around to see if there's something we can use to pad this out." That said, he headed off down a worn pathway slicing through a field of wavering, thigh-high grass.

Turning to the matter at hand, I felt another whiff of panic blow in.

"Buddy... what's with this battery plate?" I asked, flashing back to his story of having purchased "a new system" to avoid lugging around a ton of heavy batteries. "Buddy," I repeated between clenched teeth, "Didn't you test it before we left? This battery won't stay attached to the plate which means I can't power the camera, which means I can't shoot, which means we're screwed."

"I thought I installed it properly," he answered meekly. Out on an uninhabited island, miles from any semblance of technical assistance, it was not the answer I wanted to hear.

Fortunately, more through laziness than foresight, Buddy had left the old battery cartridge in the accessory case. The last screw to re-install it was just being tightened as Rob returned from his scouting tour.

"Problems?"

"Nothing we can't handle," I bluffed, glancing at Buddy as the old battery clicked solidly into place. "All in a day's work for 'bicycle repairman'."

Half an hour later, we were retracing our route across the rippling waters to re-join our somnambulant trio. Brasov lay to the north and getting there required passing through the Ploiesti oil fields, noticeably odorous long before they were visible. Memories of Grade 12 history reminded me that these same oil fields had been one of the main reasons Nazi Germany was so interested in maintaining Romania as a puppet state during the war. As strategic as they might have been, then as now, scenic they were not. Truth be told, the landscape had been boring ever since leaving Bucharest. Making the flat, desolate plains even more wearisome was Dimitri's peculiar capacity for dawdling. It felt as though we'd been trailing a slow, fume-spewing truck since the times of Shakespeare. It wasn't that there hadn't been countless opportunities to pass. Entire housing sub-divisions could have been erected, occupied and abandoned on the highway during the gaps in on-coming traffic, yet Dimitri steadfastly refused to overtake. What with a mutually comfortable language still largely untested, it felt pointless to offer any suggestions. I was also discouraged from commenting by the realization that I seemed to be the only one bothered by our lack of speed. Buddy had had his nose buried in a cheesy thriller since Snagov, while Bob kept himself busy randomly jotting down notes. Desperate to distract myself from our glacial pace, I decided to try conversing with Howdy.

"Rob says you worked in film and television here in Romania," I started off in German, over the loud rumble of the engine.

"Yes," he replied, visibly surprised at my sudden interest. "This is correct. But we speak in English. Need practice."

"Fine with me... Wasn't that a hard profession to have had before 1989?... I mean living under a dictator and all, you couldn't just do whatever you wanted, could you? Weren't you censored?"

Howdy paused.

"I make films," he boasted, pretending to crank the handle of an invisible camera with his closed hand.

"Yeah, that part I got. But what kind of films could you make?" I asked, as my eyes drifted to his still attached headgear.

"No make no more. Now retire."

Tell me this is worth it, I thought, glancing back at Buddy who was now either fast asleep or faking it.

"You worked during the Ceausescu regime."

Howdy nodded.

"So didn't you have to kow-tow to the censors?"

"Kow-tow?"

"They told you what you could and couldn't do. Weren't you restricted in the kinds of films you could make?"

At the end of another lengthy pause, Howdy casually pushed back the brim of his hat before breaking into a Cheshire cat grin.

"I make romantic films."

The remark took a moment to register, partly because Howdy's gesture with his hat had reminded me of another Vlad tale I'd picked up somewhere. This one revolved around a visiting group of Turkish dignitaries who had apparently been asked to remove their Fezzes before being ushered into for an audience with Vlad. Citing their religious tradition, they had politely declined to do so. Perturbed over their refusal, but not wishing to belittle their culture, Vlad reportedly ordered the hats nailed to their heads so the problem would never arise again.

I returned to the present just in time to notice the white highway stripes fusing into one solid line. Somewhat alarming to those of us watching, Dimitri took this development as a sign for action. Undeterred by the large hulk barreling towards us in the opposing lane, he swung out into the danger zone hoping to make it to safety before the sound of splintering glass and crumpling bodies echoed across the landscape. Jarred out of his sleep by a bump in the road, Buddy's fear-drenched scream just happened to blend in perfectly with the on-coming vehicle's blaring horn.

*

Breakfast the next morning was served in an enormous ballroom deep in the bowels of the Imperial Hotel, a bunker-like edifice built in that all-too-familiar severe East-block style. Laid out on a row of linen-covered tables in front of heavy floor-to-ceiling curtains, the buffet was being overseen by a half dozen sour-faced waiters. The "boys," as I instantly dubbed them, were outfitted in matching white jackets that looked ominously similar to the tablecloths, and at first glance didn't appear to be the kind of Romanians you'd care to meet in a dark alley, especially if you'd neglected to give them a healthy tip that morning at breakfast. Being the only patron, I was able to inch along the tables at my leisure, desperately searching for something recognizable, let alone edible. The waiters, meanwhile, remained at a respectable distance, observing my passage with little intention of interrupting it with something as unique as an offer of assistance. Cereal seemed to be the safest choice, but while filling my bowl from a milk dispenser that looked and operated like a bubble-gum machine of yesteryear, I was dismayed to see that the fluid pouring out of it was almost transparent. The subsequently soggy flakes had the consistency and taste of shredded cardboard, sufficient grounds for avoiding everything else on display with the exception of orange juice which turned out to be sweet enough to dissolve a filling. Throughout the short meal, which to my enjoyment was eaten alone, I couldn't help but wonder if hidden cameras were recording my every mouthful from behind the several large portraits adorning the opposite wall.

"So this is Transylvania," I muttered to myself, not realizing it actually wasn't, as I stepped out from beneath the hotel's towering porticos. With half an hour to kill before our scheduled departure, I'd opted for a short stroll around Brasov's picturesque market plaza, trying to avoid the puddles created by the seemingly constant drizzle.

According to a faded tourist brochure snatched from the musty lobby right after breakfast, the city was once known as Kronstadt, one of seven fortified cities built by the Germans between the 14th and 17th centuries. Their influence was still noticeable; especially in the recently renovated buildings lining the square. Whether of German origin or not, the most dominant structure in the plaza was a tall tower looming at one end. Part of the "Black Church," named so after "the Great Fire" managed to scorch its walls in the 17th century, the tower was listed as belonging to Romania's largest Gothic church. Despite that impressive label, its outward appearance was not enough incentive to lure me inside. Instead I crossed the square to seek shelter under a row of trees bordering the Old Town Hall. From there it was possible to watch several pairs of elderly gentlemen ignoring the inclement conditions to partake in an early morning challenge on life-size chess boards. Just as one match was getting interesting, a bell echoed from the top of the tower, reminding me it was time to return to the hotel.

The day's destination lay a hundred and twenty kilometres up the road, a distance I fully expected it would take Dimitri a week to cover. Dubbed Schäßburg by the same legion of Saxons responsible for naming Brasov, Sighisoara was a beautifully preserved medieval-walled city that bore witness to the birth of Mr. Tepes. Hoping to find clues as to what may have turned the lad into an impaler, the plan was to make the rounds of various houses, plaques and statues commemorating his memory. First stop was the main square, where another enormous clock tower stood guard over a half-dozen cobblestone alleyways, spreading out from the square like spokes on a bike. Each of the narrow streets was filled with wooden, mortared houses, all of which appeared to be in remarkably good condition. Honouring the tradition established at Snagov and Brasov, our trio of hirelings was in no rush to offer assistance, staying put while Buddy and I set up to capture a large bronze bust dedicated to the man of the hour.

"I think I'm beginning to understand why Vlad was so keen on impaling some of his fellow countrymen," I said to Buddy as I waited for the wind to die down before attempting a pan. "I mean, how long is Rob gonna wait before he reads Howdy the riot act? If *he* doesn't say something soon, I will."

All Buddy could do was shrug. Once we were done, it was a short walk over to the clock tower where Rob had arranged for us to attempt re-creating a time-period scene in its cellar. Set to star in the role of Vlad, was a local actor engaged by the same sinister agent responsible for providing our trio of layabouts.

"Who exactly is this guy anyways?" I asked Rob as we waited in the shadow of the tower for the actor to arrive.

"Which guy?"

"The suit at the airport, the one who gave us Howdy and company."

Rob threw a cautious glance over his shoulder before answering. "The agency back home booked him. They said he used to be a high-ranking official in the government tourism department."

"One of these 'apparatchiks' or whatever they were called?"

"Could be. The story is that not long after Ceausescu made his exit, our man managed to open a private tourist company. Not unlike many other former members of the regime, I understand."

"That certainly explains a lot," I said, partially distracted by the sight of an approaching figure.

"I feel like I need to walk a thin line," Rob added. "If he gets miffed and pulls the team, where are we gonna find someone else?"

"Not like we would miss them or anything... especially Howdy."

"I know, I know. Just do your best. I promise I'll have a word with him... I think this is our guy here."

Even though it was close to thirty-five in the shade, our budding star had shown up in a full-length, wool-brocaded coat, topped off by a long black wig. Greetings were exchanged, none of which he appeared to understand, before Vlad the Imposter was led to the darkened cellar and given details of what was expected of him. There, another local talent was awaiting us, this one a woman in her mid-twenties, dressed in a full length medieval gown. The young damsel about to be in distress smiled benignly as Rob made introductions and pointed to what looked to be an authentic "rack."

"I need you to look and sound fierce," he said, turning to Vlad. "You need to seem as though you're inflicting unspeakable torture upon our young lady. She will be strapped to the rack and you will be whipping her mercilessly, demanding she admit her guilt. Of course you won't actually be hitting her, I hope. But our camera angle will make it look like you are. She in turn will cry out in agony. Remember, all this has to look and sound authentic. Does anyone have questions?"

Rob took the silence as a "no" and guided the damsel to her place on the rack. Vlad meanwhile, fascinated by the cat o' nine tails he'd been handed, was off in a corner practicing his lines and lashes.

"Wanna bet neither of them understood a single word?" I whispered to Buddy, as Rob did a last minute script check before signalling Vlad for a run through. "This should prove highly interesting."

Once Vlad had taken his mark, Rob slid out of the frame and called for quiet. Suspended in a cloud of nervous panic as he hovered over his victim, Vlad jerked into his dialogue as "action" was called. Raising the whip, he let forth more a squeal than a screech before letting it fall to her back like a strand of limp spaghetti.

"Cuuuuuttttt," Rob groaned, striding back into the shot

"Excuse me. What's your name?"

"Yes," the befuddled actor answered.

"Right... Well what if I just call you Vlad. It'll make things a whole lot easier. So Vlad, which part didn't you get? You need to evoke a little more passion. You're supposed to be Vlad the Impaler, right? "

"Ce ai spus?" Vlad asked with a puzzled look.

"I don't think he speaks any English," Buddy pointed out helpfully.

"Oh Christ," Rob sighed. "Where's Magdalena?"

"Try the back of the van or the next cafe," I offered. "They all disappeared right after we moved to the tower."

"English not so good," Vlad quietly inserted.

But on we pushed. After a half-dozen dry runs Vlad was finally able to produce what could pass for a reasonably blood-curdling yell. Ordering him back to his mark, Rob again called for quiet, then cued me to roll. This time Vlad's actions, together with the violent surge of his whip, were convincing enough to bring a smile of satisfaction to Rob's face. That look of pleasure however, quickly faded when the damsel's reaction was several seconds late in arriving.

"Cut... Forget it. I'll fix it in post... somehow," he moaned. "I can't afford to spend all day here. We're already behind schedule. "Pack it up," he ordered. "We still have some things to shoot in the square."

Re-emerging into the harsh light of the plaza, I was dismayed to discover it had filled with dozens of tourists during our absence. Many now crowded around us on the assumption Vlad was part of the city's attractions.

"Gonna be kinda hard to film a period piece with all these tourists around," I pointed out.

"I know, I know... Do what you can," Rob said with an air of resignation. "Just do what you can."

I was in the process of weighing the options of how to shoot without a cast of unwanted extras when I felt a tap on my shoulder.

"Pardon please."

I turned to see that the gruff voice belonged to a portly, middle-aged man sweating in a dark suit. "I mayor of Sighisoara. Welcome to city. I like to meet you Miss Sighisoara."

Now normally, *"staggering"* is not a word that often enters my vocabulary. But with the dark-haired beauty standing next to the mayor, - her head and shoulders draped in a haloed arc of sunlight that highlighted the peach-fuzz hairs on her neck and outstretched arm, - it was time to make an exception. She was without a doubt one of the prettiest young women I had ever seen.

"You maybe have place for her in film?" the mayor asked.

"*If not we'll make one,*" a tiny voice echoed as I struggled to keep my composure. With my eyes still glued to Miss SS, I directed the mayor towards Rob.

"The man talking to Vlad," I blathered. "He's the one you need to ask."

Able to ogle for several minutes from a distance as the mayor repeated his pitch, I was disheartened to see Rob shaking his head.

"Are you sure you don't want to re-shoot the damsel scene?" I asked him shortly after the mayor and his protégé had departed.

"Steady, lad. I know she was pretty, but we have work to do. Besides, you're old enough to be her father."

"Probably old enough to be her grandfather... but who's counting. Anyway, didn't you know that some souls are ageless?"

"Ageless or useless?" he countered, before returning to the matter at hand.

Despite the absence of the young woman's charms, the rest of the filming went smoothly. Meanwhile word had somehow gotten back to our three slackers that we were wrapping. Within minutes of our return to the van, they all reappeared looking well-fed and rested.

"Why are these people even here?" I pondered loud enough for others to hear, as we loaded the gear. Despite his earlier promise, Rob chose to ignore the comment, preoccupied with how he was going to salvage the material from the cellar. Flopping into the front seat, he angrily tossed his notes on the dashboard and issued orders for Dimitri to "move it."

*

That night was spent at a rather shabby hotel in central Bistrita, memorable for both its bad cuisine, lumpy mattress and the murmur of a not-so-distant disco. As a result most of us were still half asleep when we hit the road early the next morning, cruising along what Magdalena informed us was "the way to Moldavia."

"I'll call the newspapers," I said, still nettled by the trio's dormancy the previous day.

On the brighter side, the landscape was finally starting to resemble the Transylvania I'd been expecting; mountainous, dark and eerie, just as the tales of horror had depicted it to be. Such scenery lasted for a full half hour before we entered into a long, narrow gorge. After several kilometres of twists and turns on the shadowy road, we emerged into a beautiful, sunlit green valley that could easily have been mistaken for northern Switzerland. Lush rolling hills dotted with quaint villages appeared, each with brightly painted wooden houses, fronted by weathered picket fences.

"Wasn't religious expression frowned upon under the Communists?" I asked Magdalena as we rolled through yet another picturesque town. "Practically every house we've passed has a cross on the gable and they look like they've been around for awhile."

Not exactly hard-pressed to perform up till now, Magdalena seized the moment to strut her stuff, sailing off into a long-winded tangent so circuitous I almost forgot my question. Fortunately, the passing vistas provided some relief from her tedious monologue. Once the villages stopped, so it appeared did time. Over the next fifty kilometres it took us to reach the Bargau Pass, not a single piece of motorized farm machinery was in evidence. Instead farmhands were out in the punishing heat, tilling the land with hoes, shovels and in some cases even a horse and wooden plough.

At first glance, it could have been a motel on the outskirts of Anywhere, USA, complete with a blood-red neon sign flashing "vacancy." We'd journeyed to this rather lame outpost of evil to film a group of Dracula aficionados who'd flown in from England solely for the experience of setting foot on the stomping grounds of their revered horror hero.

"But the guy never existed," I said, as Rob finished telling us about the group at check in. "Who would pay to come and tromp in his illusionary footsteps?"

Disappointment over the distinctly non-scary Castle Hotel was deepened upon opening the door to my room, where the only thing truly frightening was access to Romanian television. It had taken us the better part of the day to get there, so I was grateful when Rob announced that there would be a chance to rest up for a few hours before attending a costumed dinner party to be held that evening in Vlad's honour. Unlike the Dracula groupies, we'd been excluded from the obligation to "dress accordingly," a bit of a shame considering Howdy's stylistic fashion skills.

"Think Mr. Rob would mind if we get totally wasted tonight?" I asked Buddy as we rode the elevator down to a basement conference room just after seven. Quick to accept a blood-red welcoming cocktail from a fanged waiter, we retreated to a neutral corner to observe the goings on in a room decked out in chintzy red, black and orange Halloween decorations.

"Have you seen Dimitri or Heinz since we checked in?" Buddy asked.

"Who?" I mumbled back, trying to place the alcohol that was singeing my palette. "You mean Howdy? Probably in his room polishing his hat. Good thing they didn't come. They might have been mistaken for the guests of honour, or at least part of the entertainment. Can you imagine someone asking Dimitri how he managed to get his scar to look so real?" Glancing around at the costumed occupants of the room, I was prompted to add "Is it just me or is this whole thing a tad off the wall?"

"How so?" Buddy said, lifting another welcome off the passing waiter's tray.

"Where's the kick in paying money to come all this way to explore the so-called history of somebody who never existed? If you're that desperate for adventure, the organizers can tell you whatever they think you want to hear or can't disprove."

Entrenched in our little outpost, over the next half hour we managed to hear and see practically every Dracula cliché ever created, all the while doing our best to deplete the supply of bloody cocktails. In the midst of this scripted spontaneity, Rob, who had been mingling with various participants, strolled over to deliver his own horror story. Forced to stumble back to our rooms to collect the equipment, we returned to learn that his "one interview guys," had been expanded to five. Despite our rather glassy-eyed state, we nonetheless managed to set up in a small cubby hole adjacent to the main room.

"Oh man... I don't know about you, but I think I've had one too many Drac Drinks tonight," I confessed quietly to Buddy, while struggling to find focus on our first subject, - a heavy set woman whose loose fitting costume revealed more ample bosom than either Rob or I were interested in acknowledging. Buddy, on the other hand, seemed to have become temporarily mesmerized by the exposed flesh, as he attempted to attach her microphone. By the time we were ready to roll, it was evident our guest had imbibed her own fair share of liquid refreshments. Barely able to slur her own name, let alone describe how the group and tour came to be, she nonetheless made a valiant attempt to answer Rob's questions.

By eleven, the effects of drink had combined with the third dull interview to take their toll. In the midst of weighing the merits of driving a wooden stake through my heart, I was relieved to hear that the next candidate had either chickened or passed out. As fate would have it, the fifth and final guest turned out to be a Canadian university professor, complete with a 1950's beehive hairdo and cat-eye glasses, which may or may not have been part of her costume. Any interest in learning how a fellow landsman had managed to become involved with such a quirky group quickly vanished with her answer to Rob's first question.

"We're attracted to our Dracula, and at the same time we fear him."

An hour later, the party was over. Back in my room, my brain repeatedly besieged by newly-discovered pools of untapped alcohol every time I moved. I'd only been in a downward swirl for a few minutes when the unmistakable din of a blaring television startled me back to the surface. Squeezing my head out a tiny porthole of a window, I could tell the noise was coming from the room directly below mine. Re-donning pants and t-shirt I didn't recall removing, I marched down to the offending floor in my bare feet and pounded loudly on the door in question. Getting no response, I continued to knock, prompting several other residents to peek out into the hallway. Finally the door swung open and before me stood a woman from the party.

"I'm so sorry," she said, beckoning me into the room. "The remote control seems to be broken. I turned it on and it started playing this loud right away... I didn't know what to do."

"Why don't we just try unplugging it," I suggested, bending down to yank out the cable. The room began to swivel as I returned to an upright position, forcing me to brace myself on a nearby chair.

"Oh my... Now why didn't I think of that," she lamented in a high-pitched squeaky tone almost as grating as the now-dormant television. "How can I thank you?"

The idea of asking for a fresh pint of blood did cross my mind but seeing that having to explain the joke would merely prolong my stay, I settled for a simple "goodnight," closing the door behind me as several nosey neighbours did the same.

*

Looking as bright and cheerful as she likely ever did, Magdalena was already waiting by the van when we arrived the next morning from breakfast. Fearing her smile might be an indication of her willingness to ramble on from where she'd left off yesterday, I deftly managed to grab the front seat when Rob mentioned he'd like to catch some shut eye in the back. I needn't have worried; shortly after we left, Magdalena became deeply engrossed in a newspaper article. Any hopes of catching some badly needed sleep myself, were dashed when Dimitri suddenly decided to assume the role of narrator.

"We drive through south part of Carpathian mountain," he explained.

"Hmmm... m."

"Is very beautiful part of country."

"Hmmm...m."

"Your first time in this part of Romania?"

"Hmmm...m."

When several more of his comments were met with same response, Dimitri finally took the hint and silence ruled supreme for awhile. But it was far from a restful ride. Thanks to the previous night's wave of excess, a mild case of sea sickness made itself known with every sharp curve in the road. Fortunately before my digestive system could wreak its revenge, Dimitri pulled to a stop at a deserted parking lot in the middle of a thick forest.

"We here," he announced.

"And where is here?" I asked groggily.

"Dracula's Castle," Magdalena said, looking up from her paper.

"Oh Christ, not again," Buddy groaned from the back.

"No, no," Rob chimed in. "This is the real thing... There's just one slight problem."

"You mean besides Howdy? I asked. "Do I really want to know this?"

Ignoring the jibe, Rob informed us that the castle in question was still a kilometre away.

"So why have we stopped here?"

"Because much of it is straight up, I'm afraid."

"Have heart condition. I no can go further," Howdy announced at step 47 of the 1,016 we'd eventually needed to climb to reach our goal.

"Gee, what a surprise," I muttered, squeezing past him on the trail. *"What's Romanian for 'you lazy turd'?"* was a question I dearly wanted to ask at that moment, but unfortunately Magdalena had remained in the van.

By the time the 500-step mark was reached, beads of sweat had started to collect on my brow. Stopping to rest, it struck me how difficult it must have been for Howdy's forefathers to have lugged material up this steep incline in order to build Vlad's castle. On second thought, it was easier to envisage their having remained below in the ox carts, feigning a bout of bubonic plague while other fellow serfs did all the work.

After much effort however, the summit was finally conquered. Breathing heavily while perched on a stone-arched footbridge leading to the castle ruins, I gazed down at the tiny blue object that housed the lazing culprit.

"What do you suppose the prison term in Romania is for starting an avalanche?" I asked Rob as he stood up and signalled me to follow. Much to my muted joy, it took another five minutes before we actually reached our destination. According to legend, Vlad had enjoyed building castles almost as much as he did impaling. Judging by the size and structure of this one, it must have been quite the place in its heyday. Now however, it was merely a collection of moss-coated walls and crumbling brickwork, making it difficult to feel a gripping sense of history. The view on the other hand was a formidable one, with a series of mountain peaks stretching off to the clear blue horizon. Inexplicably, the panorama reminded me of a crowd of Christmas shoppers awaiting the opening bell at a department store sale, making me wonder what just what was in last night's cocktails. Thankfully, despite the spectacular backdrop, Rob vetoed the idea of doing a stand-up, limiting his request to a requisite number of beauty shots.

Magdalena was still perusing her paper when we returned. To no one's surprise, Howdy was snoozing, while Dimitri, seemingly lost in thought, was no doubt plotting another potential accident. Once underway, everyone pretty much kept to themselves, freeing me to stare out at a landscape that had once again turned dreary. Thus it came as a bit of a shock when out of the blue, Rob suddenly demanded we get a shot of it. I wasn't the only one to question his wisdom. Apparently reluctant to slow our progress by honouring Rob's request, Dimitri kept driving until a slew of unintelligible words from Magdalena made him think otherwise.

"What the hell does he want a shot of this for?" I mumbled to Buddy under my breath, while fighting off wind gusts strong enough to wobble the van.

"An hour's an hour and it's his dollar," Buddy rationalized.

Having found a stable position on the lee side of the van, I peered into the viewfinder only to discover that the countryside I'd found so lacklustre, actually looked quite moving. It didn't take long however, to realize what was moving was me. Inspired by an unknown force, Dimitri had decided to change locations, starting the motor and releasing the clutch in one rapid movement. With my jacket snagged on the handle of the side door, for a moment it appeared I was about to be dragged along with him. Barely able to regain my footing and grab hold of the camera before it crashed to the ground, a series of shrieks that would have done the fake Vlad proud, prompted Dimitri to reconsider. A number of fuses had been simmering ever since Snagov, but this time it was Buddy's that was the first to blow.

"What the hell is the matter with you, you idiot?" he yelled, leaping through the open doorway to clutch Dimitri's upper arm. "Are you completely deranged? You nearly ran over him. Where the hell did you learn to drive?"

Visibly flustered by the turn of events, Magdalena struggled to translate Buddy's flurry of abuse. Despite being known for my own capacity to "fly off the handle," it was me who remained calm. Seeing little point in joining the melee while Buddy was doing such a commendable job, it was only when he seemed ready to throttle our driver that I intervened.

"Hey Buddy... Ease up, lad. Granted, it was not his best move, but no harm's been done, so let's just let it go."

"But he could have squashed you and the camera."

"Could haves don't count. He didn't, so just calm down." Casually stroking my forehead as I glanced over to Dimitri, I quietly added, "The guy has enough on his plate, I would say."

With the crisis averted, we were soon back on the road, lost in a landscape which, thankfully, was slowly becoming more scenic again.

For the next half-hour we paralleled a fast-moving river as it wound its way through yet another thick forest. According to the map I'd borrowed from Magdalena, it should have been the Olt River. Suddenly without warning, the solid row of trees between the road and the riverbank opened up to reveal a collection of dilapidated houses on the opposite shore. Taking advantage of several recurring glimpses, I could make out a band of raggedy dressed children scurrying about on mud streets that ran up from the water's edge to the base of a steep ravine. Complete with smoke billowing out of the ramshackle chimneys, the scene resembled something straight out of a Dickens novel.

"*That can't be real,*" I thought, as I strained to maintain a view. "*It has to be a movie set.*" But before I was able to bring the spectacle to Rob's attention, the vista snapped closed as we rushed into a long, dark tunnel.

For another hour, the scenery persisted in consisting of small, desolate-looking villages, their front yards littered with overflowing garbage bins and abandoned vehicles, the makes of which I didn't recognize. In one unnamed village, the sight of a man's silhouette in the doorway of a small grocery store, the sole of one foot raised up against its frame, quickly embedded itself as a still life from a cigarette commercial.

By late afternoon we were back within striking distance of Bucharest. Our inimitable tourist guide, however, had seen fit to arrange overnight accommodation in a small town fifty kilometres shy of the capital. Another surprise in store for us was that rather than booking a hotel, he'd billeted us into a large private home.

The first impression upon opening the door to my room was that I'd landed in the storage room for an upcoming flea market. I'd only begun to take in the magnitude of this assemblage of tawdriness when there was a knock at my door.

"We've apparently been invited to a local festival," Buddy informed me as I let him in. "Rob says we don't have to film anything. It's just a 'must attend' PR thing."

"Can't possibly be as bad as our evening with those Dracula loonies. Hey… just out of curiosity, is your room as nice as mine?"

"This? This is nothing," Buddy scoffed, as he surveyed the room. "Mine is a shrine to bad taste. I didn't think it was physically possible to jam so much kitsch into one small room. Do you think all Romanian households are like this?"

"Perish the thought lad. But it wouldn't surprise me to find out this place is owned by the guide's second cousin twice removed."

"Yeah, no kidding… Anyway, we should get going. Rob said they're going to meet us downstairs."

"They" turned out to be Rob, Magdalena, Dimitri and the mysterious tour guide, who had re-surfaced to oversee the proceedings. For reasons unknown, Howdy had absconded to places unknown. On our short walk up a country lane, accompanied by a chorus of yelping dogs, we were observed by several inquisitive neighbours puttering in their yards. None bothered to wave. Purposely dragging our heels, Buddy and I watched as the rest of the group turned into a yard scattered with construction materials, before disappearing through the open door of an unfinished concrete building. Nervously awaiting us inside was a group of twenty young Romanian children, dressed in what presumably were traditional costumes. Standing stiffly at attention on a makeshift stage, they listened politely as a short man attempted to welcome us in a blend of his language and ours.

"This is embarrassing," I whispered to Buddy. "There's more people on stage than in the audience."

"Clap louder and maybe no one will notice."

As the MC's speech finished to sparse applause, he then proceeded to bark an order into his microphone. Somewhere a needle dropped haphazardly into a groove and music came scratching to life, prompting the twenty figures to start shuffling around the tiny stage in a rather uncoordinated fashion.

"Didn't they say something about feeding us?" Buddy muttered, when a lengthy third number showed no sign of ending.

"What? Who's they? Since when do you understand Romanian?"

Hunger was starting to gnaw at my own innards as well, but the memory of various meals over the past week dampened any expectations of a lavish dinner. In the meantime, lulled into oblivion by the tedium of the continuing concert, I couldn't help wondering how royalty endured the multitude of cultural displays held in their honour. Breathing through a perpetual smile must be rather difficult and take some getting used to.

Finally, after two more drawn-out numbers, the show was over. The instant the last song faded out, another group of teenagers rushed the stage, avidly removing speakers, microphones and all other sources of evidence. Simultaneous to the action onstage, a second troupe entered from a back room armed with pots, plates and what looked to be the evening's main course. Setting their cargo down on several hastily erected tables, they beckoned us to come forth before running off.

"Do they know something we don't," I asked, making

note of the fleeing caterers, while accepting the honour of being first in line. Despite the strange looking particles afloat in it, I suppressed the urge to ask precisely what liquid was being dished into my bowl. Whatever it was, it turned out to be quite tasty. As I was slowly working my way through it, Howdy shuffled in to take the seat directly across from me. Interestingly, neither he nor Magdalena, who was seated next to him, showed any interest in taking advantage of the buffet.

"We have question for you," Magdalena announced after several minutes of consultation with Howdy.

"Hmmm," I murmured, dabbing the corners of my mouth with a serviette.

"You know Germany politics, yes?"

I nodded and shrugged at the same time, curious where this might be headed. "I try to follow what's going on. Not that it does me much good. As a foreigner I'm not allowed to vote."

"Germany member of Common Market for long time, no?" Howdy asked.

"As far as I know it was one of the founding members. Back in 1957 or so. Treaty of Rome or something. Why do you ask?"

"Romania make much progress since Ceausescu killed."

"I'm afraid you've got me on that one."

"Romania show it good country. Many good people, many good workers, but many no find work. Life better when Romania in Common Market," he continued. "Why Romania no in Common Market".

"*So that's where this is going,*" I thought to myself, stalling for time by methodically folding my napkin and setting it next to my empty bowl. I was about to attempt an answer when Howdy snarled, "Why Germany block Romania?"

"You'll have to ask Helmut Kohl about that one."

"Why Romania no allowed join Common Market right now?" Magdalena echoed.

Judging from the intensity of this coordinated attack, it was clear the issue had been percolating with them for some time. It would have been nice to provide them with an answer, but all I found myself thinking was that Howdy's hat was missing. Finally, raising my hands in mock innocence, I pushed my chair back and excused myself.

"You've got me. Haven't got a clue... Now if you don't mind I think I'll get some fresh air."

Joining Buddy outside for a much needed drink, I wasted no time in getting to the point.

"You don't happen to have a mirror on you do you?"

"A mirror? What do you want a mirror for?"

Aw, forget it. I could have used one inside a few minutes ago, but it's not important. Tell me," I asked between sips of a beverage the label claimed was beer, "How many more days do we have left with this lot?"

"Unless Rob adds something at the last minute, there's just one interview tomorrow morning. It'll just be us and Magdalena. Dimitri will drop us off at the location in Bucharest and get us back to the hotel once we're done. Howdy, is officially finished as of today, but he won't be leaving us till tomorrow."

"Not that anyone will notice."

"Ahhh, and one more thing," Buddy said with a raised finger.

"Rob also said he wants to capture some b-roll of the city, so we're probably going to do a mini-tour tomorrow afternoon."

"When did you learn all this? Why is he telling you all of this and not me?"

"A little while ago. You were busy talking with Magdalena and Howdy."

"And defending Europe's integrity. Don't remind me."

"Anyway, be happy. The day after tomorrow, we're done here."

"And none too soon," I grumbled, pondering whether my half-empty beer was worth finishing. "At least we'll be rid of that freeloader so he can go back to making romantic films."

No sooner had this remark faded, we were joined by Dimitri.

"I drink beer with you?" he said, hoisting an opened can. Buddy, rat that he is, seized the interruption to make tracks.

"You live Frankfurt, yes?" Dimitri asked, before tilting his head back for a long slug.

"Not far from there," I answered hesitantly. "Where you hear that… I mean where did you hear that?"

"You talk Rob, I hear," he explained. "My daughter. She study Frankfurt. She nice girl. She teach me German each time she come home holiday. Little more each time. She study now three years Frankfurt. Maybe you meet her?"

"What is she studying?" I asked, unsettled by the thought she might somehow resemble her father.

"She nice girl. She become doctor. Move back Romania."

Having accommodated Dimitri's proud boasts to this point, there was little choice but to accept the sudden offer of her telephone number.

"You call. Maybe meet," he said, scribbling on a scrap of paper he'd retrieved from his shirt pocket. "She nice girl."

"For sure," I lied, feigning a yawn with a glance at my watch. His mission accomplished, Dimitri retreated inside for another beer, but not before slapping me hard on the shoulder and bidding me goodnight.

*

"So this is what they mean when they say a place has gone to the dogs," I remarked, as the old Peugeot entered the Bucharest city limits the next morning. As the cityscape gathered momentum, dozens more canines started to appear. Some were spotted trolling alone in open lots, while others roamed the streets in menacing-looking packs. Dimitri paid little heed to the flocks of strays, other than to occasionally bleat his horn if one or two dawdled in getting out of his path.

As Buddy had prophesied, upon our arrival at the location, it was clear we were about to jettison a portion of our weeklong excess baggage. Somehow it felt appropriate that the final image of Howdy was to follow his rump out of the van. Maintaining the tradition he'd faithfully adhered to during the shoot, one minute he was there, the next he was gone. No one, least of all me, appeared traumatized by his abrupt departure.

"Must have spotted there was work to do," I said to Buddy as we both cast a glance towards an old Gothic house that was our designated destination. Conjuring up memories of *The Munsters*, the dwelling came complete with a creaking iron gate, overgrown yard and sets of eyes behind every bush. There was even an oversized iron knocker on the front door that echoed down an imagined long corridor as Rob announced our arrival.

"Ten bucks says it's opened by a bald hunchback in a shabby suit," I wagered, setting down the tripod on a moss-covered porch. "Dragging a game leg."

"Either that or Dimitri's cousin," Buddy said, struggling to stifle a laugh.

"Gotta be named Igor," added Rob, belatedly getting into the spirit, as the end of this madness approached.

According to the morning's breakfast briefing, much of which I had dozed through thanks to another restless night, we were there to interview the alleged great, great, great etc. grandson of Vlad. How someone could prove or disprove such a claim of heritage escaped me, but then again, since when had credibility played a role in this show? With such colourful expectations, there was a trace of disappointment when the door was opened by a distinguished looking gentleman, exuding the aura of a college professor. Following a round of introductions, during which he insisted on shaking each and every hand, we were guided down a dark, high-ceilinged hallway, past various coats of arms and pieces of armour that shared wall space with the stuffed heads of a dozen former animals.

"At least it's animals and not former enemies," I whispered to Buddy, wondering whether a fetish for impaling might be hereditary.

Much to my chagrin, our interview subject led us into what must have been the smallest and darkest room of the house.

"Shit, it'll be like shooting in a closet," I grumbled,

while reluctantly setting up. Meanwhile, Rob was busying himself briefing our guest, not an easy task considering the man spoke limited English. Not surprisingly, having taken over Howdy's customary role, Magdalena had disappeared to find a bathroom.

Once back at full capacity and rolling, our host quickly showed himself to be quite knowledgeable, dredging up lengthy dissertations in Romanian, in response to each of Rob's questions. Despite his verbosity, Magdalena's translations remained close to monosyllabic. Having noticed the discrepancy, Rob called a short break and took me aside. "Is it just me or is there something strange about Magdalena's translations?" he fumed with a feigned smile in her direction. "I get the feeling she's leaving out half of what he's saying."

"Maybe you need to spread some Baksheesh," I suggested. "Tell her you'll pay by the word."

"Dream on son. She's already pulling in a figure you don't want to know. Not that it matters, not that anything matters anymore," he said resignedly. "This show is already doomed to tank and my career along with it."

After a polite but pointed request to Magdalena to produce better results, the rest of the interview went smoothly. Back outside, packed and ready to go, the imminent farewell to our translator was not destined to be a tearful one. Obviously pleased to be getting paid in cash, Magdalena's eyes remained fixed of the fist-full of dollars, as each of us prepared to submit the obligatory parting remarks.

"*Been a slice, Mag*," I wanted to say. "*If you want a tip, I'd use some of that dough to visit a hairdresser and fashion *advisor.*"Instead I settled for a quick handshake and nod.

"I dare you to give her a hug," I whispered to Rob, stepping aside to offer him space for his own salutation.

"Not part of the equation," he said through a glazed smile. "But just so you know, I wrote your phone number on one of the bills."

To my ever-lasting relief, Rob's sinking spirits prompted him to cancel the quest for b-roll, claiming, "What is there to shoot besides dogs and a former megalomaniac's monstrosity of a palace?"

"Point taken," I said without objection.

It hadn't exactly been a strenuous day but I was nonetheless dragging by the time Dimitri pulled up to a large, red-brick building, fronted by a lawn last cut in 1956. While unloading at the entrance, it didn't escape anyone's notice that the hotel had a gigantic beer garden. Citing family obligations, Dimitri declined to join us for a drink and made a speedy exit, followed by chorus of snapping dogs. After depositing the equipment in my room, I was the first and only patron to take a seat in an establishment capable of holding five hundred. Despite those rather favourable odds, it still took a mole-like waiter a good ten minutes to deem me worthy of service. Gesturing to the list of local brands on the menu, I asked for a recommendation.

"Beer is good."

"Glad to hear it," I answered, noting that local brew sold for seventy-five cents while imported rang in at four dollars a pop. "Is this stuff drinkable?" I asked, pointing to one that read like Superman's arch foe, Mister Mxyzptlk.

"Beer is good," he repeated.

"See you've made a friend," Rob jibed, as he and

Buddy joined me.

"Ask him for a good beer," I challenged, before signalling the waiter to fetch three of the "gooder" brand.

"What makes you think he'll tell you the truth?" Buddy asked, as he searched for a less wobbly chair.

"So Gents," Rob said with a sigh as deep as the Marianna trench. "We did it."

"Here's to having survived the crew from hell," I toasted as our beverages were delivered. One sip quickly confirmed the error in not having asked the waiter precisely what the "beer is good" for. It certainly wasn't drinking.

"Please," Rob said with a grimace, a result of either the beer, the prospect of reminiscing or both. "I can't bear the thought of re-living any of that. Not yet. Not so soon."

"Ditto," Buddy echoed, forcing down another swig of the murky liquid.

Deprived of the chance to poke fun at our departed trio, much of the remaining time was spent in sullen silence, occasionally interrupted by comments about what still lay in store for us. Rob was the first to excuse himself, begging off a mutual dinner with the claim of having to finish up some paperwork.

"I need to firm up some things with Hamelin and Prague," he told us. "I don't need any more surprises, thank you."

As arduous as the task was, Buddy and I managed to suffer through another two or three equally dismal brands before heading back to the hotel reception. Wandering through the dingy lobby, I couldn't help noticing two thuggish-looking men lurking near an unused fireplace.

"Now there's a couple of upstanding citizens if I ever saw any," I commented as we awaited the elevator. "Any idea who they are? If they're secret police, subtlety isn't their forté."

"You didn't get asked?" Buddy said as the doors of the elevator squeaked closed.

"Asked what?"

"If you wanted company..."

"Company?"

"Of the female persuasion."

"You're joking. Those guys are pimps?"

"I take it that means you weren't asked."

"No," I said in semi-feigned indignation.

"Shheeesh. I was asked twice even before I got to my room."

"Good thing Dimitri didn't pick up on your interest in Romanian women."

"Huh?"

Following a night of solitude, a barely edible breakfast, and a smoke-filled taxi ride through a slumbering city, our "Adventures in Romania" officially ended as the plane lifted off. Although it was only eight in the morning, all three of us felt obliged to order a drink as soon as the seat belt signs were extinguished. Shaking the last drops out of a mini-wine bottle, Rob displayed his first genuine smile in a week.

"How the hell did we get through this intact?"

"What makes you think we did?" I answered.

His smile gradually dissolving into a smirk, Rob shifted his gaze to the window before adding, "I don't know about you guys, but I feel like I can finally breathe again." Turning back to face us, he raised his glass for a final tribute. "I just want to say thanks for a job well done. It's definitely one for the record books. I'm just not sure which category yet... Good God, what a collection! You don't suppose all Romanians are like that do you?"

"God, I certainly hope not," Buddy answered.

Watching the clouds blot out the last vestiges of Romanian, territory, Rob let out a wry chuckle. "Guys, look at it this way... At least we know now it can't get any worse, right?... Guys?"

CHAPTER 26

The Pied Piper

It was only a rough guesstimate, but whenever asked how many quaint villages lay scattered across the German landscape, I usually answered, "*somewhere around fourteen billion.*" Having visited what seemed like half of them over the years, it was with a shiver of apprehension that I read in a flight magazine, that Hamelin was supposedly one of the quaintest.

Several hours after landing in Hannover, Buddy, Rob and I were killing time in a richly wood-panelled office at Hamelin's city hall, impatiently awaiting the arrival of the illustrious "Pied Piper," already forty-five minutes late. During the lull, I found my thoughts wandering to the scene from *Annie Hall* where the camera slowly pans across a classroom of grade-schoolers, as each stands to recite what has become of them in the intervening years. Ever since learning we'd be traveling to Hamelin to cover the legend of the Piper, I'd wondered how the spectacle of a grown man walking around dressed as a court jester could be stretched into a twenty minute documentary. Then again, nobody had said anything about an interesting documentary.

Despite the fact this was his day off, when our subject did finally show, it was in full costume. Following introductions, we retreated to an imposing, high-ceilinged room on the second floor. Gathered around a heavy oak table, we listened as the Piper unleashed his practiced "Spiel" (*routine*). Mercifully, fifteen minutes in, the meeting was cut short when a secretary interrupted to inform us the room had been booked for another group.

"That was sure worth the wait," I said in a low voice to Rob as we shuffled out into the hallway.

"Look. Just be glad we don't have to listen to any more of that monologue. Besides, it was only meant to be a get acquainted meeting," he answered before agreeing to reconvene the next morning back at city hall.

Early the next morning, I was absent-mindedly flipping through a copy of "Sights & Sounds - This month in Hannover" when an article on the very man we'd come to film caught my attention. According to legend, the townspeople of Hamelin had hired the original "Piper" to rid the town of a plague of rats. He had accomplished the task by using a magic pipe to lure the rodents out of town and into a nearby river where they subsequently drowned. That in itself should have been a tip-off to all those hearing the tale, for unless the Piper had taken the time to attach tiny lead weights to their feet, it's a well-known fact that rats can swim. Be that as it may, when time came for payment, the town felt obliged to renege, perhaps thinking anyone who dressed like that could easily be taken advantage of. Peeved but devoid of a plan of action, the Piper had simply disappeared, but not without first vowing sweet revenge. Then in June, 1284, 130 children from the village simply vanished, never to be seen again. Three children however, - one lame, one deaf, and one blind - somehow managed to get left behind, and it was these three who purportedly informed villagers that the Piper had something to do with the children's disappearance.

As subsequent events were never fully clarified, the door was opened to a horde of waiting conspiracy mongers.

Over the ensuing years, the Piper had been portrayed as everything from a saviour from the Black Death to a psychopathic pedophile, the latter of which was not being mentioned in the "Sights and Sounds" article. Somewhere along the line, someone took notice of the fact that the Pied Piper saga had the potential for big business. Since that discovery, officials in Hamelin have been in no hurry to besmirch the mystery with too many details. Nowadays dozens of souvenir shops and guided tours cater to curious tourists; there is even a parade in which the morbid event is re-enacted once a week during high season.

"Ten bucks says a bus load of English Piper freaks will pull up any time," I told Buddy, as we were setting up in an austere conference room on the third floor of the "Rathaus," the highly appropriate German word for City Hall.

As the interview began, the current Piper, who'd again shown up in full costume, revealed himself to be an Australian in real life, complete with a wife and two kids. Despite such dedication to the job, the man unfortunately did not have a lot of interesting things to say, although that did not prevent him from talking for well over an hour. With great effort and persistence, Rob diplomatically managed to bring the interview to an end. In the general banter that often accompanies breaking down the set, I was tempted to ask the Piper what he did before ascending to his current role. That is until I noticed he had refused to disengage from his role even though the camera was no longer running. Fearful of provoking yet another soliloquy, I limited myself to inquiring what part of Australia he was from.

"Me cometh from a land far thither. It be known as…"

Needless to say there wasn't a second question. Packed up and ready to depart, goodbyes were exchanged as I stifled the urge to tell him I thought the bells on the tips of his curled shoes were a nice added touch.

On our final morning in Hamelin, the first item on the agenda was an interview with a so-called Piper "expert," a profession or calling that struck me as being almost as silly as the main one itself. Thankfully, this discussion proved a tad more interesting, if only for the finesse with which the "expert" managed to adapt his theories to each probing question. The man appeared to be in his late 60's and judging from the number of charts, books and leaflets in his office, he must have started dedicating his waking hours to Piper research shortly after turning ten.

From there it was on to a wooded hollow outside of town, where the expert stood atop a rocky outcrop to drone on about how the children had reportedly last been seen entering a nearby cave.

"So where is this cave?" I asked myself, *"And why aren't we filming there instead, you old dingbat?"*

To no one's surprise, the following day we exited Hamelin without a shred of evidence that anything remotely similar to the legend had ever taken place. Now on our way to Prague, I refused to glance through the new in-flight magazine, fearing it might contain yet another article on the much-ballyhooed piper. Instead I found myself pondering which profession was less laudable… being the Pied Piper, or simply filming him to help perpetuate the tale of woe.

CHAPTER 27

The Golem

In the summer of 2000, a visit to the city of Prague brought to mind the image of a young, spirited colt enjoying the freedom of its new found legs. Brimming with the youth of Europe, exploring, experiencing and excessing, it virtually oozed dynamism and unlimited potential. In the midst of it all was Lenka, the young woman Rob had arranged to serve as our production assistant for the last leg of the tour. Her innocence and free spirit captured the essence of the city, and her bubbly personality and considerable network of contacts, helped open doors that a normal, regular visitor could only dream of entering. Twenty-three, but with a worldly demeanour far surpassing her years, she'd made a strong impression right from the start, introducing herself in an accent that was a preview of mischievous times to come.

Done with Dracula and relieved of the Piper, we'd come to the architectural marvel that is Prague, to examine yet another legend. This time it was the turn of the "Golem," a mythical character in Jewish folklore, alleged to have been created from an amorphous clump of clay taken from the banks of the Vltava river. The man most often associated with the myth's creation was Judah Löw ben Bezalel, a 16th century rabbi, who had been seeking ways to help protect the city's Jewish population from anti-Semitic attacks. Despite the Golem's reputed usefulness in doing so, at some point the creature turned violent and had to be eliminated, a task that was accomplished by having the rabbi simply rub out the first letter of the word written on the Golem's forehead. According to the legend, "emet" meant reality, while "met" meant death.

"*If only it was only so easy with obnoxious neighbours,*" I thought as I continued to listen to Lenka's brief recital of the Golem's history in the hotel lobby. According to our young assistant, following his demise, the Golem's remains had been deposited in the attic of Prague's main synagogue, believed to be the oldest in Europe.

"Who comes up these ideas for the show?" I asked Buddy, after Lenka had concluded her mini saga.

"Who watches them?" he answered, having a point.

While Rob and Lenka excused themselves to discuss details of the week's itinerary, I withdrew to the hotel coffee shop. Nursing my java as I stared out at the bustling street life, I was drawn back to my first visit to Prague in December of 1986.

The trip had been a spontaneous one, initiated by my then girlfriend's cousin, Boris. Having recently received official permission to leave the DDR, Boris had asked Gundula and I to join him on what he presumed would be his last chance to visit his old flame, Martina. Although Prague was only 160 kilometres from Boris' flat on the outskirts of Karl Marx Stadt, winter road conditions were such that we didn't arrive in the Czechoslovakian capital until late morning. Driving through snow-covered streets, past row upon row of dismal, unpainted buildings, many with W.W.II bullet holes still visible in their crumbling facades, it felt as though we had slipped into a time warp. As arrangements had been made for us to stay with Boris' ex and her current boyfriend, Theo, we drove straight to the family villa after registering with the police.

"My father was a successful businessman before the war," Martina explained, once we'd all been introduced and the five of us had settled in the living room for afternoon tea. "After the Communists took over, I think it was in 1948, they confiscated the house and turned it into a cooperative, telling my parents they would have to share it with other families. Four families live here now. My parents are both dead so it's just Theo and I in our section, but we have to share the kitchen and bath."

"Our section" consisted of one room, allotted to serve as both living and sleeping quarters. Later that evening, we saw an example of just how "intimate" these imposed living arrangements were, when in the midst of our post-dinner conversation, a man entered through a side door without knocking and walked through to the adjoining kitchen.

"You get used to it," Martina offered, having seen the look on my face. "Sometimes there are problems, but for the most part we all get along. It's not great but what can you do?"

That night, bedded down between the sofa and a wardrobe, I lay staring up at the ornately carved ceiling, listening to the intermittent snores of my four roommates, as I tried to conceive what it would be like to suddenly be told you now had to share your living space with complete strangers for an indeterminate period of time.

Over breakfast the next morning, Martina issued the invitation to accompany her to her workplace. Arriving at the gates of a huge dilapidated factory, we shuffled through security with the rest of the shift just after six a.m. Once Martina had punched her time card, she suggested we retire to the cafeteria for a morning coffee, despite the fact we'd just finished breakfast.

"What do they make here?" I asked, as we entered a room clogged with people and cigarette smoke.

"We are in the business of manufacturing windows," she said, her last words drowned out by a noisy burst of laughter. Standing at one of the circular tables as I waited for my scalding coffee to cool, I couldn't help gawking at the jumble of overall-clad workers, many of whom appeared inebriated and in no hurry to get out on the factory floor.

"Martina, I have another question," I said. "Judging from the smoke in the room, I get the feeling some of these people have been here for awhile. Just how long a break do these guys have?"

Martina smiled before answering, taking a deep puff from her own cigarette before adding to the thick smog.

"As long as they like. They cannot be fired. Did you not know there is no unemployment in a Communist country?" she added with a grin, flicking her ashes in a butt-filled metal ashtray. "Some will stay here for a good part of the morning. Then maybe, if they are in the mood, they will go make a window or two and then break for lunch."

"And this goes on every day?"

"Every day."

※

With the rest of the afternoon off and our hotel only a five minute walk from the Old Town Square, I decided to explore what changes Prague had undergone in the intervening years. One of the first things to attract my attention was the absence of the "helpful" money changers on every corner. Also missing were the enumerable sets of unmanned scaffolding which had hidden so much of the unique architecture during my first trip. Paint, it seemed, had also been rediscovered in the interim, turning many of the formerly soot- coated buildings into brightly coloured wedding-cake facades. Most notably absent however, was the sense of gloom that had pervaded the city in 1986. Streets were now alive with an aura of inspiration; undeniable evidence that people can recover from almost anything when given the chance.

The next morning, we learned that our first full day of work would involve gathering what Lenka called "LowKall Collar." The humorous expression reminded me I'd yet to ask Rob just how he'd managed to land Lenka. Whatever the source, there could be little doubt it had been a wise decision. Springing into action at the merest hint of a new request, Lenka was able to organize matters down to the finest detail within minutes. A perfect example of her influence and efficiency was our first destination, the famous astronomical clock of Orloj, located in the Old Town square. Built in 1410, it was reportedly the oldest of its kind in the world to still function; playing host to hundreds of tourists, who assembled each day to witness a parade of figurines trotting out when the clock struck twelve noon. According to local legend, the clock was built by a man named Hanus. So impressed had the Prague City Council been with his finished work, they allegedly ordered him blinded, thereby guaranteeing the clock would remain one of a kind forever. Lenka, bless her heart, did not have much regard for legends, informing us that in fact the clock was designed and constructed by Mikulas of Kadan and Jan Sindel, whose subsequent fates were not nearly so dire.

Initially dismayed at the thought of having to film the clock in the midst of a throng of tourists, I was pleased when Lenka informed us she had arranged for a different perspective. Guiding us through a tiny door at the base of the tower, she proceeded to lead us up a narrow, winding staircase to a small platform directly behind the clock's intricate workings. From there we had a direct view down to the hundreds gathered in the square, who unknowingly, were gazing up at us. Unable to convince Buddy to gain instant notoriety by taking the place of one of the figures and waving naked to the crowd, I nevertheless managed to get great footage despite the deafening chiming of the bells.

The next location was the equally renowned Charles Bridge. Here, Lenka's "string-pulling talent" had gained us special access to the Gothic tower at its eastern end. Whereas most tourists simply flocked through its arch to fend for themselves amongst the musicians, street art vendors and statues in residence along the cobblestone walkway, thanks to Lenka, we ascended through a secret stairwell that led to a small terrace atop the tower. Looking west, we were treated to a spectacular view of the river and distant Prague Castle on the hill. Turning south, offered an eye-level display of the numerous church steeples that dot the Prague skyline. After filming numerous other elaborately decorated buildings in and around the Old Town, our daylong quest ended with a trip to the Citadel, an ancient fort built on a steep cliff overlooking the Vltava.

"Forget about the Golem," I told Rob that evening at dinner. "We've got enough great footage to do an hour-long documentary just on Prague."

"We have Lenka to thank for that," he said with genuine gratitude. "Maybe it will make up for the fiasco in Hamelin… Just so you guys know, don't make it a long night. I know the Czech beer is tempting but we're looking at one long day tomorrow."

※

Whatever methods Rob had employed to cast the Golem, they proved to be successful, as the winning candidate was waiting for us when we arrived at the old New Jewish synagogue the next morning. The fact the facilities were closed to the public for the day, made it easier to actualize the re-creation scenes, without the disruption of curious onlookers. The one detail Rob had overlooked though, was the consequences of engaging an actor bent on giving an Oscar winning performance. Suffice to say that by questioning every instruction issued, the Golem-wannabe succeeded in creating an increasingly tense atmosphere within the first hour. By the time we'd managed to grind out the needed footage, the letter "e" on the burly actor's forehead wasn't the only thing Rob was ready to rub out. Once his services were no longer needed, the Golem was dismissed with instructions to meet us later that evening.

After agreeing to skip lunch to make up for the time lost to the Golem's perfectionism, the next task was to film "his" remains. Although I knew said remnants were housed in the synagogue's attic, I was not pleased to learn the only of getting there was by climbing the steel rungs of a ladder cemented to the outside wall. What was even harder to swallow was the discovery that the entrance to the attic was a small, "Alice in Wonderland" arched doorway some thirty feet off the ground. Faced with no feasible alternative, I made sure that the camera was securely packed into a knapsack on my back before beginning my ascent, all the while reciting the mantra, "*Don't look down, don't look down, oh shit, don't look down*".

    I got to the top rung only to realize the opening was still some distance away. Reaching it would require stretching one leg over to the ledge of the doorway while still hanging on to the ladder. If that could be managed without plummeting to my death, I would then have to grab a handle above the opening and swing myself over. As luck would have it, at the exact moment I made my move, the synagogue's caretaker, who'd gone up ahead ostensibly to help, stuck his head out to see what was keeping me. Caught in a moment of mid-air panic and the belated recollection that a good climber never takes a step he can't retrace, I somehow managed to latch on to the handle and struggle my way inside.

    Pretty much as expected, what there was to film turned out to be a disappointment. There was no shortage of dust and dirt on either side of a two-plank walkway running the length of the attic, but certainly nothing that could pass for earthly remains. In other words, it was like a thousand other attics, all of which could have been reached without such death-defying antics. Having come this far, I made the effort to turn a stunningly, dull scene into something remotely interesting, all the while preoccupied with images of my imminent descent, which hopefully would be a controlled one. Once safely back on Mother Earth, no thanks to the caretaker, who insisted on letting go of my hand before I had a firm grip on the ladder, it was off to the neighbouring Jewish Cemetery. Unlike the attic, it was hoped that there would actually be something of relevance to film there.

For those who've never had the pleasure of visiting a cemetery in Europe, it's safe to say that by and large, they tend to be well kept sanctuaries of natural beauty and solitude, that offer a welcome escape from the hectic melee often found just outside their gates. Prague's main Jewish Cemetery was all that and more. Surrounded by a high brick wall, it took visitors into another world, filled with hundreds of moss-covered headstones, tilted at various angles beneath a canopy of towering trees.

"According to the information I have, the rabbi should be buried somewhere around here," Rob mumbled, glancing up from a map, while trying to get his bearings amidst the myriad of gravel footpaths dissecting the compound. Lenka however, knew exactly where the grave was located and within minutes we'd achieved what we came for. Hoping to prolong my exposure to the tranquil atmosphere, I managed to persuade Buddy to haul both camera and tripod back to the hotel, and spent the next hour strolling the cemetery grounds.

Just after eleven that night, our group was approaching a bridge in the city centre.

"We don't need a Bowatt," Lenka advised.

"Bowatt?" I repeated. "Why don't we need a Bowatt?"

"Because there is a stairway down to the island," she said matter-of-factly.

"How can it be an island if there's a stairway?"

"It's from the bridge… Don't be so pecky with details," she scolded.

"Pecky? I think you mean 'picky'".

"It is your silly language, not mine."

Under normal circumstances, wandering through a park in a strange city in the dark is not something high on the tourist board's list of things to do. Fortunately, the citizens of Prague seem to have shared that view, allowing us to make our way down the concrete steps and through the park to the river bank without spotting another soul.

With no disruptions to worry about, other than the Golem's recurrent career aspirations, the next two hours were spent on the banks of the Vltava, re-creating his birth. Unfortunately, it was a difficult delivery, even more trying than his death that morning at the synagogue. After filming the same scene for what felt like the 80th time, largely because the Golem flubbed or altered his lines in the previous 79, I whispered to Buddy, "Why don't we just take poetic license, toss him in the river, and be done with it?"

Rob also appeared to be contemplating alternative ways of making the scene more authentic. Being the seasoned producer that he was however, he at least had the patience for a few more takes before finally calling it a wrap shortly before four.

Partly due to the stress of the previous night's

riverside debacle, as well as the accumulated insanity of the last three weeks, Rob decreed that our last day in Prague would be one of recovery. Eternally grateful, I spent most of it sauntering through the streets of the old city, visiting bookstores, cafes, galleries and other places of interest that didn't have to be filmed.

In the late afternoon, Lenka showed up at the hotel to announce that she wished to take us all out to her favourite pub to help celebrate the end of a successful shoot.

"Oh?" I said with a smirk. "Which shoot is that?"

Thoughtfully, she had not included the Golem on her guest list, and it was a little after eight when the four of us stumbled through the door of a small establishment a few blocks off the Old Square. Up to this point, none of us had given much thought as to what Lenka's "favourite pub" might entail, but it's safe to say that a room full of beat-up sofas, complete with the occasional exposed spring, and a mishmash of wobbly, plastic and wooden chairs dispersed around a sawdust-covered floor, hadn't been on anyone's list of probabilities. Lenka's bursting pride however, quickly erased any doubts we might have had, as she showed us to our seats in a corner of the dimly lit room.

"I want you all to try what is my favourite drink here in Prague. Do you know mojito?"

I didn't, but by the end of the evening, we would certainly be well acquainted. Lightening an atmosphere already boosted by the knowledge the shoot was over, Buddy sprung for the first round. Despite the temptation to reminisce about the recent cast of characters, the subject of work was strictly avoided. Instead banter turned to comparing lives in a different culture. I was content to lean back on the sofa and reflect on the pleasures of sheer survival, while Buddy, Rob and Lenka continued to trade anecdotes. Time passed quickly and we were already on what must have been our fifth or sixth round of mojitos when our waiter came over to whisper something in Lenka's ear.

"I am sorry," she said, covering her mouth to stifle a chuckle, as he hovered expectantly. "We are not able to drink any more mojitos."

Buddy, who enjoys a drink as much as the next man, and the next, and the next, objected vehemently.

"Speak for yourself, sister. I'm still capable of a few more. Besides, nobody is drunk... yet."

"No, no. He don't think we are drunk," Lenka laughed. "He says we drink so many mojitos he has no more mint leaves."

Forced to switch to Lenka's second favourite drink for the rest of the evening, it was shortly after midnight when Rob started showing signs of wanting to leave.

"I've got an early flight, so I'm afraid I have to be the first to say adieu," he said, before giving Lenka a long, heartfelt hug. "What can I say lads?" he said, turning to Buddy and me. "Gonna be awhile before we can forget the capers of the last three weeks, but God knows I'm gonna try... But I think the network will be happy with what we managed to get."

"Hopefully," I told him, accepting his hug with a mutual slap on the back. "If they only knew what it took to get some of it. One thing you have to promise me though. If it turns out they're not pleased and want to send you back, you know who not to call."

"You got it," Rob answered, aiming a smile and cocked finger at both of us. "Been a slice lads." And with that he was gone.

An hour or so later, following a couple more drinks and a tearful goodbye with Lenka, partly assuaged by the alcohol-primed vow to keep in touch, Buddy and I were careening back to the hotel, our footsteps echoing off the cobblestone streets.

"Weren't we in this movie already?" I stammered. "This feels like that scene from The Third Man. "

"The Third Man was in Vienna. Even I know that," Buddy noted, somewhat surprised by his own knowledge.

Following a script that had been acted out on so many previous occasions, I was standing in the hallway, room key in hand, drifting in and out of a sentimental daze, when I felt spurred to offer a parting thought.

"It's gonna be hard to top these last three weeks, don't you think?" I said as we both lingered in a moment of silence, "Any idea where I can get my hands on a hat like Howdy's?"

CHAPTER 28

Surviving the Hindenburg

Anyone who has taken the time to look, knows that the annals of history are littered with stories of people who found themselves in unique life-threatening situations only to be rescued at the last minute. One of the benefits of having been in the right spot at the wrong moment, was the opportunity to turn such close encounters into revenue, providing the world with a unique, first-hand glimpse of the circumstances of the ordeal. One such individual was Heinz Schön, a survivor of the Wilhelm Gustloff marine catastrophe in 1945. Another was Franz Werner, a fourteen year old cabin boy who was on board the German airship, Hindenburg when it caught fire and crashed while attempting a mooring in Lakehurst, New Jersey on May 6th, 1937.

Our rendezvous with Franz Werner took place in the southern German city of Friedrichshafen, a fitting venue since it was here on the northern shore of Lake Constance in 1900, that Graf Ferdinand von Zeppelin had successfully tested the prototype airship he had designed and built. Airships of similar design had gone on to be used by the German military at the beginning of the First World War, but in the years that followed, more focus had been placed on the development of passenger-carrying models. With the crash of the Hindenburg, however, what had looked to be a promising future for airship travel came to a sudden and abrupt end. Unlike thirty-five of the ninety-six crew and passengers aboard the fateful flight of the largest airship ever built, Franz Werner lived to tell his tale.

Seated in a nondescript hotel conference room not far from the Zeppelin museum, Werner spoke of the calamity with a confidence born of repetition; describing how he'd been in the kitchen that morning, preparing for the landing, when he felt a shudder pass through the airship. Shortly afterwards, a large ball of fire had appeared, prompting Franz's short life to flash in front of him. To his lasting fortune, a ballast tank directly above his head burst open seconds later, extinguishing the fire that had threatened to consume him. In the midst of the subsequent chaos, Franz managed to kick open a hatch normally used to load food on board. Dropping five meters to the ground, he looked up to see the airship slowly collapsing above him. What ultimately saved him from being crushed under tons of metal were the inflated tires of the airship's gondola. As the ponderous hulk struck the ground it bounced upwards briefly, allowing Franz to scramble to safety, just seconds before the blazing structure crumpled to the ground.

Despite having listened to this detailed personal narrative, it was difficult to draw a direct connection between the famous, grainy footage of the crash and the man seated in front of us.

"Don't you want to ask him anything about the cause of the crash?" I asked the producer once Franz had briefly excused himself to go to the washroom. "From what I've read, speculation has stretched from sabotage to a random spark."

"It doesn't fit the concept of the show," she replied, clearly unappreciative of my unsolicited input.

"Not even for his opinion... Off the record?"

Unaware of the cloud of resentment that had descended between myself and the producer during his absence, Franz jovially agreed to accompany us to the nearby Zeppelin museum. There, against the backdrop of a life-size mockup of a section of the Hindenburg's passenger gondola, he continued to offer details of the tragedy. Although the museum's exhibit only included the reading lounge, dining room and observation deck, visitors were given a glimpse of what it must have been like to fly in one of these enormous machines. A further sense of its immensity emerged with information that the airship had contained twenty-five double berthed cabins, washrooms and shower facilities, as well as a bar, writing room and even a promenade. But at $450 for a one-way ticket in 1937, one would have had to have had very deep pockets to enjoy such luxury.

Although we had no way of knowing it at the time, we would be back in Friedrichshafen within two years, this time to experience our own mini- version of that luxury. Handed the assignment to document a modern airship christened the Zeppelin NT, we had travelled back to the lakeside city to interview its designer and owner. We did so against the backdrop of a hangar where a second airship was under construction. As fascinating as it was to hear about all the technology that went into the building of the NT, the highlight came when the owner suggested we climb aboard for an hour-long trip over Lake Constance. Seated in one of the twelve, plush leather chairs in the glass-enclosed gondola, I was treated to a spectacular view of the snow-capped Alps in the distance. Able to walk around freely during the flight, it was also possible to capture vistas of the red-roofed towns and villages of Germany, Austria and Switzerland, as well as the numerous miniature boats crisscrossing the lake below. What was particularly noteworthy was how quiet the airship was. Other than the soft hum of its two engines, one had the feeling of being ensconced in a moving cloud.

As if the first circuit hadn't been thrilling enough, shortly after we landed, the owner approached us to ask whether we'd like to go back up, this time as ballast for a pilot trainee about to conduct his first solo flight.

"I'm not so sure I like the sound of 'first solo,'" I said to Buddy, after stowing the camera in the car and clambering back on board. "I didn't see any parachutes did you?"

"I wouldn't worry too much about a parachute if I were you. We won't be high enough to use one, and you'd probably hit the ground before the chute even opened," he said reassuringly.

So with little or no wind to throw caution to that day, it was back up we went, this time for almost three hours. With no obligation to film, and visions of Lakehurst held at a comfortable distance, I'm glad to say I survived to recall every idyllic moment of a truly unique experience.

CHAPTER 29

The Legend of Sparta

"So like what... it's against the law to put garbage in a bin here?" I asked Buddy, as we inched through downtown Athens traffic in the throes of an oppressive heat wave. "I thought this only happened in Rome or Naples. I mean, have you even seen a garbage can? I didn't spot a single one at the airport. At this rate I may end up taking this bottle back to Germany."

If initial impressions of the lay of the land so far, were an accurate barometer, one adage the Babylonians apparently never got around to passing on to the Greeks, was that cleanliness is next to Godliness. Either that or there are an awful lot of atheists in Greece. Like many visitors, I too had been led astray by those awe-inspiring images of the Parthenon and Acropolis, pristine beaches, crystal blue lagoons and charming white-coated villages slotted into coves or along the mountainside. What had not graced the pages of those glossy brochures, at least for Athens, was the immense amount of litter soiling the landscape.

As it happened, widely strewn garbage had not been the only item that had helped get things off to a bad start. Minutes after arriving at our hotel, located on a major thoroughfare, I discovered that my knapsack had somehow gotten left behind in the process of loading equipment into a cab at the airport.

"Great... just bloody great," I sneered, angry at having taken more notice of Buddy's camera than my own belongings. "Didn't either of you guys notice there was something left on the trolley?" I asked, aware I couldn't come right out and accuse Buddy, or our young assistant, Jan, for what was at least partially my own oversight.

"What was in it?" Jan asked cautiously, sensing that preventing such scenarios fell into his jurisdiction.

"A couple of books and a new pair of sneakers I bought especially for the trip. Those can be replaced. What really hurts is that my old Nikkormat was in there. I've had that camera since the mid-eighties."

Although both expressed the obligatory dosage of empathy, neither was prepared to accompany me back to the airport for what we all suspected would be a futile attempt at recovery. Instead, the two of them retreated to the rooftop pool to enjoy the cooling waters, while gazing out at the distant Acropolis. I, on the other hand was left to spend the next hour crammed into a hot, crowded bus, returning to the scene of the crime. Once able to locate the Lost and Found in the main terminal, I quickly became embroiled in a debate with an airport employee, who I was convinced had already put my camera in his locker. Tensions rose even further when I attempted to locate someone who could speak at least a smidgeon of English. Finally, after what felt like an hour-long slide towards insanity, I left my negotiating partners with a few choice words and headed back to the hotel without my beloved apparatus.

That evening at dinner, still miffed at my colleagues, I did my best to control my smouldering resentment as we were introduced to our producer. A large, gruff American with an underlying friendly demeanour, Rick instantly won my respect when he informed me that a close colleague and friend had recommended me for the shoot.

"No shit. He described you as a 'master of composition,'" Rick said. "You did a shoot with him in Italy about a year ago."

"Ah yeah… Il Barro in Tuscany, right? John… something."

"That's him. John Stavers. John and I have been buds for years. When he heard we were planning this shoot, your name came up right away."

"Nice of him to say so," I told Rick, neglecting to point out that John had spent the entirety of our Italian adventure testing wines in the villa with the owner, while Buddy and I traipsed through stone alleyways, not having a clue about what he wanted or needed. Fortunately, the scenery in the restored medieval village and surrounding hills had been so spectacular, it was virtually to impossible to deliver a bad shot.

As we were continued to get acquainted over our meal, aided by a few tolerable Greek beers, Rick provided an outline of the week's agenda.

"We're shooting for a program called *The Legend of Sparta*," he explained. "At least that's its working title. It will end up being a four-hour documentary split over several weeks."

"Four hours?" I echoed, somewhat stunned. "And we're here for only a week?"

"Sounds like a lot, I know. But we've already shot a lot of the period battle scenes back in LA. What we need here should be doable as long as the weather plays along. And with that in mind, we should probably call it a night. I'd like to be in Sparta by early afternoon so that means an early start."

✳

The next morning, having dragged ourselves away from one of the most well-stocked breakfast buffets ever seen on Planet Earth, we were met in the lobby by the driver the US production company had hired sight unseen. George, however, turned out to be very accommodating, helping us lug equipment and suitcases to his van while explaining in passable English, that we were facing a five-hour drive to Sparta. Once underway, it didn't take long for a less positive trait to emerge. George happened to be one of those people with that unfortunate habit of snorting up excess mucus into their nasal cavity every few minutes. Seeing as we'd just met, I struggled to remain silent for the first while, hoping the tendency might just be a passing phase. But an hour later, with the snorting symphony still in full swing, I decided to broach the subject; a task about as pleasurable as telling a complete stranger they have body odour or bad breath.

"So George… How long have you been doing cocaine?" I asked, straining to maintain some civility, as we swung up the entrance ramp to the highway that would take us west to the Peloponnese isthmus.

"Please?"

"The nose, your nose… the way you've been snorting. It sounds like your mucus membranes are in bad shape. You should see somebody about it. Could be serious."

"Mucus?"

"Not so important… I guess what I'm trying to say is that it kinda grates after awhile, especially when awhile might last another four hours," I said, before glancing into the back seat for some sort of moral support. But with Buddy's head buried in a magazine and Jan affixed to a video game on his phone, the only one to respond was Rick.

"It's not sooooo bad, once you get used to it," he said with pragmatic politeness.

"You mean like chewing tin foil or staring at the sun?"

"Whatever."

But fortunately for all concerned, George managed to get the message, and in the ensuing silence, there was a chance to update myself on "the legend," we'd come to film.

According to a brochure I'd picked up at the hotel's antiquated business centre after last night's dinner, a man by the name of Lycurgus was largely to blame. Tapping into the experience and knowledge gained from his travels to leading nations like Persia and Egypt, Lycurgus had attempted to create what he considered to be the perfect state, based on the guidelines of equality, military fitness, and austerity. In line with that goal he had formed a Senate that was to rule on equal standing with the King. In addition Lycurgus introduced land reform, splitting the country up into small plots in an effort to abolish poverty and encourage the population to become self-sufficient. In what was seen as an attempt to prevent stealing, he then proposed doing away with money, going so far as to ask all residents to give up all their collected valuables. As a result, life became rather "Spartan," with most people learning to provide for daily necessities by themselves. Military training and discipline, scant food portions, and frequent floggings were also instituted in an attempt to teach young boys to be brave, endure pain, and value hardships. On top of these measures, young soldiers were also discouraged from bathing, not supplied with proper clothing or allowed to complain. So rigid was their regimen, going into battle was often seen as something to look forward to. Why anyone would have viewed Lycurgus' achievements as something to be admired escaped me for the moment.

Much to Rick's satisfaction we arrived in Sparta early enough to get in a few hours of location scouting.

"According to the legend," Rick recited from a guide book as we stood at the edge of a gorge not far from the centre of the city, "It was here that the Spartans were in the habit of tossing 'unfit' children off a cliff."

"Nice habit," I proffered, cautiously peering over the edge of the gorge. "By the way, any idea on what can we shoot to go with that element of the story? Care to volunteer by any chance Buddy?"

With resolving that dilemma put on hold for the moment, we headed off in search of another location that hopefully could provide more interesting footage. Driving south on the main highway, we eventually turned off on to a dirt road that led into the mountains; continuing for several more kilometres until reaching a sandy plateau. Leaving Buddy in the car to keep an eye on the gear, I followed Rick down a footpath through the bush, until we arrived at the edge of a cliff. Waiting for Rick to decide if there was any point in shooting the plain we had just driven through several minutes earlier, I just happened to look down to see irrefutable proof of how modern day Greeks were carrying on their version of a Spartan tradition. There directly below us, was the evidence that previous visitors had seen fit to empty their pockets, car trunk, and quite possibly a whole week's worth of household refuse before departing. Still, as unsightly as it was, better garbage than children.

Day three in Greece was to take us to Mycenae, an archaeological site that housed the ruins of a segment of ancient Mycenaean civilization. Arrangements had been made for us to meet up there with a professor of Greek mythology, who according to Rick, would lead us through the grounds, offering a condensed version of Mycenaean history and its connection to the Spartan era. Unlike many other mono-themed academics I'd worked with, this one did not have an inflated opinion of himself. Instead, he expounded his knowledge in a clear, precise and above all, down-to-earth manner that made it interesting even for those of us not particularly enthralled with Mycenaean folklore, especially when being dispersed in suffocating heat. Also lightening the weightiness of the subject, was the man's appearance. With oversized reading glasses, wild, unkempt hair and rumpled khaki safari suit, he was a dead-ringer for the archetypical "nutty professor."

The morning of the fourth day saw us travel to a Greek military installation, a half hour north of Sparta. Obliged to undergo a thorough security check before being allowed on base, once cleared we were taken directly to the heliport to be briefed by a solemn-faced army lieutenant, whose job it was to ensure that we didn't film any secret facilities during our flight.

Within minutes of being air-borne, the rugged Greek

coastline came into view. Witness to what seemed to be an almost endless series of small rocky coves and isolated beaches backed by a breathtaking azure sea, I was at a loss as to what this spectacular scenery had to do with the legend of Sparta but was not about to complain.

After following the coastline for what felt like hours but in reality was only twenty minutes, we turned inland. Almost immediately, a heated discussion broke out between the army officer and the pilot. Judging from the head-shaking and finger-wagging going on, it was apparent we were nearing one of the aforementioned "forbidden zones." When the officer glanced back in my direction, I raised my hands in mock surrender, an indication I was perfectly content to enjoy the landscape rather than film it. Several minutes later, during which time I failed to spot anything that could remotely fall into the category of "restricted," I felt a tap on my shoulder. I didn't know what to make of the "thumbs up" the officer was flashing, until he suddenly pointed down to announce we'd arrived over our destination. .

"We gotta get lower," I shouted to Rick over the roar of the rotors. "You can hardly make anything out from this height and if I try zooming in, it'll look like we're filming in an earthquake."

"No, no, stay wide," he ordered. "I need to see the entire ruins."

"But it's gonna look like I'm shooting from the moon. It's almost impossible to tell what it is. Look in the monitor."

"Trust me," Rick insisted. "I can explain it in the narration. I need to see the whole complex and its position in the countryside."

"Okay, if you say so... But I still think it's a good idea to fly lower after the wide shot, just so you have some closer cutaways."

As Rick was not about to be contradicted, I took the precaution of making sure these last comments were recorded for protection against an irate editor. Although we continued to circle the area at the higher altitude, I also made sure to include a couple of zooms as evidence of how impossible it was to hold a closer shot steady from such a height.

Once done, it was on to refuel in the port city of Kalamata, a location Rick said had been some importance during the Spartan era.

"Is there something to film here?" I asked as we climbed out to obtain some much-needed refreshments at the airport cafe.

"No," our officer interrupted. "Here no film allowed. Also not on trip back to base."

"Does that answer your question?" Rick said.

With filming denied, the return flight was spent revelling in the rolling vistas, a "great to be alive" moment if there ever was one.

The morning of our final day on the peninsula was spent driving to Olympia, the site of the ancient Olympic Games. An astounding work of architecture, it would have made for amazing television had it not been raining so hard we could barely see any of its numerous statues. With filming there quickly deemed a literal washout, it was on to the city of Thebes, where for reasons that remained unknown, we documented a seemingly neglected ruin smack dab in the middle of a busy commercial district.

Back in Athens that evening at dinner, Rick appeared satisfied with what we'd accomplished, saying there was a good chance he'd be returning in a month to pick up anything still needed. Claiming he had an early plane to catch, we parted company, fully convinced we'd never see him again.

*

Two months later however, just as memories of Greece had all but faded, things took an interesting twist. A call from the LA production company revealed that Rick had been relieved of his duties with the project; something to do with the helicopter footage having been useless because it was shot at too high an altitude. Rather than sending a replacement, the company had decided to trust sending us back on our own.

Packed for another week-long stay, this time we chose to grant Jan unlimited time to play with his cell phone from the comforts of home sweet home. A second figure missing from this leg of our Greek saga was to be our driver, George. Already booked for another job, he recommended his son, Alex as an alternative.

After an uneventful flight, we emerged from the airport terminal just after 9:00 a.m. to be greeted by a strong gust of dusty, hot air, out of which strolled a short, stocky, dark-haired Greek in his mid-twenties.

"So, Alex I presume," I said, shaking his hand and double-checking to make sure all the luggage was aboard. "It's nice to meet you. Your dad says you speak English."

"Yes," he answered with a brief nod.

"Did you study it at school?" I continued as we took

our seats.

"Yes."

"And how long have you been speaking it?"

"Yes"

"Buddy…"

In addition to exaggerating Alex's language skills, George had also neglected to inform his son that he would be with us the entire week.

"Not drive only to hotel?" he asked, somewhat perplexed upon hearing the apparent change in plans.

"Correct. Not drive only to hotel. Drive whole week."

Fifteen minutes later, we were pulling up to a house in an Athens suburb. Alex sprang out and disappeared into a small, white-stuccoed building, to presumably pick up some extra clothes.

"At least he doesn't snort," I said to Buddy as we waited. "And his English is top notch as well. Bound to be an interesting week."

Ten minutes later, Alex reappeared carrying a pouch the size of a cosmetic bag.

"That's it? No suitcase?" I asked, as he climbed in and slammed the door hard enough to shake the whole van. "That's all you're taking? No change of clothes?"

"Yes"

"Yeah, okay… We've already covered that."

"No… Clozezzs are here," he corrected, holding the bag aloft. "No need more".

"If you say so," I said, turning to Buddy. "Do me a favour…Make sure you sit next to him this week at breakfast, lunch and dinner."

Despite the minor detour, it was just after 11:00

when we hit the highway, early enough for us to try and get the requested footage of Marathon before heading further north.

"You know where this place is eh, Alex?"

"Place?"

"Yeah, Marathon... Where the guy ran 42 kilometres to tell the Athenians the enemy had landed or something."

"Ah, yes, Marathon I know... Not far."

Two hours and multiple, "Are you sure this is the right road?" inquiries later, there we were inching our way up a steep mountain path more suitable for donkey-driven carts than vans.

"Tremendous view from up here Alex, but it's not exactly what we need. How much further is Marathon?"

"Soon, soon," he answered, trying to unfold a map as we edged precariously close to the side of the cliff. Unable to see the benefits of careening down the mountainside, I suggested we might be better served if he concentrated on driving, especially given that rocks strewn on the narrow trail had reached the size of small boulders, all but eliminating chances of turning around or backing up. Miraculously, the road eventually descended to rejoin a main highway and a short time later we arrived at what Alex claimed was the famous Marathon.

"Didn't we come this way about an hour ago?" Buddy asked, making no attempt to suppress his displeasure.

"Are you sure this is the place?" I asked. "I mean, there's nothing here. No signs, no monuments, no information stand, no McDonald's. It's just a field full of, what else... garbage. This can't be what we've been looking for."

And it wasn't. As a subsequent search for the real Marathon proved to be both futile and time-consuming, we decided to look for a hotel nearby rather than drive to the next location in the dark. Upon arrival at a decent-looking inn, it was quickly apparent that George had also forgotten to inform Alex that his duties extended beyond just getting us lost.

"Hey Alex... Can you give me a hand with this case? We can't leave any of this stuff in the van overnight."

Acting as if he was performing the ultimate sacrifice, Alex pitched in before announcing he wouldn't be joining us for dinner.

"But we haven't had anything but a snack today," I said. "You gotta eat something."

"I bring food with," he answered, pointing to the small bag that up to now we had assumed contained only "clozzezz."

That evening at dinner, shortly after the waitress had delivered our wine and taken our orders, I turned to broach a pressing subject with Buddy.

"We gotta talk Monsieur. I'm not gonna make it through the week with this guy. If he has as much trouble locating the other sites as he did with so-called Marathon, we'll never cover half of what they want. If it's gonna be hit and miss every day, I'll lose it. Isn't there any way he can meet with a mysterious accident or something?"

Always good for a surprise, Buddy made a call to George directly from our table. Without hearing a specific complaint, George was telepathic enough to understand the situation, explaining this wasn't Alex's usual line of work and that he did tend to get easily confused. Despite my urging to ask what Alex's real line of work was, Buddy simply thanked George and hung up.

"So we're done," he announced. "Alex is history. George is going to call him."

Fifteen minutes later history put in an appearance. If Alex's ego had been bruised by the change in plans, he didn't show it. If anything, his smile suggested he had been enjoying our company about as much as we his. With everyone now in a buoyant mood, Buddy proceeded to disperse the remaining wine before ordering a second bottle. By the time I was ready to call it a night an hour or so later, Buddy, who was pretty well oiled, insisted on showing his gratitude for the turn of events by offering a exorbitant tip to our waiter.

"Wait a second," he said to the dumbfounded man. "Here's a little something for the cook as well."

"Geez… While you're at it why don't you tip those other patrons as well," I challenged, pointing to the sole couple sitting off in a corner.

"That's great idea," he announced, suddenly getting to his feet.

"Easy lad. That was a joke… If you feel the need to toss money around, toss some of it my way."

Somehow able to register the absurdity of his gesture through the blur, the smile sagged from Buddy's face as he slumped back down in the chair and refilled his glass. Not wishing to observe any further descent, I bid the two of them a pleasant "Kalinychta" and left for my room.

"So, how'd it go with Alex last night?" I asked the next morning over a breakfast of greasy ham, stale cheese and a bun with the consistency of a shot-putt.

"Ohhh," Buddy mumbled, straining to recall the

occasion.

"It was fine. He's not a bad guy actually. He even helped arrange for a rental car this morning before he took off."

"What the heck did you talk about? The guy knows like three words of English."

"Uuuhhh... I guess I did most of the talking. Now that I think about it, he didn't say much."

"I hope you at least gave him a big tip for being such a good listener."

Left to our own devices, we managed to locate the site of the famed Battle of Thermopylae in just under two hours. We might have found it in only one, had there actually been any signs indicating that a momentous confrontation had taken place there in 480 A.D., between an alliance of Greek states under the leadership of King Leonidas of Sparta, and the much larger army of the Persian King, Xerxes.

"Maybe they don't want to advertise the fact that they lost," I quipped as we stared down into the narrow canyon our primitive map suggested must be the place. Bordered by steep, rock-covered inclines on both sides, the canyon wound its way up from the nearby Gulf of Lamia via an old, dried up creek bed, before disappearing into the distant mountains. It looked like a great place for an ambush, as anyone attempting to move through it would have been a virtual sitting duck. Given their home turf advantage, the Spartans might have won the battle had they not been betrayed by a local turncoat who reportedly tipped off the invading Persians to an alternative route through the gorge.

"Where's Rick's helicopter when you need it?" I griped, having realized the only way to obtain an overview of the gorge meant clambering up one of the steep slopes. With the camera in my knapsack and instructions for Buddy to follow with the tripod, I set off towards a plateau half way up a nearby hill. Getting there under the blazing midday sun was no easy feat, but the location was exactly what I was looking for. A quick glance back down to the valley floor however, revealed no sign of Buddy, nor did my echoing shout. Aware that Buddy was more an expert in multi-slacking than in tasking, after waiting for almost fifteen minutes, I left the knapsack half-hidden behind a large boulder and retraced my steps. Backtracking part way along the creek bed, I rounded a bend to find him sitting in the shade, and in the process downing a Coke.

"What… Coffee time already?"

"It's so friggin' hot here. Had to take a break."

"Too hot to answer me? I was calling you to bring the tripod."

"I didn't hear anything."

Thoroughly irked at his laziness, I simply grabbed the tripod and took off back to the plateau alone. After taking at least a dozen shots of the canyon and its surrounding mountains, I descended again to discover Buddy had conveniently abandoned his hideout, leaving me with the prospect of schlepping both camera and tripod all the way back to the parking area. Doing so however, meant overcoming a series of mini-cliffs, the creek had formed in its drop to the sea. Each miniature precipice had to be conquered in stages, a tiresome process that involved setting the tripod and camera down on the upper ledge, hopping down to the lower level and then retrieving them before heading for the next drop. Despite the burning heat and anger, I was making good headway until I got to a ridge that, unbeknownst to me, had my name on it. Having already scrambled down to the lower ledge, I was about to retrieve the equipment when I heard a noise I thought might be Buddy. No sooner had I turned away to investigate, the entire front section of the rock face snapped off and fell to the creek bed with a sickening thud. It took a second to realize how close I'd come to becoming a one-legged cameraman. Had there not been the momentary diversion, my foot would have been resting under a three or four-hundred-pound boulder. With no way to remove it, I would have been stranded and likely expired before Buddy or anyone else got around to looking for me. Shaken but safe, I was making my way across the last hundred metres to the parking lot when it came to me that had an accident taken place, searchers would have eventually discovered two bodies. Foot or no foot, revenge would have propelled me to find Buddy to mete out justice for not having helped me.

*

According to that grumpy, old German philosopher, Arthur Schopenhauer, "*The quantity of noise anyone can comfortably endure, is in inverse proportion to his mental powers.*" It's a phrase I'd often thought of employing whenever checking into a hotel. Most of the time however, I tried to keep matters simple, informing the receptionist of the curse of being a light sleeper and requesting a quiet room as far as away as possible from elevators, ice machines, kitchen fans and adjoining rooms. Oddly enough, the bane of my nocturnal existence didn't apply to traffic. Often louder than the annoying white noise stemming from a humming fridge or air conditioner, traffic could in fact lull me to sleep. Having heard my plaintive plea a hundred times, Buddy had made a habit of rushing to reach check-in before me.

On our first night back in Athens, I again made a point of asking for a decently quiet room. As luck would have it, a series of noisy neighbours forced me to switch rooms several times. Finally at two a.m., the frustrated night clerk agreed to put me in an executive room on the fourth floor as a last resort. The second the heavy door swung closed, I knew the problem had been solved. Outfitted with far better soundproofing, the room was the bubble of tranquility I needed to get a good night's sleep.

Much to my delight, the next morning I discovered the room also came equipped with access to a private breakfast nook down the hall, exclusive to all "executive" guests booked on the floor. Later that evening, I learned there was an additional benefit to residing on the fourth floor. Accessible only to those holding a fourth floor key card, was a reading room stocked with a free bar. At least we assumed it was free, seeing there was never anyone around to serve us or collect our money. Ready and willing to take advantage of the unexpected perk, we just helped ourselves, "we" being myself and Buddy, who proved an exceptionally eager candidate.

With the shoot now completed, it was time to discuss how we could make use of the extra days we'd tacked on for our own enjoyment. Despite my earlier impressions of the Greek capital, exploring the sights and sounds of Athens on the first free day turned out to be reasonably pleasurable; that is if you didn't mind the heat, the smells, the dirt, the noise or the constant battles to keep taxi drivers honest. Every so often you also had to overlook the occasional dead dog decomposing outside a derelict phone booth. Having said that, the city also had a number of high points to offer, Filapappou Hill being a prime example. Hoping to avoid the pressing throngs on our visit to the famed Acropolis, we ascended the nearby Filapappou Hill, from where we could marvel at the majestic beauty and symmetry of the Parthenon, light years from the bustling hordes. Another memorable moment came right after we had purchased tickets to a museum in the park below the Acropolis. That drachma drama began when I suggested that Buddy double check the change he had blindly accepted from the ticket vendor.

"You gave her a hundred, and I swear she only gave you change for a twenty. Count it."

Normally quite lackadaisical about money matters, this time Buddy wasted no time in commandeering a nearby picnic table to examine his funds. Carefully sorting the bills and coins still in his hand, he suddenly burst into a rage and stormed back over to the ticket booth. Brushing aside the current customer, he dispensed with niceties to bring the suspected infraction to the vendor's attention.

"You're a bloody thief," he screeched. Interestingly enough, instead of reaching for an alarm button or firearm, the older woman merely eased the proper due amount under the barred window without the slightest flinch of indignation or protest. Under the eyes of several shocked tourists and their children, I managed to drag Buddy away from the window before he attempted to seek any additional compensation. In stark contrast to the events at the entrance, the museum itself turned out to be a dud.

Having had our fill of historical and hysterical sites for the moment, we headed for the district of old Athens known locally as the Plaka. After wandering aimlessly through its crowded streets for an hour or so, we stopped for lunch at what looked to be a typical Greek restaurant - typical in that it came with plaster busts of every Greek God known to mankind, a series of fake white pillars attached to each and every wall, garish paintings of island beaches and Zorba the Greek's theme music blaring from tinny speakers. But the food was superb, and while feasting over a genuine Greek salad of tomatoes and herbs, a plate of gyros and a bottle of Retsina, we had the chance to talk over options for the rest of the afternoon, before settling on the idea of using the car to escape the city for more natural terrain.

"What is it with this place?" I asked a short time later, as we were cruising through a dried-out forest that looked ready to incinerate the second an errant smoker tossed a cigarette its way. "For the last few miles, the whole bloody highway has been lined with plastic bottles. I mean what is this? They're everywhere."

Eventually tiring of the trail of trash, we pulled off the main road to try and clarify our whereabouts. In the midst of examining our map, we happened to catch sight of several people lounging beside what appeared to be a pond at the edge of a wooded glen. Getting out for a closer inspection we discovered it was in fact a natural, thermal bath, completely unmarked and untouched by a developer's hand. Most of the patrons appeared to be truck drivers, who had simply parked their lorries nearby, to chill and relax in the warm waters. As inviting as it looked, the pungent smell of sulphur was almost enough to drive us away; that and the fact that one needed to walk across a teetering board spanning a grimy drainage ditch to reach the pond.

"Can you believe this?" Buddy sighed in mild disbelief, after we'd stripped down to our underwear and slipped into the soothing water. "If this was Germany somebody would have already turned it into an exclusive spa and be charging 50 Marks to get in. Here you just pull off the road, lose your "clozezz" and jump in. No signs, no fees, no rules and regulations… It's incredible."

"Enjoy it while you can lad," I told him. "What with the odour and Greece's track record with garbage removal, we're probably frolicking in the drainage lagoon from a huge chemical plant and will both be dead in a few hours"

"At this point, who cares? There's worse ways to go," he countered before paddling away to deeper waters.

*

As it happened, water was to play a significant role on our last day in the Greek capital as well. Despite the lure of remaining on the executive floor for one more day, we checked out that morning to find a more reasonably-priced alternative closer to Vouliagmeni Beach, a seaside resort area located on the western edge of the city. In spite of its name however, when we asked at the new hotel where we might find said "beach," all we got was a look of incomprehension.

"I'm sorry but I am not from here," the receptionist admitted. "All I know is there's a private club up the road. You can try there."

"How can somebody not know whether there is a beach?" I asked after we'd thanked her and exited into the blistering heat.

Private in this case, meant really private and it was only after we concocted a cock-and-bull story about being visiting travel journalists, that the the guard at the entrance agreed to let us enter on a "one time basis." It didn't take long to discover we'd stumbled upon a hangout for members of Athens' "in crowd," most of whom were congregated around the pool patio, sipping on colourful cocktails despite the early hour.

"Doesn't it seem kind of odd there's a swimming pool when the Mediterranean is only a few yards away?" I asked Buddy, once we'd staked a claim to a patch of grass. Too hyper to merely lounge in the sun, I left Buddy to sort out his rented beach paraphernalia while I went off to get the lay of the fenced-in-land and grab something to drink.

"Man, we gotta give this a try," I exhorted on my return. "This place offers tubing and water-skiing. Shit, I haven't been waterskiing for centuries… And never on the sea. Wait till you get a look at the boat that takes you out."

An avid car nut to begin with, Buddy was suitably impressed by the 375 horsepower outboard Corvette engine jammed into the rear of a sleek, bright red speedboat, but not impressed enough to actually join in. Instead he jumped into the back of the boat, promising to keep an eye on the singular tuber, namely me. Laying alone atop a tube built for two, I wriggled myself into a comfortable position, my legs dragging in the warm, salty water as the driver slowly guided the boat past rows of docked sailboats and expensive-looking yachts.

Once free of potential obstacles, and no doubt encouraged by Buddy, the driver offered a small taste of what the boat was capable of. Bouncing wildly across the waves, you could feel the boat's awesome power as the tube crested over one wave and was pulled straight through the next by sheer force. After almost twenty minutes of this pleasurable torture, I signalled to Buddy that I was ready to call it a day after one more loop. Looking forward to a leisurely return to dockside, I began to relax my white knuckle grip on the handles. Buddy however, had other ideas. Perhaps as potential payback for the wisecracks I'd been delivering over the last few weeks, he'd secretly challenged the driver, claiming I had boasted earlier he wouldn't be able to dump me from the tube. At first I assumed the sudden increase in speed was an aberration that would soon be corrected. But rather than slowing down, we kept going faster. After reaching what he no doubt considered a suitable speed, the driver slowed and cut sharply to his left letting our wake catch up with us just before entering the bay. He then looped around behind me and cut sharply to the right. The slick figure-eight manoeuvre forced me to cross over his ever-deepening wakes, which were now starting to collide with each other. Just as I passed over the threshold of one wave and descended into a hollow of the next, the driver hit the throttle, catapulting the tube high into the air. Within those brief seconds of suspended animation, I flashed back to the streets of Winnipeg, where while driving north on Main street, I had watched a television set in the back of a pick-up in the neighbouring lane, wriggle free of its moorings and leap to freedom. As I observed it tumbling through the air in slow-motion, a small voice interrupted to tell me to let go of the grips before it crashed to the ground. The second I did, the tube shot out from beneath me, leaving me to flail in free-fall as Greek gravity dropped me into the ocean like a stone. Spewing a mouthful of salt water as I surfaced, I swam to the boat and dragged myself over the gunnel, only to see Buddy on the floor, clutching his gut in laughter, as the driver looked back at me with a "mission accomplished" smirk on his face.

*

That evening, having already returned our rental car, and not interested in taking public transportation, we splurged on a cab to take us back down to the Plaka for dinner. Still wallowing in the memory of instigating my afternoon's airborne adventure, Buddy offered to pick up the tab as a gesture of quid pro quo.

"Not necessary, but appreciated," I told him, declining the invitation to share a bottle of wine. At the end of another excellent meal, Buddy's buoyant mood was momentarily diverted by the arrival of the bill. Looking as though he was swatting at a plague of invisible mosquitos, he desperately searched his pockets for a wallet that wasn't there.

"Could you have left it back at the hotel?" I asked.

"I don't know," he said with a note of rising panic. "I must have had it in the cab or I couldn't have paid for the ride. Man, I had over $300 in it… And shit, my passport's missing too."

With no other choice but to return to the hotel on the remote chance he'd been wrong, we paid the bill on my credit card and hailed a cab. The moment we pulled up to our hotel, Buddy jumped out and made a frantic dash through the lobby to the elevator. After settling the fare, I walked over to reception to ask the night clerk whether there was a number we could call in case someone had found the wallet and turned it in. Without replying, the man leaned down behind the counter and emerged with both wallet and passport in hand.

"Where the heck did you find that?" I asked, examining it to confirm Buddy as the owner.

"The taxi driver brought it back after another passenger found it in the back seat."

A quick inspection revealed that someone had already helped themselves to a hefty reward.

"At least all the credit cards are still there," I said. "I have a feeling my colleague will want to thank you."

Upstairs, the door opened to a look of stone-cold dread.

"It's not here," Buddy moaned, waving me in before heading to the mini-bar for more support. "What am I gonna do? Without a passport I can't even leave the country."

With the wallet and passport tucked firmly into my jacket pocket, I decided to let Buddy dangle a tad longer.

"We can always give George a call and see if you can stay with Alex for a few months."

With a second mini-bottle downed in several gulps, it was as Buddy reached for a third, that I decided the time to end the charade had come.

"Have a question for you."

"Just what I need," he said, holding off opening the new bottle.

"What did you learn from this evening?"

"What is that supposed to mean?"

"Okay, so you lost your wallet."

"And passport," he added.

"And passport. Why do you think that happened?"

"Because I'm a blithering idiot who didn't watch what he was doing… What is this?" he grumbled, twisting off the cap and taking a deep slug.

Seeing as he was clearly not about to draw any conclusions from the situation, I took out the missing items.

"Why not use these until you can have yours replaced," I said, tossing them both on the bed.

Caught in a moment of utter disbelief, Buddy simply stared at the source of his woe.

"How… Where… Who?…" was followed by shriek of pure delight.

"The taxi driver, probably the only one in Greece who would do something like that. Consider yourself, one lucky guy."

"It's not luck," he corrected with a grin. "I've told you that before. It's 'Welcome to Buddy's World.' Things like this happen all the time… This calls for a celebration," he shouted, jumping up from the bed. "Come on. the bar's still open, drinks are on me."

I chose not to join him, but did manage to persuade him to at least leave his wallet and passport in the room. Armed with a single credit card and a toothy smile, he waved adieu from the elevator as I slipped my card key in the door. A half-hour later, there in the darkness, with the open window letting in the sound of far off night-time Athens, I realized there's never a dull moment… Ever.

CHAPTER 30

Long lost Brother

"You're joking!" Buddy reprimanded, momentarily taking his eyes off the road to glance in my direction. "You've never heard of Dr. Ralph? How is *that* possible? The guy has one of the most watched programs on the tube. That's amazing."

"Yeah, so it's amazing. I still haven't heard of him. What's the big deal anyway? What kind of name is Dr. Ralph? Doesn't exactly inspire confidence. Sounds like one of those New-Age goofballs with a cure for virtually everything."

For those as ill-informed as I that day, a step back in time. Initially a clinical and forensic psychologist, Ralph had been a feature on a popular prime-time show, whose role it had been to listen to those afflicted with life's trials and tribulations and dispense advice to them and the millions of empathetic viewers at home. The success of his segment was such that Ralph had felt compelled to cut loose from the mother ship and start his own spin-off. Despite reviews that accused him of providing simplistic and ineffective solutions, the show had been what North American pundits would call a smash. Airing several times a week over ten seasons, it had delivered sage guidance in hundreds of episodes during its lengthy run. Nominated for a daytime Emmy every year since 1998, it had never won once.

For better or worse, none of this was known to me when we arrived in the German town of Böblingen, to meet with one of the producers for Dr. Ralph's show. Sitting together in the hotel lounge, shooing away a string of waiters bent on serving us free coffee, we listened as Sarah introduced herself and immediately launched into a story, describing how she had cut her teeth in the business seven years ago on a popular US television show.

"What was that all about?" I whispered to Buddy as the chit-chat ground to a halt and we followed Sarah into the breakfast room to meet the subjects of that week's episode.

Seated in a corner booth, finishing up their morning meal, were Martin and Karen, and their translator, Bess. As if we hadn't already had enough with Sarah's self-promotion, shortly after introductions, Bess saw fit to unleash an unprompted soliloquy, the highlight of which was the revelation that she had been an actress in her younger days and occasionally worked on national television.

"Hey, what's with all the in your face resumés today?" I asked Buddy, when Bess's poignant speech had ended, and she went off to refill her juice glass at the buffet. "These people act as if they should be patients, not participants."

Seizing the lull in the Elizabethan lore, Sarah commenced with details on the story we'd come to cover.

"It revolves around Martin's journey to Germany to meet his step-sister and visit his father's grave. Both for the first time," she explained.

Twenty minutes later, we were pulling out of the hotel parking lot to head for the first location, the rest of the group following behind in a separate car.

"Do you figure they get paid for stuff like this?" I asked Buddy.

"Who?"

"The Australian couple. Who else?"

"I thought you were talking about Bess. I mean, what do we need a translator for? We all speak English and you speak German. If you're talking about Martin and Karen, you can be sure the production company is picking up the tab for their flight and expenses. Not bad. Come up with a heart-wrenching saga and get a free trip to Europe."

The skepticism that had been nipping at our heels since the breakfast briefing was let off its leash shortly after we arrived at the town cemetery. Miking the couple for what was meant to be a spontaneous walk through the cemetery and discovery of the grave, Sarah was giving the couple their final instructions when a light snow started to fall.

"Hang on a minute," Buddy called out just as the action was set to begin. "I've got some interference somewhere in the line." As he struggled to locate the source of the problem, Karen and Martin wandered off to another section of the cemetery, unaware that with the help of their live microphones, they were no longer keeping their opinions to themselves.

"Who does this Sarah think she is vetoing our weekend sightseeing on the Rhine?" I heard Karen growl over the camera headset.

"I didn't like her from the get go either, but look... Let's just grind our teeth and get this over with."

Never mind the fact there were no boat tours in the middle of winter, the Rhine was at least two hundred kilometres away, and that Dr. Ralph and company had paid for their entire trip, Martin, it seemed had placed a higher priority on things other than visiting his long-lost step-sister. As if the candid comments hadn't raised enough doubts about his sincerity, no sooner had we started to roll, then Martin revealed an uncanny ability to conjure up tears at the drop of a hat or click of a camera. To be fair, there may have been other reasons for his teary performance. It seemed that nobody in production back in Australia had deemed it necessary to warn the couple that Germany got a real winter. Dressed in light clothing and sandals, neither were really equipped for a stroll in the midst of what had now become a developing snow storm. To make matters worse, Martin's reaction to the "spontaneous" discovery of the grave had to be repeated several times because of snowflakes melting on the camera lens. By the time the scene was completed with a smattering of authenticity, the lingering tears probably had less to do with the sight of the grave, than his relief at hearing we were off to film in warmer surroundings.

According to Sarah's script, the decisive scene where the two siblings were to meet, was to be captured at the step-sister's home.

"I need to show as much spontaneity as possible," she told me, as we stood huddled on the porch. But prospects for capturing uninhibited emotion during the climactic encounter were slim, given that the entire encounter was to be shot with a single camera. Normally such a scene needed to be plotted out and shot from several different angles so an editor could cut it together more dramatically. Because no such planning had taken place, the better part of an hour was spent in the hallway and living room, shooting various looks, hugs, tears, and stifled sobs, over and over. Despite my efforts, it came as a surprise when Sarah accepted a dry-eyed take that seemed both forced and artificial. Breaking for coffee and cake before heading off to our next location, it was hard not to notice the awkward lapse in conversation that had descended between the main characters.

"Hey," I mumbled to Buddy as he reached for his third piece of Apfel Strudel, "Is it just me or do these two long-lost souls not have a lot to say to each other?"

"What did you expect?" he answered. "You made them act thrilled and overwhelmed at least thirty times."

"Just want to deliver top quality stuff to Dr. Ralph. By the way, where is the man of the hour? I get the feeling these people could use some advice on getting to know each other. Isn't there an emergency hotline?"

With the break at an end, Sarah announced she wanted to pick up a few shots of Martin and Karen walking through the town.

"But it's still snowing," Karen pointed out in mild protest.

"That will add to the Christmas effect we want to give the show."

Ten minutes later, I was following the couple down the street as they scurried from shop window to shop window, casting wayward glances at each other and the products within.

"Old Martin doesn't exactly come across as being thrilled to be here," I advised Sarah, as we stopped to change tapes. "He's got a frown you can see a mile away."

"Stay wide then," she ordered. "I'll cover it in post with some narration about his being overwhelmed... and speechless."

"Nothing like truth in advertising."

Grateful to be back in warmer climes that evening, Martin and Karen nonetheless politely declined an invitation to join the rest of us for dinner. Considering the lack of rapport that had existed for most of the day, nobody appeared greatly disappointed at the news, especially given that it meant more wine for Sarah, Buddy and myself, likely to be in great need if Bess persisted in regaling us with any more stories of her fleetingly famous past. Sure enough, once we were all seated in the restaurant, Bess wasted no time in following that script. It was only when there was a slight break in her monologue, that I tried to derail further torment by quizzing her on the concept of Dr. Ralph's show.

"So, let me get this right. People go to him for help and share their innermost problems and secrets in front of twenty million people?"

"A simple way of looking at it, but basically correct," she answered, visibly chomping at the bit to return to her own saga.

"Isn't that sort of milking the misery-loves-company theory?"

"I don't see it that way and neither do a lot of other people," she said, taking the question for the rebuke it was meant to be.

With that conversation having reached a dead-end, the rest of the evening proceeded in small talk as the wine continued to flow. Finally, just as everyone was shuffling hints that they wanted to call it a night, Bess reached across the table to hand me her business card.

"My e-mail address is on it," she said with a broad grin.

"*What am I suppose to do with this?*" I thought as I sat staring at the card. At a complete loss as what to say or do, I simply thanked her and smiled. A short while later, as the conversation shifted in another direction, I took the opportunity to scribble "you're cute Buddy, please give me a call," on the back of the card, and slipped it into his jacket pocket as he was refilling his glass.

CHAPTER 31

Sparta in Sicily

Just when I thought it was safe to go back in the water, another call came from the "Sparta people," this time requesting that the legend coverage be extended to include Sicily. Three days later, we barely managed to land in the port city of Catania in the early evening. I say barely, because that morning we had come within a hair of missing the plane.

Accustomed to Buddy's perpetual tardiness, I didn't panic when he failed to show up on time at our regular meeting point. With no answer on his cell phone fifteen minutes past the designated time, I still saw no cause for worry. Chances were he was on his way, hurtling through a no-service zone. But as the clock moved a half-hour past the agreed-upon rendezvous, there was little choice but to drive the thirty kilometres to his home... just enough time to build up a full head of steam.

The car in the driveway narrowed my suspicions to either having slept in or an untimely death. But with just over two hours before our scheduled take-off, I was not pleased when the door eased open and there stood a groggy-faced Buddy, still in his pyjamas.

"Are you out of your mind?" I said calmly. "We gotta be outta here in fifteen minutes or we'll never make check-in. I suggest you get moving... Fast."

Rather than watch him dawdle, I returned to the car to fume. With less than a minute left on my self-imposed deadline to head for home, a disheveled heap slumped into the front seat beside me without uttering a word. Breaking all speed records and laws, we somehow managed to make check-in with ten minutes to spare.

    Despite his many idiosyncrasies, Buddy was not the kind of person you could stay angry at for long. Silent resentment might have still been lingering when we changed planes in Rome, but by the time we landed in Catania, we were once again on speaking terms. Following a quick dinner near our hotel, we strolled down to the central piazza, hoping to check out the night life in Sicily's second largest city. As in so many southern European cities on a warm evening, the plaza was packed. Casting aside bad memories of Bologna, we ordered a couple of Italian beers from a kiosk and took up residence on the stone steps of a pillared government building to observe the constantly moving throng weave its way around the piazza.
    "First one to spot a real Mafioso gets the next beer free," Buddy suggested over the sound of frantic mopeds speeding up and down the narrow alleyways.
    "If you're talking this brand, I wouldn't exactly consider that a prize worth striving for. This stuff is barely drinkable. Besides, I'll spring for half a dozen beer if you go up to the person and tell them you think they're Mafioso."
    With Buddy unwilling to accept the challenge and neither of us able to render a guess with any confirmable accuracy, it wasn't long before exhaustion from the long day sent us lumbering back to the hotel.

❃

Early the next morning, a brand new, gleaming black Mercedes sedan was waiting for us outside the hotel, complete with a suited driver. With the scenery on the hour-long drive to Syracuse less than enthralling, a portion of the journey was spent engaging with our native Sicilian driver in small talk.

"Mario, this will probably sound like a weird question, and maybe you've been asked it a hundred times... But is it true there's Mafia all over the place here?"

There was a long silence, accentuated by the soundproofing abilities of a Mercedes limousine.

"There are Mafia everywhere," he said finally. "Not only in Sicily. You have seen too many movies."

"Maybe so, but if everywhere includes where I come from, they manage to keep themselves well out of sight."

With the exception of Buddy's whispered advice to "quit while you're behind," the rest of the trip's soundtrack was dominated by the quiet swish of the speeding auto. Unlike our Greek friend Alex, Mario actually knew where he was going. At least that was our assumption when he veered off the main highway to venture down a narrow gravel road so overgrown with bushes that branches scraped both sides of the car as we passed through. After a few minutes of light screeching, the road opened up to reveal the sun-sparkled waters of the Mediterranean off to our left.

"We are here," Mario announced, pulling to a stop.

"We are? So where is the amphitheatre?" I asked, glancing around at the arid terrain.

"Behind the wall," he said, pointing to a white-brick rampart a hundred yards from where we'd parked.

"Isn't there any way of getting closer so we don't

have to schlepp the gear so far?" I protested, noting that the scrub land appeared to be filled with thorny looking bushes. "I don't even see a path."

Mario simply shrugged, as if to say, *"Do what you want. I brought you here. My job is finished."* With that he exited the car to inspect the damage the branches had caused.

"It's probably revenge for your crack about the Mafia," Buddy said as we loaded up and tramped off in search of an entrance.

"There's gotta be another way in," I complained, in the midst of our thorny dilemma. "What tourist is gonna want to scrape and scratch their way through all of this?"

A hundred yards on, we discovered an opening that led to the missing amphitheatre. Once we'd managed to make our way through what amounted to a back-door entry, we were confronted by an impressive piece of work, especially when you consider that it was carved into the hillside in the 5th-century BC. While many, if not most Greek and Roman ruins tend to be exactly that, this structure had somehow eluded the ravages of time to the point that it looked like it could accommodate the masses for an event that afternoon. Fortunately there were no crowds present, only a handful people, all of whom had presumably taken another route to get there.

"Remind me to insult Mario when we are back in the car," I said to Buddy.

"I think you already did quite well in that department. Like I said, that's why we had the pleasure of coming this way."

As intriguing as the amphitheatre was, it only took us little more than an hour to capture its ambience and position in the surrounding landscape. Rather than retracing our tortuous route to the car, a loud whistle and wave from the wall, persuaded Mario to meet us on the other side, where to no one's surprise there was a road and main entrance. Wanting to keep the tentative truce intact for the return journey, I didn't bother mentioning anything about the alternative passage. Instead I merely sought Mario's advice on what other sites we could visit on the extra day we had at our disposal.

"Taormina," was his only reply.

*

The view from my hotel balcony was simply phenomenal. Set against a solid blue sky, the plume of smoke rising from Etna's smouldering summit reigned over the surrounding countryside like some… dare I say it… Mafia don. The southern panorama was equally spectacular, displaying Sicily's rugged eastern coastline and several small villages dotting the shoreline. The town of Taormina itself rested on a plateau below Mount Tauro, its picturesque alleyways and piazzas delivering a further array of breathtaking vistas. But as impressive as these sites were, they paled in comparison to the ancient Greek amphitheatre, less than a two-minute walk from our hotel. Climbing to the top of one of several worn-stone stairways, we were presented with a view so astounding, it felt like it couldn't possibly be real.

"Why didn't they just ask us to film this one instead?" I wanted to know. "It would have saved a lot of hassle and even comes with a view of a live volcano."

Intrigued by the distant Etna, neither of us were

willing to accept the finality of "so near and yet so far." Getting there however, would involve following a winding road through a pine forest where traces of earlier Greek civilization were visible. There amidst a thicket of trees, miles from any habitation or furniture store, sat an abandoned red sofa, looking for all the world like an inexplicable work of conceptual art.

Once we were out of the proverbial woods, the landscape was transformed into one of lunar proportions, with waves of hardened lava spread across the entire mountainside in patterns that resembled an impressionist's view of a black, windy sea.

Judging from the crowded parking lot, we were not the only ones who'd had the same idea. We were however, the only ones who hadn't taken into account that Etna's summit was considerably higher than the Greek amphitheatre. Still dressed in shorts and t-shirts for the +27 degrees registered on the hotel lobby's thermometer, it came as a shock to open the door and be greeted by a stiff wind, chilly enough to recall a Winnipeg November. The only way to keep warm, besides staying in the car, which seemed rather pointless, was to move towards a bank of smouldering rock. Doing so meant being engulfed in an occasional cloud of sulphurous fumes, not to mention the possibility of being buried alive should Etna decide to throw a sudden tantrum. Protected from the wind and warmed by the heat emanating from a ten foot accumulation of Etna's recent expulsions, I thought it the perfect opportunity to go souvenir hunting. Reaching down, I grabbed hold of an interesting looking rock only to discover the under side still faintly glowing.

"Shit, this thing is still on fire," I shouted, nearly

dropping it on my sandalled foot.

"I wouldn't put that one in my pocket just yet," Buddy advised.

Between the recurring fumes and intermittent wind, we made our stay a limited one. Once we'd retrieved a few solid specimens that were not likely to burn a hole in the trunk of the car, we departed for warmer climes. Choosing to take a different route back to Taormina led us through a number of old stone villages, one of which we decided to grace with our presence by stopping for a drink. Walking across the sun-scorched cobblestones of an empty piazza, we accepted the friendly waves from a pair of Don Corleone look-a-likes sitting on a stone stoop. Having acknowledged our arrival, they quickly returned to their animated discussion, hands flying in all directions as local and world issues were deliberated between sips of red wine. Taking refuge under an umbrella at the far end of the piazza, where a tattered Italian flag fluttered overhead, we scoured the taverna's menu before ordering two glasses of Chianti. Relaxing in the warm shade, we toasted the success of our whirlwind tour through Sicily. All that was missing in this near picture-perfect scenario, was the Godfather theme playing from the tin-horn speakers atop several wooden poles.

*

As any foreigner who has traveled to Italy knows, one of its less appealing attributes is the tendency of store clerks, traffic cops or airline personnel to render non-Italians invisible whenever a homegrown native saunters into view. My own exposure to such a drama began while we were cruising northwards through Italian airspace on the way back home. According to the co-pilot's announcement, a fog bank had rolled into Milan earlier that morning, causing major disruptions and cancelling many flights, including ours to Frankfurt. Oddly enough, the same fog that would prevent us from taking off allowed us to land. After de-planing, we were advised to collect our luggage and make our way to the departure area to await further news. After nearly four hours of not-altogether patient waiting, word came down that passengers booked to Frankfurt should gather in a hall on the lower level. Full of hope, we obediently moved to the designated area only to wait anew. At ten-thirty that night, eight hours after we had been scheduled to land in Frankfurt, Alitalia officials finally got around to informing us that the flight would not leave until the following morning, suggesting we be back at the airport at 8:30 a.m.

"And tonight?" someone asked. "Where are we supposed to stay tonight? Has the airline booked us into a hotel?"

The answer was not what anyone wanted to hear.

"Alitalia," said a short, uniformed attendant, "does not consider arranging overnight accommodations as part of their mandate." And with that she gathered up her papers and promptly disappeared.

Fortunately, with the aid of several fellow passengers, as well as thinly-veiled threats to less-than-accommodating hotel clerks, we managed to find rooms twenty kilometres from the terminal. Sharing a cab with several Americans, it was agreed we would one day look back on this and laugh. In the meantime, of more importance was convincing hotel reception to re-open the bar.

Back at the same check-in counter bright and early the next morning, we were pleased to learn that the fog had lifted sufficiently to allow for some flights. Ours however, was not one of them.

"Why can't you book us on another flight?" I asked a flustered looking attendant behind the counter. "One that is actually leaving. I mean fog is fog or? Why can some leave and others not?"

"I do not know, sir. (airline speak for "*stop bothering me, you creep*") If you would like more information, you must talk to the people at the Alitalia desk."

"I thought I was talking to people at the Alitalia desk."

"I am just a service rep for the airport, sir." (airline speak for "*I told you to get lost, pest*").

Leaving Buddy to watch the luggage, I made my way to the "proper" Alitalia counter upstairs, only to find eight other pests ahead of me.

"First time in Italy?" a friendly voice behind me asked.

"No, but probably the last," I said, before easing back on the sneer. "At least if it means flying with this horde of fools again."

"It's not the first time this has happened," the middle-aged man told me. "Milan is known for getting fogged in. Last time I was stuck here for thirty-six hours."

"Oh hey. Please don't tell me that right now," I pleaded. "I know you're just trying to make conversation, but I need to hear that about as much as I need to contract the bubonic plague. I'll start walking before I wait that long."

Suddenly, with only three pests left in front of me, a well-dressed woman darted into my peripheral vision, and made a beeline for the front of the line. Without excusing herself, she demanded something from the clerk in Italian. Rather than pointing out that other people were waiting in line ahead of her, the clerk began to answer her question, leaving it up to others to rectify the injustice.

"End of the line, *bella donna*," I said loud enough for the clerk, the perpetrator and half the hall to hear. "You think we're standing here for the view? Here's an idea. Why not wait like everyone else?"

Whether she understood English or not, the look on my face needed no translation. Dropping her quest with a glare of disgust that I sent right back at her, she quickly made her exit. When my turn finally arrived, I was not thrilled to hear that my question regarding our departure could only be answered back at the very desk where I had left Buddy.

For some inexplicable reason, possibly the armed policeman standing several metres away, I refused to take the bait and simply returned to the original desk to take my place in yet another line. An hour or so later I was face to face with yet another bland-looking clerk. Not interested in a repeat performance, I immediately asked to speak to the office manager. Requested to stand aside, another ten minutes passed before a tall, lanky man in a shiny suit swaggered up behind the counter. A few words were exchanged with the clerk before before an accusing finger was pointed in my direction. Unaware his well-being was dangling by a thread, the manager adopted a rather condescending attitude when I asked why other planes were leaving and ours not.

"Ees a question of safety, sir." (*See previous airline speak*)

"*Wrong answer pal,*" I thought, and repeated the question to make sure he had understood it.

"We must follow rules. We cannot fly until we receive permission."

"And who gives that permission?"

"Airport authorities."

"Okay, I'll bite… Airport authorities… And why are these airport authorities giving permission to other airlines and not to Alitalia?"

"I do not know, sir."

Intentional or not, his "sir" was slurred just enough to push me over the edge. With all semblance of decorum now lost, I simply looked at him and hollered, "Because Alitalia sucks! That's why."

No… I didn't go to jail, and they did eventually get us home that day. But you know what? Years later, my opinion still stands.

CHAPTER 32

Safe Food in Salzburg

What with its myriad of cafes, museums, churches, music festivals and castles, Salzburg has the reputation of being one of the prettiest cities in Europe. The more time spent there however, the more the place begins to take on the characteristics of a North American one company town. But rather than having an inordinate amount of economic activity wrapped around a huge steel factory, car plant or nickel mine, it's the figure of Wolfgang Amadeus Mozart that has become the all encompassing influence. Prompted by the fact that the child prodigy was born there, over the years entrepreneurs have borrowed a page or two from same playbook used by the English royals, to insure that Mozart's name and image have been plastered over everything that moves and doesn't.

Having passed through the city on the banks of the Salzach as part of the requisite "go to Europe and find yourself" tour in the early 70's, I had long been familiar with its Mozart-related "attributes." Never a big fan of monogrammed coffee mugs, fridge magnets or other knick-knacks, I was happy to learn my return to Salzburg this time would have nothing to do with the famous composer. This visit was to revolve around a "food security" conference scheduled to take place in a 18th century castle that overlooks a small lake in the centre of the city. Originally built by the Salzburg prince-archbishop, Leopold Anton Freiherr von Firmian, and restored by the Austrian impresario, Max Reinhardt in 1918, Schloss Leopoldskron had seen a number of inhabitants pass through its portals since the Nazis had forced Reinhardt out of his native country in the 1930's.

One of those inhabitants was a trio of graduate students from Harvard University, who in 1947, decided to start what they called the Salzburg Seminar for American Studies. Their idea was to gather some of the top minds from around the world, place them in a secluded, serene environment, and have them reflect, discuss, and debate important issues of the day. With time, the seminar matured to the point that formidable intellectual forces gathered there numerous times a year. This particular seminar, sponsored by a large US corporation, had attracted sixty experts from forty different countries, many of whom were organizers, activists and people working at the grass roots level in non-government organizations(NGO's).

Requested to attend the opening plenary on "sustainable agriculture," but without filming it, we learned that food security was defined as the supply of constant and nutritional food for every person on the planet. We watched as speaker after speaker mounted the rostrum to encourage participants to use the conference to share their experiences and the difficulties they faced in achieving that goal. According to statistics delivered by one presenter, an estimated eight hundred million people, many of them children, did not have access to adequate nutrition. Sustainable development through the use of community-based systems, in other words, focusing on educating individual farmers as opposed to pouring money into huge projects, was to be a primary theme.

"Interesting stuff eh," I said to Buddy as the opening ceremonies came to an end and attendees broke off into working groups to explore potential solutions applicable to their respective lands. Seeing as core issues such as comparing which models had been successful and whether their usage could be replicated in other lands were likely to be debated in these seminars, it came as a surprise when the producer said there was no need to film them. Instead we were directed upstairs to the luxurious top floor living quarters of the seminar's director and asked to set up for a number of interviews with selected guests. Although the apartment offered a multitude of eye-pleasing settings, I was not displeased when the producer announced that all of the twelve interviews could be shot with the same background.

Following a quick scouting of the various rooms, we settled on the living room, placing a high-backed, upholstered chair near a window to make use of the available light streaming in.

"Buddy, can you do me a favour? Take a look in the monitor, and tell me if it improves the shot when I turn on this table lamp?" I asked, hoping to make a few final tweaks before the arrival of our first interview subject.

"It looks okay," he said with a degree of uncertainty. "But I think the lamp is a bit too bright. I think we need a dimmer bulb."

"Volunteering?"

The brief exchange was indicative of the relationship that had developed between the two of us over the years. Not many bosses would have taken such a wisecrack so lightly, especially when delivered in front of a producer. But Buddy, as I had come to learn and appreciate, was not your typical boss. Although most offhand remarks were nothing more than a harmless, but irresistible cheap shot, at other times they were a reaction to his not pulling his weight. But even in circumstances where tempers did flare, we could usually sit down and talk about the problem without any accompanying hysterics or power plays. If he *had* ever taken something as a personal insult, he hadn't let on. Having born witness to our antics on various shoots, several producers had commented that our rapport made us look and sound like an old married couple. The truth was, our two personalities just functioned well together. With his outgoing manner, an art he liked to call "the schmoozathon," Buddy would create a comfortable atmosphere for the client, freeing me to concentrate on fulfilling my end of the bargain. Despite numerous trying moments, it had largely proven to be a successful combination.

Thanks to the articulateness of the participants, two cancellations, and the expertise of the producer, all ten interviews were "in the can" by five o'clock. That left plenty of time to restore the room to its original status and still attend the formal dinner in the large banquet hall. With a no-filming policy in place during the meals, we had the chance to observe and mingle with guests, all of whom had been asked to dress in the traditional clothing of their respective countries. As interesting as various costumes were, it was the African women who made the most indelible impression. With the intensity of their colourful outfits, their quiet grace, and unassuming strength reflected in their faces, they were simply in a league of their own. Following a sumptuous but not extravagant meal, after-dinner drinks were served on the terrace, where people could engage in casual conversation while enjoying a view of the lake and surrounding forest. Seated at a lakeside table, waiting for further instructions, Buddy and I were relaxing with an after-dinner coffee, when I looked up to see the institute's director walking over to join us.

"Everything to your satisfaction gentlemen?"

"Couldn't ask for more," Buddy replied. "This is some location for a seminar".

Accepting the compliment with a nod, the director began to pepper us with questions about life in the video lane. His own interest in the field, he explained, stemmed from having worked on a documentary about a former Nazi concentration camp.

"It must be great to travel so much and be involved in so many different things every day. I'm kind of envious," he said, leaning forward for a closer look at the camera at my feet.

But despite the friendly tone and sincerity of his comments, something felt out-of-whack. Here was the head of a world- renowned think tank, whose guests had included such luminaries as Prince Charles, former German Chancellor Helmut Schmidt and author Saul Bellow, and it was he who was expressing admiration for our field of endeavours.

"I think it's us who should be envious of you," I replied. "How many people have the opportunity to immerse themselves in such a level of intellectual stimulation, and in an environment like this? Tonight for example, we've had the chance to talk with people from Cameroon, Nigeria, Argentina, Mexico and the Sudan about the food issues plaguing their countries. How many people can do that?"

Before the director could respond, the conversation was cut short by the announcement that guests were requested to return to the plenary hall to share their thoughts on the day's sessions.

"I'm afraid duty calls gentlemen. Nice talking with you," he said before rushing off.

With informal discussions on the terrace winding down, guests began making their way to the hall. Fully expecting to film the proceedings, we were following the crowd in when the producer stopped us in the foyer.

"No need to film this guys," he announced, casting a quick glance at the camera. "I got all I need from the interviews."

With nothing left on the official agenda, Buddy decided to return to his room. Made curious by the glimpse I had had of the castle's library during our introductory tour, I handed Buddy the camera and headed off there, hoping to browse through some of the hundreds of books stored in the wood-panelled room. A half hour later, hidden away in one of the ornate little cubby-holes pocketed around the main room, I was flipping through a book on the history of Schloss Leopoldskron when Buddy found me.

"Listen to this," he said in a voice loud enough to attract the glares of several other patrons. "The producers in LA were really happy with the stuff shot in Sicily."

Setting his laptop down on the desk in front of me, he urged me to read the email on the screen.

"*Everybody involved feels it will greatly improve the quality of the show. Great working with you guys. Look forward to doing it again. All the best.*'"

"Not bad," I said, eager to return to my book.

"That's not all. Remember the shoot in Sindelfingen?"
"In the Jewish cemetery?"
"That's the one. The client just sent news that the program is up for an Emmy in the documentary category and will be broadcast nationally in August."
"Does that mean I can raise my prices?"
"If all you're going to do is get a swelled head, maybe I shouldn't show you this last one."
"Last one?"
"Someone is looking for a camera team for a shoot in Italy, Turkey and Bosnia-Herzegovina. Man, are we on a roll or what?"

After a series of not so hushed "*Sssshhh's*" from fellow readers, the blowing-your-own horn session was brought to an end.

The next morning, Buddy and I were standing in the parking lot, waiting to say our goodbyes to the producer and conference director, when I happened to spot a grounds-keeper atop a sit-down mower, weaving his way through a group of trees as he trimmed the expansive lawn.

"Now there's a job with a purpose," I said with more than just a twinge of envy.

"Should I just leave you here?" Buddy asked.

"Tempting offer. But even if the grass is always greener, you still have to cut it."

Leaving the man to his enviable task, we said our goodbyes and departed. An hour or so later, as we crossed back over the frontier back into Germany, I was surprised to notice that despite the "dodge-em-car" atmosphere of the autobahn, much of the tranquility that had permeated our brief stay at Schloss

Leopoldskron, still lingered. Inspired by the intellectual stimulation generated by those so committed to a cause, it seemed likely that even the most cynical had left the seminar with a renewed sense of optimism about the future of the planet.

CHAPTER 33

Nuggets on Tour

It's not everyday that one finds oneself strapped into a Black Hawk helicopter, skimming across the treed hilltops of Bosnia-Herzegovina at 150 kilometres an hour. But in the spring of 2002, there I was staring out the open door of a U.S. military chopper, enjoying the agreeable scenery, as my heart pounded and adrenaline coursed through my veins. Only occasionally did the thought cross my mind that there might be someone with a grudge and a Stinger hiding in the woods below. Fortunately, there wasn't; either that or they were incredibly bad shots. As a result, the sleek, dark, and without a doubt, appallingly expensive machine was able to race us along to our destination unhindered.

Two weeks prior to being en route from Sarajevo to Tuzla in one of four "birds," Buddy had received a call from the National Basketball Association headquarters in New Jersey, confirming we'd been booked to accompany members of the Denver Nuggets basketball team on an overseas promotional tour to U.S. bases in Italy, Bosnia-Herzegovina and Turkey.

We flew into Naples on the morning of May 17th. Met at the airport by an NBA staffer, we were driven directly to the Grand Vesuvio Hotel, a fancy 5 star inn near the city's harbourfront. Once checked in, we came down to the lobby for what turned out to be the briefest of briefings with the producer and several high-ranking individuals of the NBA.

"Did you get the feeling nobody was particularly interested in talking to us?" I asked Buddy, after we'd been duly dismissed and told to meet back at the hotel the next day at noon.

"They weren't the friendliest guys in town, but maybe the players will be better. At least we've got a light schedule."

With our first appointment not scheduled until the following afternoon, the decision was made to spend the rest of the day wandering through the labyrinth of narrow alleyways that make up the old city, many of which were cluttered with lines of laundry hanging between the closely-connected balconies. Filled with the noise of daily life, not to mention pleasant and disturbing odours, it was surprising to see how energized the whole area was, displaying a liveliness and pride seldom seen in more modern neighbourhoods.

"Excuse me, but what is that?" I asked the waiter in the small restaurant we stopped at for lunch.

"It's the steak you ordered, sir."

"A steak?" I repeated matter-of-factly. "But it's almost black and hard as a rock. I've seen fire hydrants more tender than this."

Refusing an offered replacement, I selected a ham omelet, hoping it would arrive before Buddy finished devouring his lasagna. Ten minutes after leaving the restaurant, a wave of nausea started to make its presence known.

"Either that guy put something in my meal as revenge for my comments, or the eggs were from last century," I groaned, clutching my rapidly bloating abdomen. Fortunately, I remembered having passed a pharmacy on our earlier rounds, so it was only a matter of minutes before I was taking a slug of an analgesic I hoped would soothe my rebellious stomach. Back out on the crowded street, and doubtful whether extended walking would help my threatened intestines, I suggested we return to the hotel, pointing to a stone stairway that appeared to lead down to a lower section of the old city.

"I think this way will get us back to the hotel. If I'm going to fit for work tomorrow, I should probably lay down and let my guts have a rest."

Walking several metres ahead of Buddy, I hadn't descended more than a few steps into the stairwell when I heard him call out. Turning to investigate, I saw a young man in his late teens, apparently quite desperate to discover the time of day. In a flash I was back in the restaurant, querying Buddy as to why he had insisted on wearing such an ostentatious watch in a city well known for its criminality. Between his shiny satin shorts, sleeveless T-Shirt and LA Lakers baseball cap, someone aboard a passing plane would have been able to tell he was a tourist ripe for plucking.

Despite everything happening so fast, it felt like I was watching a movie in slow-motion. Realizing the young man had ripped the watch from Buddy's wrist, I started back up the stairs with what felt like leadened limbs. Pushing Buddy aside, the thief ran around the stairway's retaining wall with me in hot pursuit. Once having recovered his balance, Buddy moved to the opposite side of the stairwell hoping to block his attacker's path. Just as it looked like we had him trapped, the robber leapt over the wall and dropped down onto the stairs. Somehow able to maintain his balance despite the six or seven foot drop, he took off like a shot. Faced with a split-second decision and no apparent alternative, I instinctively tossed my plastic bottle of analgesic, only to see it explode on the steps less than a foot from the fleeing figure. Taking two steps at a time in hot pursuit, by the time I got to the bottom of the stairwell, the watch's new owner was half a block away, his bobbing head barely visible through the crowd, as he glanced back to see if anyone was on his trail. Knowing I wasn't likely to catch him in this lifetime, I pulled up short alongside an old man lazing on his first floor balcony.

"Problemo?" he asked with a knowing grin, before drawing deeply on a self-rolled cigarette.

"Si... problemo. Watch... gone," I explained, holding up my bare wrist.

"Ah... si, ees Napoli," he said with a shrug.

On the walk back to the hotel, the scene just witnessed was replayed a dozen times, each with an altered ending of should have's, could have's and would have's.

"Why didn't you try beaning him with a brick or something?" I grumbled.

"I dunno... Where was I supposed to get a brick?" Buddy mumbled. "It all happened so fast. Why didn't you just throw up on him? "

"Never thought of it... Not a bad idea though. Would have made for a memorable finale... Hey, for someone who's just been mugged, you don't seem terribly perturbed."

"It's because the laugh is on that guy."

"How so?"

"It didn't keep proper time."

"Somehow I doubt if the guy is planning on keeping

it or giving it to his girlfriend. The real hammer will come when he realizes he's stolen the only Rolex spelled with two 'L's'."

Considering the afternoon's adventure, Buddy was surprisingly buoyant that evening at dinner, insisting on relating the entire encounter to the maître de as he seated us at a table in the hotel's restaurant. Such verbosity however, came with a price. Next morning at breakfast, we were approached by two men identifying themselves as police officers. Buddy's story had apparently spread amongst the hotel staff overnight, with at least one member having considered it their civic duty to report the crime. Requesting we accompany them to the local precinct to peruse mugshots, the officers assured us we would be finished in time to be back at the hotel by noon. With that settled, it was not an altogether unpleasant experience riding along in the back seat of a police car through the city's narrow streets.
"Which one of us do you think looks more like a crazed killer?" I asked Buddy as we stopped at a light, and one elderly pedestrian leaned down for a closer look at the criminals.
At the police station, a ramshackle building at the end of a darkened alleyway, we were escorted into a small, windowless room and informed that a thief had been apprehended the previous evening in possession of three watches and a gun.
"A gun?" I asked. "I don't think our guy was carrying a gun."
"Most thieves don't commit a robbery without a weapon," the officer assured me. "It's a good thing you

didn't catch him because if he didn't have a gun, he probably had a knife."

"Or a bottle of Pepto Bismol," Buddy quipped.

"Com'è quello?"

"Forget it... non importanto," I answered.

As none of the scruffy individuals in the police line-up fit our assailant, the next two hours were passed poring over hundreds of photos. Less than a quarter of the way through the first book, all of the seedy characters started to look the same.

"We're never gonna be able to identify this guy," I said to Buddy. "Let's just fake it and get out of here. We're due at the hotel in less than an hour."

Buddy however, was quite enjoying himself, feeling it his solemn responsibility to do what he could to see justice served.

Fifteen minutes later, "I've found him," he blurted out. "That's the guy... I'm sure of it."

"You're kidding," I said, glancing over at an image that bore no resemblance whatsoever to our missing culprit. The police officer who'd been guarding the door (as if we were likely to try to escape or steal a mug book) wandered over to inspect Buddy's conviction. Adamant he had fingered the thief, Buddy was crestfallen when the officer pointed to a small red 'D' next to the name.

"He is dead," the officer said in a heavy Italian accent.

So much for beyond a reasonable doubt.

Although refused a "police escort" back to the hotel, we nonetheless managed to get there in time to be introduced to the five members of the Denver Nuggets who'd come on the tour.

"I feel like a midget," I whispered to Buddy as we sat in the lobby encircled by men all pushing seven feet tall. "Too bad none of these guys weren't with us yesterday."

In a continuation of the relaxed pace we'd enjoyed so far, the tour manager outlined the day's schedule, which called for filming the players as they strolled through the old city, stopping to sign autographs and posing next to famous landmarks. Following a short break for dinner, the action picked up again that evening, when we traveled to a naval base south of the city to film a basketball clinic and autograph session held for military personnel and their families.

"Wow! Do they really still have things like cheerleaders?" I gasped, gawking at a group of heavily made-up teenagers performing their routines in semi-coordinated fashion. "I've obviously been away from North America for too long."

Unlike *my* reserved judgement, the audience loved their routine, greeting each stanza of "sis boom bah, rah rah rah" with a thunderous round of applause and whistles.

Twelve hours later, we were back at the same base, this time at the military airport terminal, waiting to board a flight that would take us to Sarajevo. Standing in the small nondescript departure lounge, glancing at a photo of George W. Bush on the wall, I couldn't help but notice the lone aircraft parked on the tarmac, no more than a hundred yards away.

"Is *that* our plane?" I asked in astonishment, as I accepted my passport back from the tour manager.

"That's her," he confirmed with a broad grin. "Courtesy of the U.S. government. Just for us... How's them apples?"

"Last night it was cheerleaders and now it's 'them apples.' What is this 1964?" I mumbled to Buddy as the group made its way towards the boarding ramp. Following the players up the stairs, I was able to get a close-up view of the logo on the fuselage.

"It's Air force two," the tour manager explained from behind. "Well not really. It's the plane used by the first lady. Pretty nifty eh."

Tempted to tell him I thought it was *"peachy keen,"* I decided there was no point in encouraging him. Once seated in one of twenty-five large leather chairs in the main compartment, it struck me that given the U.S.'s current reputation in the Balkans, flying around with what amounted to be a Presidential bullseye on the side of the plane might not be such a great idea.

As we arced away from a shrinking Mount Vesuvius, and out over the Gulf of Naples, my first inclination was to order a bottle of champagne and some caviar and put it on the First Lady's tab. The second was to jot down some derogatory remarks about her husband, and stuff it down one of the seats for some political big wig to discover at a later date. Instead I settled for browsing through several outdated American gossip magazines crammed into the pouch on the side of the seat.

Other than a hastily called interview with one of the players, conducted in the private office at the front of the plane, the flight was uneventful. Shortly before landing in the Bosnian capital, a member of the tour staff came over the intercom to request everyone's undivided attention.

"Just so you know folks. We are about to enter an area that not too many years ago was a war zone. That means there are certain precautions that need to be undertaken, mostly for your own protection."

"Buddy, are you getting this?" I asked across the aisle.

"Huh..." he answered, removing his nose from a cheesy crime novel. "Oh yeah... sure."

"Once we're on the tarmac," the voice continued, "under no circumstances are you to walk where there is no concrete, unless that is, you hope to save on shoes in the future. Does everybody understand? We don't want to be taking you back in pieces... assuming we can find any."

"Pleasant thought," I murmured, eliciting another "Huh?" from Buddy.

Presumably for security reasons, the plane parked at the far end of the runway, a considerable distance from the main terminal. Allowed to disembark, we had a few minutes to glance at our new surroundings before a van was scheduled to arrive to take us to the hotel. Looking up into the hills that overlook the city, it was easy to imagine what a shooting gallery snipers must have had during the war, as they took a bead on innocent civilians going about their daily chores.

"Where's the sound guy?" the tour manger suddenly barked. A quick scan confirmed Buddy was not amongst the huddle of players, nor could he be back on the plane as the walkway had already been removed. Moving around to the other side of the plane for a better view up the runway, there was still no sign of him. It was only when I turned to rejoin the group that I spotted a brightly clad figure lurking in the grass, fifty yards from the tail of the plane.

"Can I have your pin ball machine?" I called out, trying not to attract the others' attention.

"Just want to grab a shot of the plane so I can prove to everyone we flew on Air Force Two."

"I'll see to it that's engraved on your tombstone, and besides it's Laura's plane, not Air Force Two."

Before being dropped at the hotel, the group was treated to a short tour of "Sniper Alley," - that is if you can call driving past bullet-riddled buildings and a high-rise apartment block with sections of the upper floors simply blown away, - a treat. Also noteworthy were the occasional patches of grass in the city centre, all of which had grown several feet high because no one had been brave or crazy enough to cut it. Overall, Sarajevo still appeared to be a functioning city, but one very much on edge. Given that more than half the population was reportedly still armed, there was a good chance it would remain that way well beyond our short visit.

Shortly after unpacking and freshening up, we were whisked off to a home for autistic children, where team members were scheduled to hand out gifts and sign autographs. Few of the guests gathered in the run-down hall appeared to have any idea whose autographs they were collecting, but were grateful for the free T-shirts, buttons and baseball caps being dispersed. From there it was straight on to a U.S. military base where more than 400 adults and children had been jammed into a gymnasium for the much anticipated meeting with NBA stars. Made up entirely of military personnel and their relatives, all of whom started whooping and hollering upon our entry, the frenetic audience was forced to listen to a round of introductory speeches before an abridged basketball clinic got underway.

Early next morning saw us back at the same base, huddled outside the mess hall for a scheduled breakfast and autograph session with soldiers. Whether common practice, or merely a sudden urge to be filmed in the bravado mode, many soldiers had brought along their M-16's, presumably loaded. Following the meal and a short impromptu ceremony where the camp commander thanked the NBA for bringing a bit of America to Sarajevo, we were escorted out to the heliport. Sitting there in the brilliant sunshine were four Black Hawk helicopters, seconded to transport us to the International Forces (IFOR) base in Tuzla. As final preparations were being made for our departure, Buddy and I decided to carry out a brief inspection of the "birds."

"Didn't someone say these things can carry twelve people plus a crew of four?" I asked him, surprised at how small the Blackhawk actually was. "Can we get one of these for our next aerial shoot?"

"Only if they take Visa."

"This baby can cruise at 175 mph," one of the pilots interrupted. "That, I can tell you, is fast. And you won't feel a thing. With four blades it is a super smooth ride, which makes it great for shooting… If you know what I mean," he added, with a wink in my direction.

The flight out of Sarajevo followed what seemed to be an incredibly low-level path, continuing that way until the cityscape gave way to the hilly countryside. Despite the sense of power and speed of the Black Hawk, one remained very aware how vulnerable it was, should somebody decide to take a pot shot.

"One of the reasons we're flying so low," an accompanying soldier informed us, "is that it's harder for someone on the ground to get a bead on us."

Our first stopover was an off-base sub-station, where the entire staff had assembled to meet and greet the NBA celebrities. After a few more speeches, a condensed clinic, and presentation of gifts the Nuggets organization had brought along, we were once again airborne. Unlike the departure from Sarajevo, which had been at spaced intervals, this time all four Black Hawks cruised in tight formation. Feeling much like commandos storming a foreign beach, immediately upon landing at the main base in Tuzla, we were transported to yet another packed gymnasium, where following a round of welcoming speeches, the raucous crowd was entertained by a scrub basketball game between Nugget team members and a half dozen military personnel. Egged on by the screams and cheers of off-duty soldiers and their families, the latter group actually managed to hold their own for awhile. In an attempt to heighten the atmosphere, the Nuggets had brought along their own team mascot. Dressed as Rocky the flying squirrel, the mascot's main duty during the game was to race up and down the court sidelines, inciting and provoking both players and members of the audience; pausing only to shoot another T-shirt into the crowd from his specially designed bazooka. When the shortened game ended in a tie, Nugget players broke up into small session groups to offer tips to interested players. As we weren't required to film all five sessions, someone came up with the idea of having a little fun with Rocky to help pass the time. A few inquiries were made up the chain of command and within minutes we were back out at the helipad, this time accompanied by

Mr. Squirrel and several heavily-armed colleagues. Once I was set up, Rocky was handed an M-16 and given the instructions for his "assignment." After attempting a menacing grimace for the camera, he sprinted across the tarmac and jumped into one of the copters, which immediately took off to circle the field. A minute or so later as the chopper swooped in for a rapid landing, Rocky leapt out in a ready-for-action combat pose. The group of soldiers who'd gathered to watch were loving it, so a repeat performance was quickly arranged, this time with Rocky donning a red bandana. As I watched the copter loop around for a second landing, all I could think of was the fair chunk of money our little stunt was costing taxpayers. But better on us than more weapons.

Events in the gym were just coming to an end when we rejoined the troupe for the short drive to the next scheduled meeting. Once again our arrival was met with an uproar of applause and whistles, this time from hundreds of Implementation Force (IFOR) soldiers, who had assembled in an enormous tent to meet the team and enjoy a few hours off with varied refreshments. Wandering through the crowd to capture some footage of the soldiers as they listened to yet another round of speeches, I had to endure numerous slaps on the back, presumably in gratitude for having helped break up the monotony of their day.

The flight back to Sarajevo that evening was unexceptional, making it easier to rest up for the next day's planned junket to eastern Turkey. Early next morning we were back aboard our moving target, flying over the rugged terrain of south-eastern Europe, before crossing into an endless array of orange and brown desert and mountain vistas that make up much of Turkey. Upon landing at Incirlik air base, the site from which US and British forces were then enforcing the no-fly zone in Iraq, we were picked up and driven directly to the mess hall for a pre-arranged luncheon.

"What the hell was that?" I asked, as a deafening roar shattered the relative silence just as we were entering the building,

"That gentlemen," said the Colonel accompanying us, "is the sound of freedom," pointing to a jet fighter taking off, its afterburner kicking in as it lifted off from an unseen runway.

"That gentlemen," I said to Buddy once we were inside, "could be the sound of a blowhard."

Thin tasteless chili, a plate of bone-dry french fries and a glass of watered-down cola, illustrated the lengths the military was prepared to go to make their soldiers feel right at home. The questionable food appeared of no concern to our group of giants though, who returned to the buffet line for second and third helpings. During one of the lulls in table talk, there was a chance to ask the Colonel whether we'd be able to add a brief diversion to our itinerary.

"It's my first time in Turkey and I wouldn't mind seeing some of it other than from a plane," I explained as a hair-netted waitress came to clear our table. "Any chance we could drive into the neighbouring town sometime later today?"

"Sorry son, but I'm afraid we can't let you off the base. Too big a risk of possible terrorist attacks."

Ignoring the "son" reference as well as the green jello dessert, I shrugged and excused myself to visit the washroom. An unsettling image was awaiting me on my return.

"New photo for the company web site?" I asked Buddy, watching in disbelief as he stood there with an M16."

"Nah… just a new method for crew control," he answered with a grin.

With lunch wrapped, it was on to the base auditorium for more of what had started to feel like an endless series of speeches, clinics, and giveaways. Rocky was on hand again, but for some reason this time his antics fell flat with the fans. Unable to venture beyond the fences of "anywhere USA," the evening was spent roaming between a Burger King, the bowling alley and the PX, where one could at least purchase a few emergency beers to relieve the boredom. Sentenced to spend the night in cramped office quarters that had been quickly re-fitted for VIP guests not really that important, I was amazed to make it through till morning without strangling several loud snorers.

With the whirlwind tour of Turkey having lasted less than twenty-four hours, breakfast was served onboard the flight back to Naples. Beyond having to bid farewell to our prestigious plane, nobody seemed particularly heartbroken to be parting ways, and there were no hollow promises made to keep in touch.

As was often the case with foreign shoots, Buddy and I had tacked on a few extra days, this time with intentions of taking in the famed Amalfi coast. After picking up a rental car in downtown Naples, we decided to include a quick visit to Vesuvius before heading south. Unlike Etna however, the entire upper region that day was fogged in with zero visibility. With nearby

Pompeii suffering the same fate, we headed for Amalfi sooner than planned, witnessing breath-taking scenery along the serpentine coastal highway. With high season yet to kick in, we were able to find a cheap hotel right on the sea with a balcony view that extended all the way up the coastline. The town of Amalfi itself was intriguing. Built right into the side of the cliffs, its steep streets, were littered with small groves of lemon trees amidst a profusion of tourist shops. Content to spend the afternoon as aimless "turisti," that night at dinner, we were in the midst of our meal when a man seated at the next table struck up a conversation. Claiming to be a former restaurant critic for the New York Times, the longer he droned on, the more Buddy and I suspected it was a "Lonely Hearts" column he wrote for. More immune to occasional spells of misanthropy than I, Buddy made the generous but fateful offer of asking whether he'd like to join us for a trip to Paestum planned for the next day.

Faced with a predicted two hour drive to the 2500 year old temple complex, we departed for the neighbouring province of Salerno right after breakfast, negotiating through a multitude of hair-pin turns along the narrow coastal highway, constantly aware of the precipitous drop to the deep, blue sea, inches from the edge of the road. Despite getting stuck behind a bus and a large truck that were impossible to pass, we made it to Paestum without overly frayed nerves. Leaving Buddy to enjoy the souvenir shop in the company of his self-inflicted wound, I wandered off to explore the grounds on my own. Thanks to a dearth of fellow tourists, due in part to a light drizzle that had begun, it was possible to stroll through the compound relatively unencumbered.

With its large temples, amphitheatre, city walls, and flagstone walkways all incredibly well preserved, the remnants of this ancient Greek site made the Acropolis look more like a poor second cousin.

"So how many fridge magnets did you buy?" I asked Buddy as we rounded a corner on the return trip to be greeted by a lengthy line of cars trapped behind yet another bus. Not in the mood for swallowing exhaust for the foreseeable future, we chose to abandon the main road and cut inland, hoping to reach Amalfi via another route. Much to our enjoyment, the detour took us through the town of Ravello where, entranced by the houses, lush foliage and general ambience, we decided to stop for an early dinner. Relaxing on the garden patio overlooking the sea, as the sun packed up and left for Canada, our quiet guest broke his silence to ask whether either of us had a business card.

"We could keep in touch," he said. "Share stories about our travels etc."

Buddy and I exchanged an awkward glance before I excused myself to the washroom, leaving Buddy to mumble something about having left his cards back at the hotel. By the time I returned, Buddy had diffused the situation by asking for one of our guest's cards. Following what turned out to be a superb dinner, we headed for Amalfi, somewhat dreading the possibility of another evening of extended tales. Much to our surprise, when back in the town our guest begged off, saying he was too tired to join us for a drink even though an invitation hadn't been issued. As a result, my last waking hours of Amalfi were spent on the hotel balcony, nursing a glass of Merlot while gazing out over a moonlit sea. As the events of the last week rolled in with the tide, the flight in the Black Hawk was the first to hit the shore, followed closely by the First Lady's jet. As clouds drifted in to diminish the moonlight, and my wine glass emptied, moving up fast to dislodge the two frontrunners in memory lane was the sweet, sweet knowledge that we wouldn't be flying home via friggin' Alitalia.

CHAPTER 34

To the Core

For better or for worse, in sickness and in health, for pretty much most of my life, I've been thin. Considering my questionable diet, non-existent exercise regimen and general method of not taking care of myself, it is rather remarkable that being overweight has always been something that other people have had to deal with.

Having never actually seen a large person close up before, at least not a naked one, I wasn't at all prepared for the expanse of flesh that was exposed when nurses pulled back the sheet covering the first patient. For some reason the sight reminded me of terraced rice fields on an Asian mountainside, the paddies quivering each time the nurse made adjustments to the patient's body.

An hour prior to having entered the operating theatre, outfitted with the standard green pants and jacket, complimented by a plastic hairnet, cotton face mask and shower caps for shoes, we'd been sitting in the surgeon's office listening to him explain. "It's a relatively simple procedure we'll be carrying out today; a non-invasive operation to tie off a portion of the patient's stomach. Normally it only takes around twenty minutes, but I'm afraid there won't be much to see. I'll only be making two small incisions, one for the camera and one for the instruments. All the action will be on the monitor and the whole thing will be over before you know it."

While in the process of donning our scrubs in the changing room, the same doctor had reemphasized the importance of sterility, warning us not to touch anything in the operating arena. Just before the electric door slid open for us to enter, I took Buddy aside to repeat the message.
   "You heard what he said right? No unnecessary movement, and don't touch a thing. I will be near the monitor so you can position yourself on the opposite side and stay wide, keeping me out of the shot. Got it?"
   Buddy's blank eyed stare was not terribly reassuring, but at this stage little could be done to alter circumstances. The decision to let him act as the second cameraman had come against my better judgement, shortly after our arrival at the clinic near Salzburg. We had been seated in the lobby, flipping through incomprehensible medical journals when the producer, a young woman from Korea, had turned to ask, "How much of a problem would it be to have a second camera in the OR today?" Sensing the opportunity for a larger paycheque, Buddy had quickly tossed aside his magazine to offer his services. Diplomacy became the name of the game when she turned to me for a second opinion.
   "It might serve just as well to set up a second camera on a tripod with fixed wide shot," I suggested, avoiding any direct eye contact with Buddy. "I can pick up close-ups from the shoulder."
   "Actually, I'd prefer both cameras be mobile so we can respond quickly to any changes during the operation," she said.
   Not wanting to challenge her or embarrass Buddy, I stifled my concerns until she had gone off to the washroom.

"Nothing personal man, but you don't have any experience. I know you've heard me say a thousand times that a monkey could be taught to operate a camera in a week... but even a monkey needs to practice."

"How hard can it be?" Buddy answered, visibly miffed by the comparison. "I can deal with it."

"Shooting from a tripod is one thing. Going hand-held needs practice. You'll be putting the whole shoot at risk."

"I can handle it," he repeated. "Besides all she wants is a wide shot. Anybody can do that."

"I'm glad you have so much respect for camerawork."

"I didn't mean you... You just tell me where you want me to stand, set up the shot and I'll figure out the rest. Don't make it such a big deal."

We hadn't been in the OR for more than a few minutes, with echoes of "the rest" still ringing in my ears, when all eyes turned to the source of a loud bang.

"Sorry," Buddy muttered, sheepishly trying to move a trolley of instruments back to its original position. "Sorry."

"Just leave it," the surgeon ordered. "And for God's sake, don't touch anything else."

Shortly after the first patient was brought in, I positioned Buddy well away from the operating table, advising him again to, "Stay wide with no zooms, and no movement. Got it?"

"Got it."

Glancing around to find the best vantage point for my camera, I'd no sooner settled on a location near the monitor, when another loud clanging reverberated through the room.

"Good Lord man," the doctor bellowed, as Buddy quickly tried to retrieve a pan he'd knocked to the floor. "This is not a circus tent. You are in an operating room full of sterile equipment. Each time you bang into something… a cart, a wall, another person, you are putting this patient in jeopardy. If you're not able to refrain from smashing into things, I'll have to ask you to leave."

The stern message hit home and for the duration of the first operation Buddy managed to avoid careening into any other objects. No further disruptions occurred during the second procedure and it wasn't until we were well into our third operation that I felt a tap on my shoulder.

"Excuse me, but am I going to be able to use any of the footage Buddy is shooting?" the producer whispered with a concerned look on her face.

It was an awkward and critical moment to say the least. Having concentrated on my own footage, I hadn't kept close tabs on the "second cameraman." What with the absence of bangs and clangs, I'd merely assumed my instructions were being followed. A single glance in Buddy's direction however, made it apparent I had erred grievously. Not only had he moved from his original position, he was now attempting some sort of pan or dolly, moving within millimetres of a tray of instruments, while I watched in silent horror. As the assisting nurse took over to complete the final stitching, I made way over to where Buddy had come to rest.

"What are you doing?" I asked, gently but firmly moving him back from his precarious perch near the instruments. "I asked you to stay put. Why are you moving around? Gimme the camera for a second."

Hoping against hope, I rewound the tape and pressed play, only to be dismayed by the series of choppy zooms, shaky pans, and out of focus shots that made themselves known.

"I think we have enough footage from the second camera," I announced, refusing to hand the camera back. "You might as well wait for us outside."

"And?" the producer wanted to know as I hoisted my camera back on my shoulder in preparation for the next patient. Giving a quick spin to the roulette wheel of feasible explanations, I settled on the claim of a technical malfunction, just as a loud crash was heard coming from the ante room. Instinctively, everyone exchanged knowing glances as the door opened and Buddy stuck his head into the room.

"It wasn't me, honest... it wasn't," he pleaded in a high-pitched voice before the closing door again.

It wasn't until we were back out in the parking lot, packed up and ready to go, that I thought it wise to offer an apology and explanation to the producer. Suppressing the strong urge to add, "*I tried to warn you,*" I simply told her, "I'm really sorry about the material from the second camera. I think it might have been a dirty head. But I shot a few wide shots of the last operation on my camera, so I think you'll be covered. You can't really tell one patient from the other from that distance."

The look on her face made it difficult to tell how soon disappointment might morph into anger. But rather than hanging around to find out, I simply handed over the tapes before bidding her adieu.

"Well, Stanley," I said to Buddy as he eased out of

the parking lot and honked a final goodbye. "That's another fine mess you've gotten us into. I think you can forget about ever working for that company again."

"That's okay," he said with a chuckle. "She probably can too."

CHAPTER 35

Lobster Boy

"What sort of food did you gentlemen have in mind?" the nattily dressed young woman behind the counter asked.

"No idea, I'm afraid," I answered.

"Seafood is a specialty here in Lisbon. There's a good seafood restaurant just a few blocks from the hotel that serves delicious lobster."

"Lobster it is," Buddy interrupted, breaking off from fiddling with his cell phone to conclude the discussion for both of us. It was not until we were out on the street that I attempted to voice my reservations.

"I don't know about this. Seafood has never been near the top of my list of sumptuous foods. Take oysters for example… or better yet, take them away before I gag. I mean who wants to eat something that looks like it came out of a nose?"

"Are you kidding me?" Buddy said, as we waited at a light to cross the street. "I love oysters. You just haven't tried them with the right sauce."

"Chopped up erasers probably taste good with the right sauce," I countered, gazing longingly at the menu as we sauntered past a cozy looking Italian eatery. But argument was futile and several minutes later we entered a crowded, noisy, smoke-filled establishment outfitted with a mixture of maritime decor that took kitsch to stratospheric heights.

"Man oh man, get a load of this place… And I

thought Germans could be loud and crass."

Any hopes of not getting a seat were dashed when a grey-coated waiter, looking like he just walked off a factory floor, waved us to a table near the lobster tank.

"At least they're not in white," I said, recalling the bane of Bologna, as we pondered the options for our meal.

"Not being a big lobster fan, I'm going to go for the steak."

"Great, all the more for me," Buddy replied, rubbing his hands with feigned glee.

"Somehow I don't think our waiter has a case full of Mr. Friendly trophies at home," I noted, as our drinks were delivered with a scowl. "By the way, did you see the size of the lobster he took out of the tank for you. The thing was gigantic."

"Not a problem," Buddy boasted. "I'm really hungry tonight. I can handle a big one."

In spite of our many hours together on the road, the stress of the shoots themselves and the shared meals or repeated retreats to the bar, conversation between Buddy and myself had rarely felt stilted. That evening was no exception, although hearing anything above the constant din and the sea shanty playing in the background did prove to be an effort.

"I don't get it," I said, raising a question that had been bothering me for much of the day. "The hotel chain that brought us in for this shoot is presumably paying big money for what is supposed to be a virtual tour of their facilities."

"And?"

"And at the moment, about three people on the planet have an internet connection fast enough to watch it online."

"That's not our problem. We just take the money and run."

"Yeah, but this is the seventh or eighth hotel we've covered so far this year. Don't you figure somebody would have noticed by now and complained?"

"Complained about what?"

"That their so-called film clip looks more like a jerky slide show. How can anyone be impressed with that?"

"Look… Nobody has even noticed that it takes us one day to film everything, yet we usually stay for three. Don't make waves. Just enjoy it. It's easy money."

The lad had a point. Dwelling for several days at five star hotels in the likes of London, Vienna, Brussels, Berlin and Amsterdam, to name just a few, hadn't exactly been onerous, especially with many having granted us carte blanche to meals and services.

"Can you remember that time at the Ritz Carleton in Berlin?" I said. "The one that Lagerfeld reportedly designed and decorated?"

"Tough to forget that one."

"And they'd given us free access to the bar…"

"And we were going to order that $10,000 bottle of Russian wine, let the wine steward open it, take a sip and say 'whoa this stuff is terrible… take it away Jeeves…'"

"Maybe we should we try it here in Lisbon."

"Only if you want it to be the last hotel on the tour," Buddy answered, raising his glass for a belated toast.

"Can you nuke lobsters?" was the first question begging an answer when a short time later, the waiter set down a crustacean large enough to have co-starred in a 1950's Japanese horror movie.

"Man… this thing looks great," Buddy drooled.

Secretly convinced there was no way he could finish such a huge portion, I turned my attention to the plate in front of me.

"Excuse me… Are you sure this is what I ordered?" I asked the waiter about to flee.

"Sim , o que mais deve ser?"

"What was that?"

"Probably means eat it and die, gringo," Buddy mused, while cracking open his first leg.

"Yes, it is steak," the waiter explained in a sudden shift of tongues.

"But why is it grey?"

"Grey?"

"Grey… like the colour of your jacket, the sidewalk, my mood."

"Eu não entendo," he answered, sharing his befuddlement with a desperate look to Buddy.

"Don't look at me pal," Buddy told him, with a mouthful of lobster.

Clearly unconcerned with my concerns, the waiter gave a perfunctory shrug and disappeared into the hazy throng.

"Do remind me to slit the receptionist's throat when we get back to the hotel will you?" I said, holding up the plate to see if there was any odour to the slice of concrete. "This thing is grotesque… I can't eat this. I need to get the waiter back. Did you see where he went?"

"Probably to get a gun," Buddy cracked, dabbing his bib at some errant sauce.

As Buddy continued to gorge himself, I alternated between the waiter's whereabouts and the culinary curiosity on my plate. When the former did reappear, it was only to remove the evidence without comment.

"No, I don't want anything else... but thanks for not asking," I said to his shrinking back.

"Funny how some people have all the luck," Buddy pointed out, shoving another fistful of lobster into his mouth with a smirk of satisfaction.

Approximately half an hour later, tired of watching Buddy dawdle over the dessert portion of his meal, I casually scanned the recently delivered bill to see if I'd been charged for something I couldn't eat.

"Say... how much was your lobster?" I asked after determining the bill had in fact been adjusted in my favour.

"Hmmmph? What?" he answered, after inserting a last slice of chocolate cake. "I'm not sure. They charge by the ounce. Why?"

"Well, I still haven't quite figured out what the Escudo is to the Mark, but unless I'm completely out of it, your giant lobster looks like it's going to cost you somewhere in the range of $60."

"How much?" Buddy blurted, sending a flurry of wet crumbs out over the tablecloth. "Let me see that."

A quick calculation on his phone revealed my estimation to be relatively close to the mark.

"When and if the waiter comes back, ask him if he was standing on the scale while weighing your lobster," I suggested.

Needless to say when the gentleman in question returned to collect his fee, a heated discussions ensued. Although Buddy didn't really have a case, in the end he was granted a minor reduction by the beckoned manager. Not satisfied with that small victory, he attempted to seek further revenge by leaving what amounted to a two-cent tip, a sum the waiter fortunately did not discover before we'd left the premises through a gauntlet of condemning stares from fellow patrons.

Out on the street, the gentle warm breeze was a welcome reprieve from the dismal atmosphere we'd just escaped. Headed back up the marble promenade towards our hotel, conversation turned to the matter at hand.

"Firing squad or mysterious accident?"

"I don't follow," Buddy said.

"Which does she deserve for recommending that restaurant?"

"Hey, my lobster was fine."

"Yeah… All 50 pounds of it."

"Okay, but I only paid for forty."

"You mean the client only paid for forty."

"Better still."

"Ten bucks says she's related to the owner."

"You blew it," Buddy said, stopping to balance on one foot as he adjusted his sandal. "You could have asked for a doggy bag for so we could have slipped that piece of meat into her purse."

Chuckling at options that might have been, we were joined by a perfectly-timed chorus of laughter erupting from a group at a sidewalk table of the Italian restaurant we had failed to frequent earlier. To add insult to injury, as we sauntered past, they looked to be enjoying themselves immensely.

CHAPTER 36

Behind the scenes

What started off as a simple five-day celebration to mark the marriage of Bavaria's Crown Prince Ludwig and Princess Therese of Sachsen-Hildburghausen in October of 1810, has changed dramatically over the intervening decades. In 2016, some 6.6 million people attended the festivities, consuming some six and a half million litres of beer, 95,000 litres of wine, 550,000 units of chicken, 140,225 sausages, 44,000 kg of fish and 116 oxen, over a span of sixteen days. The annual event has proven to be a boon for the city of Munich, reportedly pumping 1.1 billion Euros into its economy. Somewhat less appealing aspects of the event however, have been the tons of waste created, scores of fights, puddles of vomit, 100,000 attempts to steal beer mugs, and a few dozen "Bierleichen"*(Beer corpses)*. Hey, what's not to like about the world famous Oktoberfest?

Upon hearing an American food network had booked us to film a "behind the scenes" glimpse of the renowned event, I had taken it upon myself to inquire just how many people amongst my circle of friends and acquaintances had actually been there. Up to that point, I had been under the impressions that few Germans, other than perhaps a horde of devoted Bavarians, actually ventured to the festival, preferring to leave the its dubious delights to the English, Australians and Americans. The results of my private survey revealed that no one I knew had ever attended, or would at least admit to it.

During the four hour drive it took to reach the Bavarian capital that day in September, I felt myself drifting back to another era in time. It was the summer of 1963, the year I had first received permission to attend the Red River Exhibition completely on my own. The Canadian equivalent of a large County Fair, the "Ex," as it was more commonly known, was held each June just as school was letting out for the holidays. First and foremost amongst the interests of a geeky thirteen year had been the midway, with its dazzling lights, blaring music, screams of terror and joy from the thundering rides, and moans of customers being hornswoggled out of a "sure thing" prize for their date. It was simply pure and perfect pandemonium. The ultimate attraction for me however, had been the Freak Show, a politically-incorrect expression if there ever was one. There was something about watching garishly dressed barkers on a platform in front of ten-foot high cartoonish banners of the "featured exhibits," that I found utterly mesmerizing. There was also the crystal-clear memory of their growling into their microphones as if they were about to swallow them whole, as they cajoled and challenged passing patrons in an attempt to lure them in to the wonders of Lobster Boy or the Bearded Lady.

"Hey you there… yeah you… the guy with the pretty lady… how bout' bringin' the little woman in to show her the time of her life?"

Such trumpeted overtures were of course rarely successful, but that didn't diminish the fun of just hanging around listening to the rehearsed routines. Inevitably told to, "Beat it kid… go pester somebody else. You'se gotta be sixteen to gets in here," the forbidden sights remained out of reach that summer despite my new-found independence.

Having been told Oktoberfest was unlikely to have its own official "Freak Show," I harboured no expectations of partaking in the same quality sleaze as we strolled on to the grounds of the "Wiesn," the enormous field where the carnival unfolds every September. In fact it had all seemed rather tame until we entered a gigantic tent to find it jammed with thousands of people. Despite the fact the clock had yet to strike eleven a.m., all patrons were diligently consuming "Maße" (one litre mugs) of German beer, served by "Dirndl clad Mädels" with décolletés reminiscent of a mid-sized derriere. Those guests who hadn't already reached the table-dancing stage, appeared content to remain sedentary, linking arms with fellow drinking companions to sway from side to side on wooden benches, while a German brass band perched on a gazebo in the middle of the tent, cranked out an endless series of "oom pah pah" ditties.

Snaking our way through the crush of humanity, a large portion of which was already slumped over their tables, it took time to adjust to the deafening din, thick smoke and fumes of a thousand different smells. Fortunately, with our status as "media staff" we were elevated to an "VIP" section overlooking the entire proceedings. Congregated on the upper level was a sprinkling of German"Promis"(celebrities), busy enjoying themselves while keeping an eye out for roving camera teams that could document their doing so. As is often the wont of celebrities, many appeared to have gone a trifle overboard in the glamour department, coated in layers of make-up and jewelry and dressed in traditional "Dirndl and Lederhosen."

"Say, is it just me or do some of these people look rather decadent. I feel like we're filming at the fall of Rome. All that's missing are the grapes and the guys with the fanning palm leaves."

"That's a bit excessive," Buddy said. "Jealous, are we?"

"You bet… no foolin' you."

Despite the somewhat reduced noise level on this upper section, the rousing cheers that erupted every time the bandleader called for an audience response, made it impossible to conduct any interviews. Hoping to find a quieter venue, we re-located to the next cavernous hall, only to discover what sounded like the same endless song that was played at the last tent. Once again escorted to the VIP area by a buxom waitress, this time the producer insisted on filming the "Promis" as they drank, ate and joked at how ridiculous they all looked in the traditional costumes. As expected, there was the usual batch of "which channel is this going to air on?" from the crowd. Rather than offering the truth, which was, "Sorry, this is for US television," it proved easier to simply suggest they tune into the National News tonight when they got home.

Once a sufficient number of smiles, toasts, and friendly waves were "in the can," on we moved to the belly of the beast. There, in a huge kitchen, amidst the clamour of clanging pots and pans, breaking glasses and plates, and shouted orders, we were given a first-hand look of how tons of food and drink are prepared behind the scenes. Despite the high-noise threshold and sauna-like temperature, we attempted to conduct a standup interview with the main chef.

"Delivering quantity is not a problem if you're well prepared," he shouted above the din. "It's maintaining the quality that is the challenge."

After twenty minutes in this culinary hell, we switched to the adjoining restaurant, to film members of the crowd gorging and drinking themselves into near oblivion. Then in a flash, the tumult was over. Back in the relative tranquility of the hotel bar a short while later, a ringing still present in my ears, it was clearer than ever that Oktoberfest was little more than one big excuse for one giant piss up. For all those out there thinking that their lives are somehow incomplete because they have yet to attend this much acclaimed marvel... allow me to suggest, "think again."

CHAPTER 37

Island Fortress

The more thought I've given it, the more I'm convinced that the average person doesn't know very much about the Channel Islands; or probably care much for that matter. My first exposure to them came quite by accident, while on a tour of Brittany in the fall of 1986. Mildly awed to be standing on the same St. Malo jetty where Jacques Cartier had set off for Canada some 350 years before my arrival, a passing whim prompted me to book a day trip to Jersey, the largest and most well-known of the Channel Islands parked off the north-western coast of France. Unbeknownst to me at the time, the tail end of a North American hurricane had the same idea, spewing its final fury as it made its way through the English Channel, and exposing us to highly treacherous waves the minute we left the French harbour. As a result, the trip to the English outpost that day, which normally should have only taken two hours, was stretched to four and a half, most of which was spent heaving on a deck lashed by wind and rain. Seasick to the point where being washed overboard by an errant wave would have been a blessing, I hoped my second visit would prove to be considerably less dramatic.

It was on a cloudy and calm, August morning when we left for Guernsey, departing a mere stone's throw from the very pier in Cherbourg where the Titanic had set sail on its fateful maiden voyage in 1912.

"Should I be taking this as an omen?" I asked Buddy as our small chartered boat chugged past the final buoy and out into the open sea. Several uneventful hours later, a portion of which was spent trying to understand how and why people came to inhabit such a seemingly remote outpost, we were met in St.Peter Port by our producer, Dwayne, and the island's entire tourist and real estate board, a middle-aged, Belgian woman by the name of "Call me Marta." Not one to feel silence must be golden, Marta provided a running commentary on what she deemed were the island's unique features, during the short drive to the residence that was to be our home for the next five days. Waiting for us in the open doorway of a white-washed stone house, was a grey-haired lady on loan from Coronation Street. As many elderly English ladies tend to do, she insisted on calling everyone "luv" as she showed us our rooms and issued the decree that dinner would be at "six sharp."

Bright and early the next morning, as cheerful as all get out, Marta returned to fulfil her promise of showing us "the island." Given that Guernsey is little more than twenty-five miles square, it proved not to be a lengthy tour.

"The people born here are called "vaques," she explained as we passed a lone house hidden amidst a cluster of trees.

"And why is that?" Dwayne asked.

"To be honest, I couldn't tell you," Marta replied, seemingly unconcerned she was driving down the centre of the road. "It apparently has something to do with the cows here. But don't quote me."

"Don't ask," I whispered to Buddy, elbowing him in

the ribs before directing my comments to Marta.

"How many people actually live here?"

"On the whole island?" she asked, casting a glance into the rear-view mirror.

It came as a bit of a surprise to hear the population was around 60,000, seeing as we had virtually been the only car on the road several miles after leaving St. Peter Port. A short while later, as the mini-expedition neared its end, our genial hostess suggested dropping by the "yacht club" for drinks.

"Unless my watch has stopped, it's only 10:30," I casually pointed out to Dwayne, hoping he would back up my statement and suggest we use the free time to do some location scouting. Instead he agreed with Marta, saying an early lunch would give us time to discuss what the week's shooting itinerary would entail.

"What's to discuss." I said to Buddy as we made our way up a flagstone path towards a stuccoed bunker that apparently served as the main watering hole for the island's elite. "We're gonna be here for five days. We could shoot the whole island three times over in that amount of time."

"Relax," Buddy said. "It's gonna be a laid-back shoot. Enjoy... *Sheesh* you complain a lot."

"Normally, one must be ahhh membaaah," Marta joked, as she greeted and nodded to acquaintances scattered across the patio. "But today you are my guests."

Entering what appeared to be the main room, we noticed that most of the thirty to forty patrons present were nursing a drink despite the early hour. Regrettably it was not the typical quaint English pub I'd become accustomed to over the years, but rather a drab chamber with the ambience of a recently vacated storage closet. Plaques, photos, and replicas of knots adorned the walls, with the only truly interesting thing to look at being the view of the harbour through a large picture window.

"Maybe we should be filming *this*," I told Buddy as we accepted a welcoming glass of Sekt served by a white-jacketed waiter. "Seems to be in fashion again."

"What's that?"

"The waiter… never mind."

"Here's to a successful shoot, gentlemen," Marta toasted, raising her glass to take a sip before turning her attention to one of her nearby friends.

"I say lad," I said, nudging Buddy. "Check out the guy leaning against the mantel… the one in the admiral's jacket. Talk about being caught in the empire mode… Stiff upper lip and all that."

Given the admiral's flamboyant posturing, it was probably a good thing that the murmur of the crowd made it impossible to hear any of his conversation.

Over lunch, it was agreed the afternoon's agenda would include driving up to "La Citadelle," the shoot's main attraction. Little more than than a ten minute drive from the yacht club, we caught our first glimpse of the seaside garrison as the coastal road swerved inward around a wide sand-striped bay, to reveal it sitting on a high cliff above the blue-green waters of the English Channel.

"Man, if this is their holiday home," I asked aloud, "What do these people have for a permanent dwelling?"

Although nobody had specifically requested a history lesson, Marta felt compelled to let us know "La Citadelle," had been built by the English during Napoleonic times, to act as a bulwark against nations with a penchant for looting and pillaging.

"Why is it called La Citadelle if it's in English territory," Buddy wanted to know.

"Probably just to irk the French," she said with a sly smile. "It's now a seasonal home to three people. But as you may well ask, why do three people need a residence with thirty two rooms, seven bathrooms, and twelve thousand square feet of living space?"

With the clock already closing in on three, the decision was made not to disturb the occupants that afternoon, but rather to return early next day to get in a full day of shooting.

*

The fog had yet to lift as we pulled into the gravel courtyard a little after nine the next morning. The fortress may have looked impressive two hundred years ago, but decades of lashing, salt-sea breezes had taken their toll. As we were about to discover, the building would not be the only element to induce the feeling of traveling back to a distant era. Following a knock on a heavy iron plate, the large door swung open to reveal a stiff looking gentleman attired in a heavy woollen pullover, augmented by a silk-scarf tie.

"Ahhh good morning, good morning ... Do come in gentlemen... and lady. Do come in," he corrected himself as he stepped aside to expose two others awaiting us in the large foyer. Wallace, a man in his midfifties, who looked as though he'd just stepped out of a Monty Python skit, introduced himself, his wife Penelope, and his father-in-law, "the Captain," before beckoning us all into the living room where a tray of welcoming drinks lay in wait. Confined to a wheel chair, the elderly Captain declined Wallace's offer of assistance with a scowl before rolling up to the table to help himself to a glass.

"New Zealander by birth," the Captain suddenly boasted, lifting his glass in an impromptu toast. "Although you wouldn't bloody know it anymore from my accent. Lost the bloody thing after all my years abroad."

"Daadday," Penelope complained.

"Oh alright child... We *are* all adults here," he harrumphed.

"At least most of us," he added, casting a fleeting glance in Wallace's direction. "Spent most of my years in Africa, I did... even once treated Albert Schweitzer."

"Probably to a drink," I whispered to Buddy before taking a second sip of a liquid I still didn't recognize. Glancing around the room as the Captain continued his narrative, it came to me that "*an isolated fortress on a remote island... rather eccentric owners quick to offer a refreshment that will cast their unsuspecting guests into a stupor before they're hauled down to a cellar dungeon for an evening of fun and torture,*" I thought, "*I've seen this movie before.*"

Caught up in this momentary illusion, I was only half listening as the Captain explained how he had purchased the Fortress in the mid-1960's for the sum of $160,000. Slowed by either the affliction of elevated age or his second glass of the golden liquid, the Captain didn't specify how long he'd actually lived there, saying only, with an unmistakable tinge of resignation, that he now shared the living space with his daughter and son-in-law. While he continued to drone on to no one in particular, I used the opportunity to give the fifty-something Penelope an undetected once over. Outfitted in a long flowing dress, topped by a wide- brimmed floppy hat that was fastened under her chin with a sheer scarf, she could have easily passed for Blanche Dubois from A Streetcar Named Desire. Sitting upright on the sofa, her hands properly folded on crossed knees, she not so much moved as fluttered, as she diligently listened to her father's tales. When the Captain's mini saga finally drew to an end, Wallace offered to take us on an informal tour, to get "a feel for the place." Not wanting to miss a good sound bite or any spontaneous action, Dwayne suggested both Penelope and Wallace be miked beforehand. The Captain, meanwhile, announced his intention to take his mid-morning nap but not without first helping himself to a third glass of refreshment.

As we wandered through a maze of rooms, each containing a healthy portion of expensive furniture, both antique and modern, Wallace seemed to be enjoying himself immensely, narrating tidbits of history about "La Citadelle" and its fortunes. As far as the building itself was concerned, amazing or luxurious were not words that came easily to mind. Signs of deterioration were visible everywhere. Rust from the iron-framed windows and doors had leached into the plaster, while the near constant salty atmosphere had prompted paint to bubble or fleck off the walls in large chunks. It was also difficult to ignore the strategically placed buckets in one of the bedrooms, set up to trap water leaking from a roof that had obviously seen better days. Add to that the visible stains on the library's thick oriental carpet, which brought to mind an unfinished "connect the dots" drawing, and the place emoted an aura of what could diplomatically be called bygone elegance, or perhaps more accurately "long gone elegance".

We'd only managed to survey half the home's many rooms when Penelope floated back in to make an announcement.

"We absolutely must have drinks on the terrace before continuing the tour, darling," she uttered, in a thoroughly irritating, high-pitched accent that conjured up images of a croquet match with members of an incestuous royal family. Having already witnessed the prominent role yacht club activities seemed to play on the island, the invitation hardly came as a surprise. Several minutes later, the six of us were seated beneath a weather-beaten canopy, protected from the stiff sea winds by a crumbling stone wall. "Daadday's" failure to join us, we were told, was due to his currently being "indisposed." The first round of gin and tonic went down exceptionally well, and was quickly followed by a second. It was only when Dwayne politely declined the offer of a third, that Wallace got up to excuse himself.

"Frightfully sorry old chaps… a bit of business matter online. Shouldn't take long. Penelope love, be a good lass. Show the gents the remainder of the house will you dear?"

Accepting a polite peck on the cheek from her departing husband, Penelope begged our pardon to retreat to the ladies room, promising to meet us in the kitchen to continue the walk through.

"Man oh man… I could get used to these real quick," Buddy declared, about to reach for a refill before Dwayne's stern glance advised otherwise. A short while later, awaiting Penelope in the only fully modern room of the house, I was helping myself to a glass of water when I noticed Buddy off in the corner chuckling to himself.

"What's so funny?" I asked. "Besides this entire scenario, that is."

Without a word he simply handed me his headphones, instantly transforming me into an accomplice as I listened in on the conversation Penelope and Wallace were unknowingly divulging on their open mikes.

"Really now Wallace, I think this whole venture is a complete and utter waste of time. I can't for the life of me see how this is possibly going to help us to sell the house. It's so disappointing."

"Now, now, my dear. One mustn't be discouraged. After all, there's bound to be *some* benefits. It's not as though this is really costing us anything other than a few drinks for these heathens. We might as well make the best of it. I'm sure they shan't be here much longer."

"Oh Wallace, I can't help it. I'm so frightfully disappointed. I mean, what's Daadday going to think?"

"Oh Penelope."

With visions of Wallace taking Penelope in his less than brawny arms and sweeping her off for an afternoon delight, I silently handed the headphones back to Buddy. Seconds later the good lady herself reappeared, looking none the worse for wear. Gesturing for us to follow, she led us into what turned out to be the most interesting room so far. Dominated by a long wooden table capable of seating at least twenty people, the dining room's most striking feature was an enormous floor-to-ceiling picture window running the length of the room. Offering a spectacular view of the bay, locals and tourists could be seen cavorting on the beach below, with a few brave souls even venturing into the sea. Declaring the room the perfect location for Penelope to deliver a general synopsis of the house, Dwayne positioned her before a wall-covering tapestry, before advising her to just "act naturally," as she described the room.

As we started to roll, Penelope gingerly waltzed around the end of the table, her fingertips lightly brushing the tops of several high-backed chairs as she spoke directly into the camera.

"*Loretta Young,*" I thought to myself, watching her prance across the room. "*She's morphed into Loretta Young opening her weekly television show. All that's missing is the frilly gown.*"

"Ohhhhh," Penelope sighed. "This is absolutely my faayyvorrrite room in the house. I mean, just look at that view," she moaned before directing the camera to capture the vista.

"I can remember when Mommy and I were alive," she continued, stopping beside a suit of knight's armour as I brought her back into frame. "We so much enjoyed coming to this room just to sit and watch the waves roll in and people out strolling on the beach. It was ever so pleasant."

I flinched at the flub but kept rolling, glancing to Dwayne with a grimace that silently asked, "*Did she just say what I think she said?*"

Numerous rooms later, all of which were anything but remarkable, the house inspection was complete. With footage of the accompanying grounds left until tomorrow, the only item still on today's agenda before the inevitable return to the "yacht club," was an interview with the still-missing Captain.

"I saw a location yesterday that might work," I said to Dwayne. "It's on the other side of the bay. If we can position the Captain properly, we should be able to get the whole fortress in over his shoulder."

Having overheard my suggestion, Penelope interrupted to express her concern about doing the interview outside the house.

"I'm afraid Daadday is rather quite frail. I'm not certain journeying outside is at all advisable. What do you think darling?"

Wallace, who had returned just in time to hear the tail end of the discussion, strangely enough took it as a cue to slink off once again.

"Shan't be long darling. Must finish what I've started. Only wanted to fetch a drink of water."

As a compromise, it was agreed that the three of us would scout out the location, while Penelope roused her father from what she said was his mid-afternoon nap. Should the idea be to everyone's liking, she would then drive him over.

The small grassy plateau at the opposite end of the bay was exactly the shot we were looking for. Although it only took twenty minutes to set up, another half hour passed with still no sign of Penelope and her father. With an eye on the sinking sun, I suggested Dwayne make a second call to see what the delay was.

"We risk losing the light right in the middle of the interview if she doesn't show soon," I warned.

"I can't call her again," Dwayne said. "She's already looking for any excuse to cancel."

Ten minutes later, a lone car appeared at the top of the hill, driving slowly enough to be part of a royal funeral cavalcade through the streets of London. During the subsequent struggle to help the Captain out of the car, a whiff of his breath signalled that we might be in trouble.

"I have the feeling Daadday's nap may have included a pre-nap nip," I quipped to Buddy as we made final adjustments.

"Oh I do hope this won't take very long," Penelope whined. "Daadday is really not up to traveling you know."

"Traveling?" the Captain blustered. "I've traveled the world me whole bloody life. If I can't even make it across the bloody bay, then put me on a skiff, set it on fire and shove me out into the bloody Channel." Turning to us, he ordered "Let's get this bleedin' show on the road gentlemen."

In retrospect, Dwayne handled it well; maintaining a decorum and professionalism despite the Captain's tendency to slur an unintelligible answer to nearly every question.

An hour or so later, we were back at the yacht club, dutifully taking part in the traditional round of drinks before dinner. Milling around amongst what I presumed was the upper crust of the town, I took a perverse pleasure in observing the various intrigues, catching snippets of local gossip here and there about who was doing what, with whom, and where.

"Did you guys understand a single word the Captain said?" Dwayne interrupted.

"Not a word. But it sort of fits his character and the whole story don't you think? I think you have the makings of a great sitcom. You can call it "Upstairs, Downstairs & Around the Bend."

As it happened, the workload over the next few days turned out to be excessively light. In addition to filming "La Citadelle's" exteriors from various perspectives, we were able to pick up general footage that captured the special ambience of the island, including highlights such a previously scheduled mini-regatta in the harbour, which drew out half the island's population, large ocean-going vessels cruising the Channel, and gigantic flocks of seagulls brooding and crapping over a tiny off-shore island. Beyond that, an inordinate amount of time was spent at the yacht club.

"Think it'll sell?" I asked Dwayne, as we cast a final look at the harbour from the stern of the ferry returning us to Cherbourg.

"Not for the 2.3 million pounds they're asking," he said.

"Are you putting me on?" I sputtered. "Two million quid?"

"Two point three to be precise lad. Two point three."

"Who's gonna pay that kind of money for a place you can only use for a few months? It was barely tolerable in the middle of summer. What the heck is it like in winter? Must be depressing as hell what with cold, grey skies everyday."

As we were speaking, off to our left the Fortress poked its profile through the lingering fog, as if it was bidding us a fond adieu, right on cue.

"I say lads," I pondered aloud with a stiff upper lip. "Does anyone here remember that old quote from Dorothy Parker?

'If you want to know what God thinks of money... just

look at the people he gave it to.' Anyone fancy drinks and a round of shuffleboard on the poop deck ... daaaarrrrlings?"

CHAPTER 38

Heated Moments

"Sorry, but I don't get it. Why does someone wait until three days before a shoot, to start looking for a crew?" I grumbled, upon picking Buddy up at our designated meeting place. "Especially one so big. Do they think we don't have anything better to do than wait around for the phone to ring?"

"Morning to you too," Buddy answered. "Not get a good night's sleep did we?"

"Sorry... Morning to you too. But seriously, if this is a three- week shoot, they must have had to plan it."

"We were available. We accepted the job. We're on our way. Where's the problem?"

"No problem. I just would have just preferred a little more notice, that's all."

A mere two days after returning from Guernsey, the message had come through we'd been contracted for several episodes of a program called the Ultimate Zoo. Teamed up once again with our intrepid, albeit somewhat temperamental producer, Dwayne, there'd just been enough time to fill a suitcase with clean clothes before heading off to the picturesque, Swiss city of Zürich.

According to Dwayne, who we subsequently picked up at the train station in Frankfurt, the Zürich city zoo had won a slot in the series because of Masoala, a Madagascar rain forest they'd re-created under a huge transparent, climate-controlled dome.

Able to sail through southern Germany without encountering a single "Stau" (traffic jam), we checked into a fancy, avant-garde hotel near the university, rid ourselves of our personal possessions and made our way up to the Zürichberg, a section of Zürich that overlooks the northern end of Lake Zürich and is home to the city's zoo. Prior to leaving for Switzerland, Dwayne had suggested I preview several episodes of the program to familiarize myself with the style producers preferred. I was less than impressed, particularly with the rapid staccato style of editing which barely gave you time to identify an animal, let alone see what it was doing. Memories of those screenings were still with me when we arrived at the zoo's administrative offices to meet its director.

Although the main premise of the show was to revolve around Masoala, Rod, the zoo director, was eager to show us around other components of the zoo. Not really in the position to object, and feeling we could take advantage of the fact the facilities were closed to the public that day, ten minutes later we were trudging along through a series of empty walkways, accompanied by a cacophony of unseen animals acknowledging our presence. Our little troupe came to a halt outside a large enclosure where several "Brillen Bears" (spectacled bears) were sharing space with a group of friendly-looking animals Rod told us were "Coatis." Although the natural-looking landscape was split in two by a deep, water-filled trench, both species could venture back and forth in their mutual territories via an automatic "tree trunk bridge" that swung into place at the flick of a switch. In order for us to film without being mangled, Rod had kindly arranged for staff to isolate the bears on one side of the trench before removing their causeway. Following Rod through a double set of barred doors, the second of which did not open until the first had clanged shut, we were instantly accosted by a group of curious Coatis, whose most distinctive feature was their elongated tail that stuck straight up in the air as they strutted around the compound.

"The Coatis are native to South America," Rod explained with a smile. "They're a friendly lot, but you don't want to get them riled."

"Don't ask what it takes," I warned Buddy, only half jokingly. Despite Rod's assertion of their friendliness, it was still somewhat unnerving to be standing in the midst of these "wild animals."

"I assume he wouldn't have let us in here if there was a risk of us ending up as tomorrow headlines," I said to Buddy as Dwayne and Rod wandered off to discuss the zoo's special feeding techniques, which required animals to discover their food hidden in hollowed out trees or stumps, rather than have it merely spilled to them out of a bucket. In the meantime, I started to scout around for the best location to begin filming. While standing on a raised ledge near the trench, I happened to glance back down to see Buddy kneeling by his sound kit, surrounded by half-a-dozen Coatis sniffing and licking at his bare legs and exploring the contents of his bag.

"I wouldn't get too friendly with them if I were you," Rod casually warned, breaking off his discussion to make the point.

"It's okay," Buddy slurred in response. "They like me."

"That may seem so, but they can turn on you in an

instant. I would keep my distance if I were you. And no sudden movements if you're fond of all your fingers."

Buddy's response was simply to chuckle as he reached out to try and pet one of the animals that was tapping at a mike windscreen. Although the exchange between Buddy and Rod had been brief, it was long enough for both Dwayne and I to recognize that something was drastically wrong in the state of Denmark.

"Tell me I'm friggin' dreamin," Dwayne growled at me, while Rod walked over to reinforce his advice to Buddy. "Is he out of his mind?" he continued with barely repressed rage. "I mean the guy's out of it for Christ's sake. What the hell does he think he's doing?"

There was not much I could say in return. Unwilling to confront Buddy in front of Rod, Dwayne guided him off to resume their discussion. The tactful move provided the chance to approach Buddy myself.

"You must be out of it in more ways than one," I said with less than veiled contempt, making sure I was out of earshot to the other two. "Dwayne knows you're loaded."

"Really?" Buddy gulped, his eyes bulging as a look of panic swept in. "How does he know?"

"How? Are you completely insane? You want me to turn the camera on you so you can see for yourself?"

"Oh shit. What am I going to do?" he said in a tremulous voice, straining to comprehend the seriousness of the situation. "Do you think Rod noticed?"

"I think someone aboard the space shuttle probably noticed. I'm amazed neither of us spotted it on the drive over. How did you get so wrecked anyway? I mean we were in the car for five hours."

"Well, I was thirsty after we checked in so I had a few of those 'Alcopops' out of the hotel mini-bar," Buddy confessed. "I didn't think we'd be coming to shoot today."

"A few? We were only there for ten minutes… Not a terribly swift move, lad. If I were you I would fake being sick. Make up a story about something you ate at breakfast or you're car sick from the drive… something. Just get out of here and sober up. The Dwayne is not pleased."

What I hadn't realized at the time was that Buddy's daily intake by that time had increased to the point where even "a few" could push him deep into his comfort zone.

Not long after Buddy made an awkward apology and departed, the three of us moved outside the fenced perimeter to continue filming. Within seconds of closing the tree bridge to re-connect the two halves of the compound, we watched as three bears came lumbering across to join their Coati roommates. The two species appeared remarkably accepting of each other, that is until one of the smaller bears happened to take a casual swipe at a Coati he felt was being a little too inquisitive. In a flash the young bear was surrounded by seven or eight snarling compatriots that had sprung out of nowhere to protect their threatened sibling. Instinctively alert to the danger, the bear quickly pirouetted and made a hasty exit back across the walkway.

"Wow… Did you see the teeth on those guys?" I said to Rod. "You really don't want to get on *their* wrong side. They looked ready to make bear burgers out of him."

"As I told your colleague," Rod said, "They appear friendly but can be very fierce if something upsets them. It's best to keep a safe distance. They have razor sharp teeth and quick tempers to match. Your friend was lucky."

That evening back at the hotel restaurant, Buddy was not so lucky in avoiding another set of flashing teeth. Despite the lack of privacy in the crowded venue, Dwayne went ahead and read him the riot act.

"No booze for the rest of this shoot unless you want me to send you home right now," he demanded. "Is that clear? Not a drop... Tell me you understand?"

"I understand," Buddy agreed meekly from behind his raised menu.

Following an ominously quiet breakfast the next morning, the three of us returned the zoo, this time headed for the rain forest we'd ostensibly come to film. Besides the extraordinary concept and construction of the building itself, the most unique feature of Masoala, was that there were no cages.

"Visitors must discover the exotic tropical plants and animals themselves, within a landscape that replicates their natural habitat as closely as possible," Rod explained as we were leaving his office. "They are only allowed to do so from designated walkways, leaving the animals, birds and plant life to pretty much have the run of the place."

As we pushed through a set of heavy, plastic curtains at the entrance to Masoala, we were met with a solid wall of thirty-five degree heat. It was so humid inside the dome that shooting had to be delayed for ten to fifteen minutes to let the fogged-up camera lens acclimatize itself. During the lull, Rod informed me I would be allowed to venture off the paved walkways, provided I stuck to the dirt-service paths.

"Don't go off into the forest itself. There are a lot of plants you could end up damaging without even realizing it."

Although real work had yet to begin, I'd already managed to use up several paper towels in a futile attempt to keep the sweat pouring off my brow from stinging my eyes and blurring my vision. Once the camera and my body had adapted to the drastic climate change, I left the trio and moved off into the jungle. Twenty or thirty feet into the foliage, I stopped to get my bearings, squatting down in the middle of a narrow path shaded by several large overhanging palm leaves. Suddenly I could feel a tongue licking at my exposed leg. Suppressing the urge to whirl around and swat it away, I managed to slowly cock my head far enough back to discover a pair of saucer plate eyes staring back at me.

"I hope you guys are more friendly than the Coatis," I told a beige-coloured lemur. The distraction of my voice was enough to cause him to stop and rear up on his hind legs, freeing me to slowly raise the camera to my shoulder without scaring him away. It was a relief to realize the viewfinder had also cleared itself of condensation and after recording a couple of minutes of the lemur's innocent and curious stare, I panned off into the forest only to discover several other sets of eyes gazing back from the protection of the undergrowth. Suddenly a fruit bat swooped down from an overhead tree, skimming so close to the top of my head it nearly sent me tumbling into a basin of water just off the path. Moving a little further along the trail, I nearly missed a chameleon perched on a broad palm leave right in front of me. Virtually invisible at first glance, if it hadn't been for the gently swaying leaf, the chameleon's complete immobility would have made the footage look more like a still photograph than video.

After spending over an hour filming various animals, including a frame-filling, 400 pound giant turtle that almost crushed my foot in slow motion, I returned to the main walkway to seek out another location. I was still in the search mode when Dwayne rushed up to direct my attention overhead.

"Up there, hanging from the roof. There's a guy trimming trees. Rod says we can get a better shot of him from the gangway, so follow me."

"There's no way I can go up there," Buddy confessed, after glancing at the walkway that arched up to the summit of the dome. "I'm afraid of heights."

"That's what I needed to hear. Have you been talking to Howdy lately?" I answered with a grin, waving off Dwayne's offer to assist. "It's not a problem. Once I'm up there, there's nothing you can do anyways, except possibly die of heat exhaustion. I'll just take my time getting there."

"You can't take too much time," Dwayne warned. "Who knows how long the guy will be up there."

Although the metal gangway hadn't appeared particularly steep from ground level, once I started up with both camera and tripod, it quickly became apparent how strenuous the climb would be. With the temperature and humidity increasing with the elevation, it was necessary to stop several times to rest and catch my breath. By the time I'd reached a point where I had a clear view of the tree cutter, I was virtually drenched, not to mention exhausted. From this hard-won vantage point, however, I was able to film the man as he dangled above a canopy of tall trees, some fifteen to twenty metres above the forest floor. Held aloft by professional mountain climbing gear attached to the roof, I watched as he shifted his position with the aid of a small electric motor that enabled him to move forwards, backwards and sideways on a grid. As he went about the business of trimming branches that threatened the support wires of the dome, he did so under the observant eyes of a half dozen lemurs perched randomly along beams under the curved roof. I was probably into my fifth or sixth minute of filming when the battery light in the camera display started to flash red. I'd picked up a spare battery before beginning my ascent, but just for the fun of it, considered calling down to Buddy to bring one up. It was as I turned to set the used battery down on the gangway, that I noticed another nosey lemur observing me from no more than five feet away. With its four paws wrapped one behind the other around the thin handrail, it remained completely motionless as it stared intently at the camera. As the display screen sprang to life with the new battery, I was able to slowly pivot around and fill the frame with his curious face. For several minutes the two of us remained static, quietly rubbernecking each other as if old, long lost friends. The lemur was the first to bore of the venture, casually twisting the front section of his body around at an impossible angle to reverse direction before simply scooting away.

Later that evening at a restaurant near the hotel, I was recounting details of the day's events to Dwayne when we were joined by a somewhat subdued Buddy.

"Hi guys," he said with forced jocularity, keenly aware of the thin ice he was still on. "Sorry I'm late. Important phone call… You guys satisfied with today's results?"

All but ignoring Buddy's comments, Wayne's singular response was simply, "Not a drop."

Buddy, who'd managed to remain relatively upbeat for much of the day, mainly by avoiding Dwayne's proximity, looked deflated by the remark. Although Dwayne's reaction was justified, if somewhat repetitive, I thought it best not to take sides, curious what other forms of animalistic behaviour we were likely to encounter over the next two weeks.

CHAPTER 39

Face Value

Truth be told, I'd never really put much faith in so-called premonitions, tending to lump them in the same credibility category as the horoscopes you find in the back pages of a newspaper. Such a stance however, has not always prevented illogical perceptions from occasionally convincing me something calamitous was imminent. The fact that two previous portents of doom turned out to be duds, was not enough to render me any less vulnerable to a third. The first foreboding had occurred in the mid 90's, the day before I was scheduled to fly to several German cities aboard a helicopter. Despite repeated mantras of logic, I was certain the trip was destined to end in a fiery crash. The second inevitable disaster was the inexplicable but unshakeable conviction I would not live to see my 50th birthday, the probability of which had been buttressed by a consistently poor diet and family genes that made me a prime candidate for arterial sclerosis.

    The stars for the latest foreseen dread began to align themselves in the middle of one of our tightest schedules in years. Barely twelve hours after returning from Zürich, Dwayne, Buddy and I were back on the road again, this time headed for a Dutch city that had previously been little more than an autobahn exit sign on the way to and from Amsterdam. Following a pre-shoot tradition, during the drive I learned that Arnhem was widely known for a bridge that was fought over by

British, American and German troops in September of 1944. While that item was no longer on the list of the city's "must sees," mainly due to the fact it had been bombed out of existence several weeks later, my travel guide did indicate another architectural wonder still worth visiting, St. Eusebius Church. Dominating what there was of an Arnhem skyline, at first glance the building looked as though it had been the product of squabbling architects, unable to agree on a common design for the planned house of worship. Judging from the edifice's bewildering facade, it seemed the awards committee had simply chosen to resolve the bickering by allowing each architect to build a portion according to his or her own style, begging the question of just how long drugs have been legal in Holland.

Several hours before first bearing witness to the foibles of St. Eusebius' creators, the second leg of our three city zoo tour had gotten underway with our arrival at Arnhem's renowned Burgers' Zoo. Located on the outskirts of the city, the zoo comes equipped with a desert, rainforest, African savannah and several other themed exhibits. The feature we had come to film however, was Ocean World, a maritime exhibit that featured what was then considered one of the world's largest salt-water tanks.

Attending what we hoped would be a short introductory meeting with officials, we were surprised to suddenly find ourselves hustled off on a tour of the zoo's facilities, on the premise it would aid in preparing a shooting agenda for the following day. Tired from the long drive, I wasn't paying much attention to our guide, until that is, we were led into the building that housed the huge tank. To help gain an idea of its enormity, we were told the glass-walled structure held nearly eight million litres of salt water, and no... I didn't know or care to ask how many bathtubs that translates into. Home to a collection of sharks, manta rays, eels, and dozens of other species of fish, it was large enough to house a life-size galleon shipwreck. Another feature offered to the visitor was being able to observe marine life from within a glass tunnel, resting on the bottom of the tank like some transparent snake. Nowadays such an attraction may be as common as dirt, but in 2004, it was still a relative novelty. In any event, it was the first time I'd ever had the experience of standing in a see-through tube, where all that kept you from receiving a prolonged salt-water shower was six or seven inches of solid glass.

Right after the mini tour had wrapped in late afternoon, we drove to our hotel, checked in, and immediately headed out for dinner in the city centre. As it happened, we ended up parking within a hundred metres of the aforementioned St. Eusebius Church. When a cursory glance of a plastic menu tacked to the wall of a nearby restaurant in the market square failed to lure us in, we ventured further into a nearby pedestrian zone oddly lacking pedestrians. Several locked doors later, a friendly passerby informed us that as today was a Dutch holiday we'd be lucky to find anything open. Forced to return to the restaurant in the square, now succumbing to the lengthening shadows of St. Eusebius' ninety-three metre tower, we seated ourselves at an outside table, placed our orders and dissolved into a discussion of plans for the upcoming week. The meals pretty much lived up to the low expectations spawned by the menu and I was halfway through my second beer by the time a waitress came to collect the plates. Still busy conversing with Dwayne, it was only on the periphery that I heard her mutter the standard inquiry about a level of satisfaction. Scraping his stool on the pavement as he edged away from the table, Buddy was the only one to respond.

"It was fine," he told her with a forced grin, pushing his largely untouched serving forward with his thumb. "You can take it. Please… I'm done,"

"You did not like it?" the voice asked.

"No, no… it's not that," he sputtered. "I had a really big lunch today. Really, I did. I'm just stuffed… really."

Still focused on Dwayne, now fumbling through a wad of papers, I was not at all prepared for the waitress's response.

"That has to be one of the lamest excuses I have ever heard."

Everybody has a face story… Everybody. Be it the glimpse of a visage in the window of a passing bus, a casual glance at a waitress's muted joys and woes as she goes about her tasks, or the blank stare of a checkout cashier held a second too long… there are simply faces that inexplicably catch your attention and draw you into their orbit.

As I turned to view the source of this voice, I was met by a silhouette, crowned with a haloed tuft of short blonde hair. Just at that moment reality seemed to shift into slow motion as the murmur of adjacent conversations and clinking dishes fell away.

"Excuse me?" I asked, shielding my eyes against the

setting sun. "Is that something they teach at waitressing school in Holland?"

"I don't believe him, do you?" she countered, resting one hand on her hip in measured defiance.

"Well I don't exactly make a habit of watching how much he eats on a given day... it's just that I've never heard quite such a response."

"Would you rather I'd simply smiled vacuously? "

"No...Not at all," I answered, shifting in my chair to devote her my full attention. "I think it's great. It's refreshing. Just so... unexpected, I guess."

Having temporarily abandoned the discussion with Dwayne, I could feel a growing urge to know just who this cocky person was. Normally unsettled by such spontaneous encounters, it came as a surprise to feel myself convening a round of small talk with unaccustomed ease.

"I know it's not something one usually asks the waitress who's serving you," I said, after we had engaged in some light banter. "But we've had some bad luck with meals in other cities in the last while, so I thought I'd ask if you happen to know whether there's a good Indian restaurant in town. "

Visibly letting down her guard, she tilted her head to one side as a faint smile bent the corners of her mouth.

"With food as good as here you mean?" she said with a sly nod. "No, it's okay. You don't have to answer that. I know this is not a place for gourmets," she added in a lowered voice. "There *is* a place a few blocks from here. I believe it is called Paradiso."

As she continued to scan her memory, her free hand swept back a clump of springy hair just as the setting sun went behind a cloud to reveal a pair of blue eyes staring back.

"El Paradiso, that's it... No wait," she said with a sigh. "That's not so good."

Grasping for another name, she reached across the table for another plate, briefly supplying me with a scent of her being.

"There's another place you could try. I think it's called the Paranda Palace or something like that. It's not far to walk from here. Ten minutes maybe. They serve Indian food and Dutch food as well."

"Dutch food?" I asked, stifling a crack about cheese and tulips.

"No, on second thought... you can forget that place as well. The food is not so good."

"Well," I chuckled. "I'm glad you figured that out before giving me the address. But if you knew the food is bad there, why mention it in the first place?"

"The India Palace," she blurted out, placing the last of the plates on the pile and hoisting them in her arms.

"That's a much better place... and it's just around the corner on Prinzen Straat. Don't ask me why I didn't think of it from the start. Will there be anything else?"

"On which street?" I asked with a frown, while searching for something to write on.

"Prinzen Straat," she repeated, her movement indicating our discussion was about to end. "Straat is Dutch for street."

As the tip of my pen finished carving a thin blue channel in the damp beer coaster, I called out to her departing figure. "Hey... how can we be sure that five minutes after we've left, it's not going to come to you that this place on... Princeton Statt."

"Prinzen Straat," she corrected, halting several feet

from the entrance.

"Whatever... That this place is also of questionable quality."

"I guess you'll just have to trust me and find out for yourself," she answered with a broad toothy grin before disappearing into the restaurant.

"Are we done?" Dwayne jibed, mildly irritated at having had our discussion disrupted.

"I'm done," I replied. "Boy, am I done."

Thwarted of the chance for any further contact, soon after we paid for the meal and left. Back at the hotel I abstained from a communal drink at the bar, hoping a restful night would offset the early call time. Lulled by the drone of traffic from a nearby autobahn, I was sliding towards sleep when a familiar face came looming out of the darkness. Fuelled by too many road movies where the stranger beckons the waitress with the promise, "Listen sister, I can take you away from all this," the face hovered for a moment before abandoning me to a night of turbulent mind games there was no chance of winning.

Back at the zoo at seven the next morning, we were introduced to Moritz, the staff member assigned to be our guide for the next few days.

"Don't know about you, but I'm looking forward to seeing what lies behind all the effects visitors take for granted," I told Buddy as we followed Moritz to our first location, a shark feeding station atop the giant tank.

"What I'm looking forward to is lunch," Buddy answered, briefly eyeing the bucket of food intended for the Great White wannabees. "Between last night's meal and not having enough time for a good breakfast, I'm famished."

"I think the best place to film from is probably the gangway," Moritz advised, pointing to a narrow metal pier that jutted out above the surface of the water. Wanting to give me an idea of what I could expect to encounter, Moritz grabbed a chunk of meat from the bucket and flung it out into the pool. In an instant several circling dorsal fins swooshed in, churning the water as they scrambled to grab their own fair share.

"You know there's not a big call for one-armed cameramen," I told Moritz as I took up a position at the end of the walkway, highly aware that one false move could send me tumbling into the water. With the camera balanced on one knee, I was able to capture a series of shots of the feeding frenzy until one piece of meat landed a little closer to the gangway than expected. As two sharks dashed for the prize, one turned away at the last moment, sending a wave of salt-water arcing up over the walkway. Reacting in what felt like slow motion, I instinctively pulled the camera to my chest, turning away to shield it from the coming onslaught. Doing so temporarily threw me off balance and it was only a well-placed hand on the railing that prevented me from becoming dessert. Although the camera had been spared any damage, I was now destined to spend the rest of the morning in a damp, salt-encrusted t-shirt.

Buddy and the sharks weren't the only creatures who'd been longing for a meal that morning. Several yards further along, just below the ledge of an open window we'd moved to, I looked down to see three or four manta rays of varying size as they treaded water, while waiting for their turn at the trough.

"These guys actually have faces," I said as one poked

through the surface before swiftly diving under in what seemed like a deliberate attempt to splash me. Unlike the sharks however, the rays were not at all aggressive, patiently sculling back and forth as each ration was tossed into the water.

As is the case with most intensive shoots, full concentration made the hours virtually evaporate. Once the feeding was finished and the technical aspects of maintaining the tank covered, the decision was made to break for an early lunch. On the walk over to the main restaurant, Moritz happened to mention that the zoo welcomed some two million visitors a year, a high percentage of whom seemed to be lined up at the self-serve buffet upon our arrival. Fortunately Moritz had made arrangements for us to dine in a separate wing so we could avoid a long wait. There was, however, still the matter of selecting our own food from the buffet. After perusing the hand-written menus on overhead blackboards, I opted for an Italian dish, scooping up a healthy portion of noodles from a large silver tureen, before turning to collect my cutlery from a nearby rack. Just at that moment a familiar figure moved in from the corner of my eye.

"Hey," I said without the slightest hesitation. "What are *you* doing here?"

The look on her face revealed a surprise equal to my own.

"Hello," she said tentatively. "What are *you* doing here?"

Beyond those two questions, the moment, which would later come to be known as the "nano-second," left both of us temporarily dumbfounded. Five seconds earlier or later, turning left instead of right and the two ships would have indeed passed unnoticed in the night. Despite the subdued lighting in the restaurant, while she spoke, I couldn't help noticing how asymmetrical her face was; the right side reflecting a much softer aspect than its hard, almost bitter-looking counterpart. Although mutual obligations limited our discussion, it was enough to water the seed of interest that had been planted at the previous night's dinner. Adrift in a state of mild confusion, I rejoined the others, only to finish my meal in contemplative silence. A short while later, under the guise of wanting a breath of fresh air, I excused myself and went off in search of the "face." Unable to locate her amidst the massive throng, I was about to abandon the quest when I happened to glance over to see her sitting several yards away. Without giving it a second thought, I approached her table.

"Hi. Sorry to bother you again... but remember that Indian restaurant you recommended last night?"

She smiled and nodded, pointing to her mouthful of meal. The pause provided the chance to quickly survey her two companions, a woman in her late thirties and a young girl of four or five.

"I managed to forget the name of it," I continued.

"The India Palace," she replied, dabbing her lips with a napkin. "As I told you, it's not far from the square. You just walk up the pedestrian mall in the direction of the train station."

"Mall... train station," I repeated slowly, trying to think of a way to prolong the conversation.

"Excuse me mate. I know you'd prefer to spend the afternoon chatting to this pretty girl, but we do have work to do."

The grip on my shoulder indicated it was more a

command than a request, leaving me with little choice than to bid her adieu.

Whether it was giraffes loping across a pseudo savannah, a rhino rolling in dirt to rid itself of pesky insects or people gaping at snakes, monkeys or tigers held in glass enclosures, all of the subsequent animals filmed in their adopted habitats that afternoon were viewed through the filter of the missing "face." But she was nowhere to be seen that day, nor two nights later at the Indian Palace. Nevertheless, she continued to haunt and hover, sentencing me to depart Holland without so much as a name.

In the week between our return from Arnhem and departure for Vienna, havoc continued to prevail. Uncertain whether I should be seeking an explanation for the against-all-odds "coincidence," of the second meeting, or simply chalking it up as "just one of those things," I realized that much of the torment came from the fact I'd been in a healthy and fulfilling relationship with Isabelle for a long time, and was not by any means on the prowl. Struggling to find a solution, on the evening before we were set to leave for Austria, I sat down to concoct a mail on the premise of discovering whether this irreverent hostess could possibly be as interesting as she had seemed. Caught up in a chaos of my own creation, I addressed the letter to the restaurant in the square, losing sight of the fact that in the swirl of inflamed interest, a subject is often granted attributes they do not possess or deserve. At this juncture however, there was no way of foreseeing that painful lesson, nor the reality that when two people's paths cross, far too often one is left in the other's wake.

CHAPTER 40

Chasing Cheetahs

"Gentlemen, as heart-breaking as this may sound, the final segment is upon us," Dwayne announced at dinner on our first evening in Vienna. "Rain forests in Switzerland, shark tanks in Holland and now cheetahs in Austria. Talk about twisted."

"What's so special about cheetahs?" Buddy wanted to know, handing back his menu after pointedly ordering a non-alcoholic beverage with his meal. Although Dwayne showed no reaction to the gesture, there was little doubt it had been registered, a signal that the underlying tension from Zürich had yet to fully dissipate.

"You'll see soon enough," Dwayne said. "Call time tomorrow is 8:30… Ready to roll."

The next morning we assembled on the grounds of what we'd been told was the world's oldest zoo. Constructed within Vienna's famous Schönbrunn Park in 1762, its advanced years belied the fact the Tiergarten rates as one of the most innovative and modern zoos in Europe, if not the world. Shortly after our introduction to several administrators, our guide, Brigitte, escorted us to what she described as the old lion sanctuary. Strange, was probably the best way to describe how it felt to be standing inside the concrete bunker where lions had previously yawned, growled and bared their fangs, while lolling their way through yet another tedious day.

"We like to think of it as a bit of a role reversal," Brigitte explained, pointing to a thick-curved window behind which several cheetahs lay lounging in the sun. "Here it's the animals turn to observe *us* in the cage."

Judging from the bored, "who gives a hoot" look on their faces, it was questionable whether the cheetahs considered these new arrangements much of an improvement.

"Not terribly exciting if they're just gonna lay there," I told Dwayne, hoping we could somehow coax them to offer a glimpse of their world famous speed. Overhearing my remark, Brigitte suggested moving to the outdoor section, where an assistant could demonstrate what she called the "predator feeding mechanism."

"In the wild, cheetahs have to hunt for their food," she informed us, as we set up outside a high, steel-barred fence. "If we just hand them the food, they tend to get lethargic, and sometimes even a bit fat, if you can imagine. So we developed a system that forces them to chase their prey. The only difference is that unlike the real world where sometimes the hunt is unsuccessful, here we eventually let them win every time."

While Brigitte was busy explaining the logistics of the system, we watched a green-clad zoo attendant enter the compound, carrying a bucket. Separated from the cheetahs by a solid chain-link fence, he made his way up a slight incline before glancing back to the trio of cats now eagerly pacing back and forth on their side of the enclosure. The anticipation in all quarters was heightened further when the attendant reached into the bucket and removed what was obviously the remains of a deceased hare. Attaching it to a hook suspended approximately six feet off the ground, he gave it a downward tug to make sure it was secure before retreating to a booth on the outside of the compound.

"As you can see," Brigitte said, "The hook is fixed to an electric motor that can be moved along a grid that runs the length and breadth of the grounds. The speed and direction is controlled from a console and can get up to nearly 50 miles per hour. We don't want to make it *too* easy for them." she chuckled. "If you're ready, we can give you a demonstration."

"Feel like volunteering for a test run?" I asked Buddy, as a small crowd began to build around us. "No? Not even if I convince the attendant to give you a ten-second head start?"

"Enough with the jokes, you guys," Dwayne interrupted. "The attendant's already to go… Start rolling."

Having strapped on a mobile console similar to those used for controlling model airplanes, the attendant proceeded to make a few adjustments, causing the suspended meal to jerk forwards several times on the line. Another adjustment sent it back to its original position, accompanied by a high-pitched whizzing sound. Aware that something was up, the cheetahs were becoming more rambunctious with each passing second.

With the unfortunate lunch still swinging on the line, the attendant gave us a thumbs up and reached for a button on a nearby pole. With a loud metallic clack, the gate opened and the three former loungers darted out into the compound. Despite having observed the goings-on, they initially seemed unaware they were being treated to an early mealtime. Finally one cheetah spotted the dangling dinner and in three or four elegant bounds, reached the bottom of the incline just as the attendant reacted. Having stayed on a wide shot, I was able to capture the hare taking off with the fastest creature on Earth in hot pursuit. Whether done for our benefit or simply part of the regular feeding routine, the attendant let the cheetah gain on his meal before suddenly reversing direction. No slacker, the lone cheetah made a flying leap at the bounty only to bat a furry leg in mid-flight. This back and forth procedure was repeated several times with the cheetah getting closer and closer to victory each time. As graceful and lightning fast as the chase was, I somehow doubted the editor would include the climax, cutting to another scene just before the cheetah tore little Johnny's Easter bunny to shreds.

"Remind me not to come back as a rabbit in another life," I said to Buddy, as we switched positions to shoot a similar scene from a different angle with the other two cheetahs. "Do you think we should ask this guy if he's got a life-sized bunny suit for Dwayne?" I suggested while the man in question was talking with Brigitte.

"You're still recording you know," Buddy noted.

I hadn't, but decided to let the comments remain as a humorous way of wreaking vengeance for his having forced an untimely exit at the Burgers' cafeteria.

With the excitement of the chases over, it was a struggle to stay motivated as we traipsed around capturing other animals. After almost three weeks of waddling penguins, lumbering elephants or lewd monkeys offering up their pink posteriors to those foolish enough to tap a finger on the glass, it had all become somewhat tiresome. Having garnered more than enough footage to flesh out the half-hour episode, I was not thrilled when Dwayne agreed to Brigitte's suggestion we make a final stop at the "big cat house."

"Have you noticed that every time we come to Vienna, we end up in some sort of cat house?" I asked Buddy as we passed an astonishingly realistic glassed-in habitat that made it appear as if there was nothing separating us from an enormous pacing tiger. Entering a darkened tunnel marked, "No unauthorized entry," we were led into a small back room where two sleek, black jaguars were being held in separate pens. Within seconds of our entrance both cats decided to take a swipe at each other through the bars, simultaneously emitting roars that virtually deafened all those within the small concrete facility.

"Yow… Am I glad I didn't have any mikes on for that little number," Buddy said, belatedly holding his hands to his ears. Hoping to find a good angle to capture an attendant preparing food for the two black beauties, I shifted position, not realizing how close I'd come to the bars of the cages. All of a sudden, one of the cats let out another ferocious roar as I felt the camera jar against my head and something wet ooze down from my hairline. Reaching up to determine whether I still had a scalp, I was pleased to discover it wasn't blood but "merely" the drool of an irritated jaguar, his subtle way of letting me know how much he'd love to rearrange my facial features.

That evening at dinner, Dwayne had an unexpected message to deliver. "I'm not quite sure how to tell you guys this, but it appears we were a little too productive for our own good today."

"You're complaining?" I asked, leaning back to enjoy my freshly poured beer.

"No. But you guys might when I tell you there's not enough work to justify staying another day. I took a close look at the script to make sure, but I'm afraid we're done lads. It's a wrap."

Early next morning, we dropped Dwayne off at the train station before plodding our way through rush-hour traffic towards the autobahn. Facing a seven-hour trip home, there was more than enough time to reflect on the shared experiences of the past few weeks. Lemurs and Coatis, sting rays and sharks, cheetahs and penguins had all been along for the ride, not forgetting Wallace, Penelope and the Captain.

Thoroughly drained by the time I got home that evening, it was all I could do to flop down in front of the laptop with a cold beer at arm's length. Hitting the icon for incoming mail, my eyes quickly focused on a name I didn't recognize. With fingers laced below my chin, I sat with my elbows on the desk, staring at the return address for several minutes, pondering what to do. Just as I was about to reach for the mouse, I heard a small voice in the back of my head warn, "Don't open it… It will bring nothing but heartache." I didn't listen.

CHAPTER 41

A Dude in Paris

The phone was halfway through its fifth ring before I could get to it. It was Buddy calling with news of what he considered to be our latest coup.

"Are you familiar with a show called The Dude," he asked.

"Heard of it, but never seen it. Is that the one where they round up twenty young women, remove all traces of cognitive powers and then pit them against each other to vie for the favours of some guy they've selected as this season's God gift?"

"That's the one. Well, get this… Next week they want us to do a behind the scenes episode of this season's opener."

"As lurid and sublime as that sounds, I'm not sure I want to work for such a dumb-ass program. I may have smudged my reputation a few times, but even I have limits."

"It means a whole week in Paris."

"Ahhhh, mais oui, monsieur… Quand partons-nous?"

Although the luminescence of Paris had been greatly reduced by the prospect of filming for a show designed primarily for dim bulbs, I knew it would still feel great to be back in the "La Ville-Lumière." Unfortunately, we wouldn't take full advantage of its pleasures right away, as to save on costs, the production company had booked us into a drab hotel in a satellite city's industrial park, thirty kilometres northwest of the capital. Not surprisingly, none of the candidates, the "Dude," or the higher echelon of the production staff were staying at the same austere "Auberge."

Upon our arrival, it was impossible not to notice the similarities between the hotel's parking area and a used car lot full of old "beaters," sufficient grounds to be concerned about what was awaiting us inside.

"Who booked us into that Bag du Fleas anyways?" I asked Buddy, speaking through the paper-thin walls of the rooms we'd been assigned. "Everything in my room is made of plastic except for the bed, and I'm not even sure about that… and going into the bathroom feels like you're entering a mock-up of a space capsule. The whole thing is painted in the ugliest shade of brown imaginable.

Fortunately, with the shoot scheduled to begin right after dark, there wasn't enough time to get thoroughly depressed at the idea of spending several days there.

Once underway to the location however, I once again pressed Buddy for an answer to the burning question.

"Hey don't look at me man," he answered. "Blame the executive producer."

"You mean the same guy who's probably staying at the Ritz, driving a Mercedes and eating at some chic French restaurant with the money saved from putting us in that hole."

"One and the same."

An hour later saw us pulling into yet another parking lot, this one a roped-off, make-shift effort in a field adjacent to a grand 16th century castle south of Paris. The front courtyard of the castle was a hive of activity and at first glance I counted six cameras, a large crane and dozens of lights furnishing the set. People were scurrying in all directions, each carrying out a task in seemingly coordinated fashion. Waiting for us in the registration tent was Roger, the same producer we had worked with in Luxembourg a few years back.

"Good to see you again gentlemen," he said, greeting us with a broad smile. "I see the ravages of time haven't take that much of a toll."

After a round of back-slapping and traded cheap shots, the three of us retreated to a smokey lounge that doubled as the catering area. Helping himself to a bottle of mineral water, Roger sat down to explain the night's agenda.

"You've seen the front courtyard already," he began. "That's where the primary scene will go down. The first shot involves following the stretch limo as it pulls up the driveway to deliver each candidate. The Dude will be standing at the front entrance to greet them one at a time. He'll present each with a single rose, exchange some small talk, plant a kiss on her hand or cheek, and graciously request she retire to the salon until all the other candidates have arrived. It's pretty straight forward. I'm sure you even you guys can handle it," he added with a smirk.

According to Roger, the magic moment was to be covered from every conceivable angle twenty-five times, hence the six cameras and crane to make sure nothing was missed. A short while later, a production assistant directed us to a spot near said crane, so we could ostensibly film without being in someone else's shot. Preparations continued at a frantic pace and it wasn't long before the crew was ready for the arrival of the first candidate. Now, under normal circumstances, one might be forgiven for assuming that opening a car door, exchanging a few words, and walking up a cobblestone pathway to the front door were not particularly difficult tasks. But in Videoville, things don't always go according to plan.

"If you're going to be talking to someone," the director told the first contestant, who had remained tongue-tied when the Dude had asked where she was from. "It helps if you have something to say,"

"I'm sorry," the young woman said in a fluster. "I'm just so nervous... I promise I'll get it right this time."

"You do know where you are from?" the director asked half jokingly, before ordering everyone back to their marks. "Okay...Let's try it again."

Over the next several hours, a remarkable number of contestants displayed the ability to either flub a line, have trouble getting out of the car or trip on the red carpet. What kept it all from getting painfully boring for us, was that the women who'd already passed the introductory rite of passage and settled in the salon to await their fate, had forgotten or not been told their microphones were still "live." With a direct feed from the main sound board, Buddy was privy to comments the "ladies" were making when they thought no one else was listening.

"God what a hunk Garrett is, don't you think? I wouldn't mind a roll in the hay with him... maybe even twice."

"Get in line sister."

"Do women always talk like that?" I wanted to know, handing Buddy back the headphones.

"How should I know?" he said with a shrug before

returning to the prattle.

"I thought anyone with a white sports jacket knew such things."

Once all candidates had been initiated, the crew regrouped in the salon where the Dude was scheduled to host a small cocktail party. Not a big room to begin with, the addition of six cameras, the crane, the crew and invited guests, made it absolute minuscule. To avoid getting into anyone's shot, I took refuge beside a floor-to- ceiling curtain, from where I could follow the Dude as he worked the room, chatting and flirting with the bevy of beauties. More often than not however, the spontaneous small talk between him and his current focus needed to be repeated, either because of a technical problem or something had not been to the director's liking. As it was, each "tete-a-tete" encounter took place under the jealous gaze of other candidates, adding fuel to an already heated competition. Having to listen to the various levels of articulateness through the camera's headset for over an hour, slowly drew me into a trancelike state; one where the only matter of importance was to learn how these candidates had been selected in the first place. While in that state, my overactive imagination soon conjured up a scenario where a gaggle of producers and writers were crowded into a smoke-filled back room somewhere in Hollywood.

"Okay, let's see now," said a balding, bespectacled, forty- something man with a large stogie in his hand. "According to my records, we've got two catty gossips, several girl next doors, a hussy or two, a vamp, and six space cadets. Are we still missing something?"

"The back- stabbing conniver?" a younger producer inserted.

"Ahhh right… the conniver. Forgot about her. Toss in an extra naive farm girl, first time in the big city and we're just about done. Gentlemen, I think we have a winning line up."

Back in the real world, the clock was pushing 3:00 am. by the time we'd finished capturing the "special moments" with each of the twenty-five candidates. Exhausted and longing to get back to the hotel, as grungy as it was, Buddy and I departed swiftly, only to soon find ourselves lost on one of the area's winding back roads.

"I'm sure I've seen that sign before," I told him, convinced we'd been going in circles. "Why didn't we take the autobahn?"

"I thought that's where we were heading. All these villages look the same, especially at night," he complained, taking a left where I thought he should have stayed straight. The longer we drove, the more apparent it became that part of French culture limits a village to one road sign, leaving it up to the town council if and where to place it within a twenty square mile area of said village. Such a lack of directions would have been troublesome enough in the middle of the afternoon, but at 4:00 a.m. it was bordering on catastrophic. Soldiering on, expectancy built as we followed the headlights through a foggy forest only to arrive at a sign that indicated our destination was back in the direction we had just come.

"This is bloody insane," I said angrily as we stopped to try and make sense of a small map found in the glove box. "At this rate, all that's missing is a handwritten sign around the next bend saying 'Good luck, Eenglish

Peeg.'"

By the time the correct route was finally located, both of us had seen a headless horseman or two galloping across the misty landscape.

The upside to last night's late shoot was that we were given the following day off. After a late breakfast of stale buns, watery orange juice and a plate of cheese and ham slices that looked and tasted like plastic, the two of us hopped a train into central Paris. Preferring to explore the streets of Paree on my own, I parted company with Buddy at the Gare du Nord station. First stop on the crowded Metro was the Eiffel Tower where instead of joining the eight million tourists standing in line for the elevators, I followed the other four million hoofing it up the steel staircase. In any event, I needn't have bothered to be in any rush, as access to the top platform was denied due to fog. Forced to wait my turn to gaze out at the hazy skyline from the second level, it appeared that things hadn't changed much since my first visit in 1972. What *had* changed in the interim was the influx of souvenir shops on the Tower itself, all flogging a variety of Tower-related kitsch. Lured into one of them by sheer curiosity, for a moment I was tempted to buy the most hideous item on sale, until realizing there were just too many awful items to choose from.

From the Tower it was on to the Arc de Triomphe, down the bustling Champs-Élysée, through the Tuileries park, past the long lines at the Louvre and across the bridge to Notre Dame. Despite having followed this same route on previous visits, this time I found myself wondering what it must be like to actually live in Paris, fending off tourist hordes and having the famous sites seem blasé after seeing them for the eleventh million time.

"*The worst thing about living in Paris however,*" I thought as I crossed the Seine to enter my favourite bookshop, would be the torture of having to improve my high school French.

Add on stops at numerous other bookstores, "*une jambon et fromage baguette*" for lunch, and a long stroll along the Seine, past ancient stands selling products nobody seemed to be buying, and before I knew it the day was done. After perusing the street-front menus of several establishments, I chose to have dinner at a noisy, crowded basement restaurant somewhere on the Left Bank. Seated at a table three inches from my neighbour's, I was attempting to get through a thoroughly disappointing meal when an elderly Japanese man next to me started up a conversation in broken French. Although communication proved difficult without a common usable language, I could tell from his facial expressions that he was equally unimpressed with the quality of his, by no means inexpensive meal. But despite our mutual handicap, there were a few minutes of shared joy spent trashing the current status of so-called French cuisine.

※

With call time set for 4:00 p.m., much of the next morning and early afternoon was spent killing time at the hotel, not an easy feat considering the drastic lack of facilities at the two-star dump.

"Today's segment will focus on showing the Dude out on the streets of Paris cavorting with five of the twelve candidates who survived the first cut," Roger began to explain, after we'd met up with him at a cafe near the city centre. Waving off Buddy's offer of a second cup of coffee, he continued. "Thank God though, we don't have to cover that. We'll meet up with them at the Eiffel Tower around four."

Although it had only been 48 hours since their arrival, almost half of the original candidates were already on a flight home.

"Any idea on how that selection was made?" I asked Roger.

"Not a clue... I can ask the network producer but I'm not sure I'll get a straight answer. I suspect it's a joint decision... I doubt it's the Dude's choice alone."

A half hour later, we were standing across from the Eiffel Tower when an open-topped double decker bus pulled up alongside. Despite the stiff, cool breeze blowing that day, the Dude and his lightly-clad companions had been chauffeured around the famous landmarks while sitting on the upper deck. The inherent joys of shivering for hours, with your every move under constant observation, was reflected on their faces as the troupe exited the bus. After downing several cups of warming coffee at a nearby kiosk, the Dude and his remaining ladies were requested to spend the next half hour having a frightfully wonderful time, strolling around the terrace and fountains of the Trocadero. From there it was a short hop over to a nearby merry-go-round producers had rented, so the Dude and contestants could gaze goofily into each others' eyes as they spun around on an otherwise empty carousel. One could only imagine what they might have been saying to each other in this brief moment of privacy.

Dusk was already rapidly approaching by the time we were instructed to make our way to the Arc de Triomphe, leaving the other teams to finish recording the contrived sentiments made astride ceramic horses. Against impossible odds, we were able to find a parking space within view of the arch. Met at the base by a production assistant, we were quickly guided to the rooftop observation deck via a tiny four-person elevator. Producers had presumably paid a bundle to have the deck closed two hours early, so the barren, windswept plateau could be transformed into a cozy rooftop brasserie, complete with candelabra, fresh-cut flowers and four or five small, round tables. It was all meant to serve as the ideal location for what was scripted as an intimate rendezvous between the Dude and his last few would-be flames. With the twinkling lights of nighttime Paris providing the backdrop, it was hard to picture a more romantic setting, and even harder to imagine a worse sense of timing. Within minutes of the candidates' arrival, a nasty rain began to pelt down. Candles were quickly extinguished, tablecloths flapped wildly and napkins and menus took flight. With everyone sheltered under a nearby canopy, praying for a let-up, the producer was finally forced to call it quits after half an hour of steady downpour, all too aware that viewers were not likely to be thrilled at watching a romantic encounter unfold in the middle of a monsoon. Almost immediately, Roger delivered the next setback. Due to budget restraints, it seemed he wouldn't be able to keep us on for another day to cover the postponed dinner. Having already had a free day in Paris, it wasn't the end of the world. Having quickly concluded that making for Germany straight away a lesser evil than returning to the hotel from hell, we bid Roger and the rest of the team adieu, and made our way back to the car.

"Besides, we'd probably only get lost again," I quipped as I slammed the trunk shut and hopped into the passenger's seat. Opting for a final cruise down the Champs-Élysée before starting the long journey home, a last glance back to the floodlit Arc brought the realization that Paris would never quite be the same again.

CHAPTER 42

Ditto in Rome

In all likelihood, I could have easily gone to my grave, content in the knowledge of only having experienced The Dude a single time. But much as it had been with the first encounter, fate intervened; this time with the lure of filming in the Eternal City.

Partly to save on costs; partly to enjoy some spectacular European scenery, we decided to travel to Rome by car, leaving early on a Saturday morning, driving as far as northern Italy before stopping for the night. Picked entirely at random, the city of Mantova turned out to be a good choice, loaded with interesting facades, yellow-lit piazzas, dark and moody laundry-filled alleyways and a good selection of outdoor restaurants. There's something to be said about dinners on a warm, summer evening in Italy, but it's not polite to talk with your mouth full of delicious home-made pasta, so suffice to say, the combined experiences left the senses satisfied despite brooding memories of Naples and Bologna.

It was early Sunday afternoon that we rolled into Rome only to roll right out again largely because our hotel was located in Frascati, a hillside enclave twenty kilometres from the centre of the Italian capital. Thoroughly unimpressed with the shoe-box rooms the production company had reserved for us, we promptly moved to a nicer hotel just up the road. With production not set to begin until mid- afternoon the following day, we decided to initiate a replay of Paris, by filling Monday with a healthy dose of sightseeing.

"So now that we've managed to cram a week of playing Joe tourist into a single afternoon, let's call in sick and drive home," I suggested after we'd covered the Colosseum, the Spanish Steps, Trevi fountain, Circus Maximus, Hadrian's Tomb, the Forum and the Vatican in the span of several hours.

"Not a bad idea," Buddy agreed. "I'd consider it if I thought we could still charge them for half-time, but I doubt if there's a clause in the contract that covers abandoning a ship before its sailed."

Despite the late call time, our old comrade-in-arms, Roger, had demanded we meet up with the network production crew at their hotel for an early morning briefing. After enduring a series of long-winded discussions that were basically a repeat of the Paris protocols, we joined a cavalcade for the short trip to a renovated 18th century villa in the hills above Frascati. There, the rest of the morning was spent hanging out or watching the production staff finish decorating the sets for that evening's grand opening gala. To our great relief, when lunch was called, we were invited to dine back in town with the executive producer and the show's current host. The former was a hefty gentleman in his late-thirties, dressed casually in a sweat shirt and dark chinos. The latter struck me as somewhat older, mid-forties perhaps. Then again, the expensive tailored suit he was wearing may have aged him somewhat. Seated at a cliffside restaurant, we were soon joined by this season's eligible Dude, attired in beige slacks, a white short-sleeved shirt and a cashmere pullover sweater draped over his shoulders. Dandy facade aside, he turned out to be a down-to-earth guy, despite having been introduced as a "real" prince. Amidst the relaxed small and shop talk making the rounds before our meals arrived, I was prompted to pose a question that had gone unanswered in Paris.

"Sorry if I sound kind of nosey," I began, aiming my words at the executive producer, when a gap opened up in the conversation. "Ever since the shoot in Paris, I've been curious how the show selects its contestants. I mean, in Paris there was quite the cross section. How do you decide one over another?"

Simultaneously sipping on their cocktails, the host and executive producer exchanged one of those "you wanna tell him or should I," looks before the host said, "It's actually a pretty simple process. Whoever agrees to sleep with us immediately gets a slot on the show."

The muted laughter however, prompted a quick response from his colleague.

"I'm not so sure it's a good idea to say stuff like that," he said. "After all, we don't really know these guys. Suppose they believe you. Cracks like that could get us into all kinds of trouble with the network. It's not true gentlemen," he added, turning to us. "Not true at all."

"It's okay," Roger assured them. "My guys aren't about to run off to the Enquirer."

"That is unless you fail to tell us how they're chosen of course," I inserted, earning a frown from Roger.

"Let's just say we try and find a mixture," the EP said matter-of-factly. "We want to give the audience characters they can relate to, bitch about, and discuss at coffee the day after the show… And if we've really done our job... the whole week."

"So looks count, maybe a little talent, but the main requirement is to somehow be memorable... for both good or bad reasons."

"You could put it that way. Something for everybody."

Much to Roger's relief, the arrival of the food brought further questions and revelations to an end.

In what was basically a replay of the morning's scripted pattern, the remaining hours before "action," was called were passed lounging in the courtyard, observing the lighting crew and camera teams jostling for position. Production managed to start on time just after dusk, but unlike its Parisian counterpart, here the opening sequence ran so smoothly, we'd already managed to film a third of the expected arrivals by 9:00 o'clock. Following one of the takes, as the crew reset for the next candidate, the director repeated an earlier warning to all those in earshot, that once cameras were rolling, no one was to walk anywhere they might be anyone else's shot. Shortly before we were about to resume, my battery light started to warn of an imminent demise. With still enough power to capture the next candidate, as a precaution, I told Buddy to make sure he had a replacement on stand-by.

"They're in the storage room," he admitted sheepishly.

"What, all of them? Don't you even have one here?"

"I forgot to charge them last night, so I put them on when we first got here. They should be charged by now."

"Okay... But when we break for the next contestant, zip over and get a couple? Just make sure you're back in time before we start rolling again."

As soon as the next candidate had been welcomed, kissed, and shunted off to a room in the villa, Buddy slipped away into the darkness. Although the storage room was not exactly light years away, he had yet to return by the time the next scene started.

"Who the hell is in the shot back there," the director suddenly thundered, calling a stop ten seconds into the action.

"Oh man, please don't let it be Buddy," Roger moaned.

But sure enough, slinking out from behind the bushes with a battery held above his head, the only man on the planet who probably couldn't recall where he was or what he was doing when he heard Kennedy was shot, did turn out to be the smiling culprit. For some reason, perhaps the loopy look on Buddy's face as he trundled across the driveway, the director chose to just laugh off the faux pas.

Over the next few hours, as we continued to listen to blithe descriptions of which part of North America each of this season's ladies stemmed from and what they were planning with their futures, I was surprised to learn one was actually from Manitoba. For a fleeting moment, I considered revealing our mutual heritage should the opportunity arise. That is until I noticed how zoned out she seemed in the opening scene, giggling non-stop at the Dude's every utterance.

Once again, a welcome distraction to the plodding proceedings, was Buddy's ability to eavesdrop on the chitchat coming from the live mikes.

"Oooooh, he is so cute! Did you see his dimples?" one woman confessed, unaware that the equipment stuffed into her gown was broadcasting her comments to a wider audience.

"Did you see the way he smiled at *me* when he handed me my rose?" asked another. "I think we've connected already."

"Stand back girls. He's all mine," chimed a third.

It was just after midnight when the last candidate climbed into the stretch limousine for the short trip up the driveway. With expert finesse, the crane swooped up one final time to capture her stepping out of the car, while the other cameras recorded her accepting the long-stem rose, sniffing it briefly, before being escorted into the villa. With no post-arrival party planned this time, it was a wrap just after the front door slowly swung shut.

With the arrivals sequence for all 25 candidates now "in the can," members of the crew headed for a restaurant in Frascati, that producers had persuaded to stay open late. Aided by excellent food and a seemingly endless flow of good Italian Chianti, all concerned seemed to be enjoying the post-wrap atmosphere.

"I could get used to this," I told Roger, savouring the last morsel of what must have been the world's best tiramisu.

"One more piece and it comes off your bill," he joked, before excusing himself to the washroom. I decided to take advantage of the empty chair to approach the visibly relaxed director,

"Went better than expected tonight eh?" I said, taking his slow nod and grin as permission to continue. "A small question if you don't mind."

"I'm game."

"Is it my imagination or did a couple of tonight's candidates come across as dullards?"

Chuckling at the assessment, he leaned back to send a thick plume of cigar smoke up into the Italian sky.

"Viewers need and want something to gossip about. Every season there has to be one or two members of the cast to complain about or else they'll tune out. It's actually quite interesting to see the reactions some candidates provoke. We try to make sure you can't spot the 'notables' in the first couple of episodes, but they'll be recognizable in a few weeks."

Surprised at his candidness, I was about to make further inquiries when a semi-feigned cough from Roger suggested I not press my luck.

In what I sense may have been revenge for the previous evening's inquisitiveness, the next morning Roger arrived with a stinker of an assignment.

"I need you to shoot photos of all the candidates," he said, guiding me into a room in the back of the villa where numerous photos were pinned to a wall. "They were supposed to do this in LA, but they didn't."

"All of them?" I asked, looking at the extensive collection of glossy eight by tens.

"I'm afraid so… and one other thing. I need all of them with a variety of moves."

So instead of relaxing in the makeshift lounge erected for the crew, the next three hours were played out in the small, windowless room, performing an endless series of push ins, pull outs, pans and drop downs for every last candidate. Well on the way to becoming brain dead by the time the unenviable task had been completed, my mood was lifted with news that the afternoon shoot had been postponed due to a major technical problem. With Buddy choosing to spend the down time back at the hotel, I was free to take off for a spontaneous tour of the surrounding countryside.

"*Castel Gandolfo... Where do I know that name from?*" I mumbled to myself, as I zoomed past a sign indicating it lay eight kilometres up the road. Following what appeared to be a newly paved road through the forest, I eventually drove into a channel of tall, elegant cypresses, behind which lay a lake off to the left. A few hundred yards on, as the road curved and climbed to enter the town, I managed to find a parking space in the shade of a high wall encompassing what I presumed were the grounds of the Pope's summer residence. A number of signs led me to the town square, and I knew I'd stumbled on the right place when I spotted two Swiss soldiers dressed in striped jackets and pantaloons, topped off with very goofy looking hats, guarding the front entrance.

"He's not here right now," a friendly fellow tourist informed me in German, as we stood amidst a crowd of curious onlookers.

"Who?" I answered in English, wondering why she'd assumed I was German.

"The Pope of course," she scolded, staying in her mother tongue. "When he's in residence, they fly the Vatican flag."

"So, you mean I've come all this way for nothing?"

Miffed by my sarcasm, the middle-aged woman strode off in a huff, muttering several German phrases under her breath. I was tempted to respond in kind, yelling, "I understood that" but let it go in the name of international relations.

Back on the road a short while later, I was made curious by a sign that told me a further ten kilometres would bring me to the ruins of Tuscolano. As it turned out, Tuscolano was nothing more than a field of scorched grass with a few square stones strewn randomly about, a site unlikely to make it to UNESCO's world heritage list any time soon.

What would soon come to be known as "Black Thursday," started off like any normal day. Told we were to be ready to roll at the Colosseum by 4:00 p.m., Buddy and I drove into Rome a few hours early, hoping to use the extra time to visit a site I'd read about before leaving Germany. Accustomed to the rather boring landscape of Canadian cemeteries, over the years I'd come to consider their German counterparts as something special. The English Cemetery however, blew the German "Friedhöfe" out of the water, taking the acknowledgement of death and mourning to an entirely new level. Enclosed behind high, roughly-hewn stone walls, stood dozens of stunningly emotive statues. Figures such as a weeping angel leaning over the back of a headstone, or a small child in the arms of a grieving mother, helped create an aura of tranquility throughout the gardens, a feat made even more remarkable by the fact we were mere metres from the hectic heart of Rome. Content to simply wander the pathways, marvelling at the beauty of the tributes to the departed, I was startled when I unexpectedly came upon Buddy watering the wilting flowers on various graves.

"What are you doing?" I asked somewhat foolishly.

"I just wanted to show my respect," he said quietly, moved by the surrounding serenity. "This place is incredible."

It was slightly past four when we arrived at the foot of Constantine's Arch, only to learn the "girls" had been delayed and were not likely to arrive before five. In a prime location for people watching, we passed the time gawking at the hundreds and hundreds of visitors streaming past the nearby Colosseum. Shortly after the five o'clock deadline came and went, Roger received news that we should now not expect them to arrive much before six.

"Our meter is going to run out by then," I warned Buddy. "Probably not a bad idea to hike back and pump it full for another couple of hours. I didn't check to see how long we need to pay. If we're lucky maybe it's only till six or seven. Keep an eye on the gear. This place is probably crawling with pickpockets and thieves."

Hoping to stretch his legs, the show's official photographer, who was there with his assistant, offered the same advice before joining me on the ten-minute jaunt back to the car. Twenty minutes later, after threading our way back through what had become an even heavier crowd, it immediately caught my attention that the camera was not where I'd left it. A quick glance to Buddy, squatted down with his back to me, initially made me assume he'd moved it to keep it under better surveillance. But as I stooped over his shoulder to confirm, I discovered he was simply busy writing postcards.

"Where is the camera?" were the words that would echo and haunt us for weeks. The colour instantly draining from his face, Buddy jumped up in a frenzy, sending the post cards scattering across the pavement.

Dashing over to where the assistant was sitting, he frantically scanned all directions before turning to me with a bleak look and going into free fall.

Recalling the scene weeks later, it was obvious we had been closely monitored from the start. Whoever had been observing us, had simply bided their time, waiting for the right moment to strike. That moment had presented itself with our departure for the parking meter. It was possible an accomplice had even followed us to the car, ready to interrupt an untimely return with an innocent request for directions. With Roger off getting a drink and Buddy busy finishing off what would soon become the world's most expensive post card, the thieves had made their move. I say "thieves" because then and now, it seemed unlikely that a single person could have pulled it off.

"Didn't you see anyone?" I asked the assistant, as Buddy continued to skitter around, hoping and praying the camera would somehow suddenly turn up. "Did anyone come and talk to you? Try and distract you? I mean it was right here by your Nikons."

"No one," he said cautiously. "Except for an elderly Polish couple asking directions."

"Directions for what? And how did you know they were Polish?"

"They had a sticker on their suitcase and spoke bad English."

"Wait a second... a suitcase? Who brings a suitcase to the Colosseum? Didn't that strike you as somewhat odd?" I pushed on, not bothering to veil my suspicions of negligence.

"I didn't think about it," he snapped back defensively. "They just asked if I knew where the train station was."

"What am I gonna do?" Buddy shrieked in the background, as he continued to pace back and forth in utter confusion.

"I guess we should contact the police," the photographer offered lamely.

"That'd be as useless as tits on a bull," Buddy snarled. "The bloody camera is probably half way to Poland by now… in a bloody suitcase," he added, casting an accusing glimpse at the assistant. Whoever *had* absconded with the camera, had at least a five-to-ten minute lead on us, making it pointless to carry out a sweep of the milling crowd. Despite the fact we were now a camera team without a camera, upon his return, Roger took news of recent developments remarkably well.

"I don't think it will help get it back, but for insurance purposes, you do need to file a police report," he advised.

"Great idea. Too bad I don't have any insurance," Buddy groaned, going through the motions of collecting the unfinished postcards before collapsing in a heap on the curb.

"Buddy," I said with some hesitation. "I know it's a blow. Worse with no insurance, but…"

"But what are we going to do for the rest of the show?" he interrupted.

"Don't worry about that," Roger advised. "That's the least of our troubles. I can pick up material from the other camera teams. One way or the other we can work it out. Just try and calm down. After all, nobody got hurt. It's just a camera."

"Just a camera with all the footage of those photos

shot this morning," I added.

"Oh Christ, that's gone as well?" Roger sighed. "They've already packed up the photos to send back to the States."

Thirty minutes later, when the Dude and his girls did finally show up, Roger was quick to inform the director what had taken place. Although no direct comments were issued, it was clear from his posture that he was not impressed. After a brief discussion, it was concluded that Buddy and I should return to Frascati, leaving the rest of the crew to film the girls cruising around Rome on Vespas, La Dolce Vita style. In spite of Buddy's earlier reservations, before doing so, on the way back to the hotel we stopped at a nearby police station to file a report. Made almost comical by the fact the policeman spoke no English, as predicted, the procedure turned out to be of little valuable.

By the time the main crew returned for dinner later that night, Buddy was well into his second bottle of assuaging wine. Even after the restaurant had closed and the crew gone off to bed, he insisted on starting a third bottle, while sprawled out on the steps of a church in the town square.

"Not gonna help the situation much if you get picked up and tossed in the can for being drunk."

"Who gives a shit?" he snapped, from a place far beyond logic. "Screw them... screw the jerks who boosted the camera... screw the 'Dude'... screw Italy... I'm never coming back to this stinking land as long as I live."

"The thieves were likely Polish," I pointed out less than helpfully. "Probably had a false-bottomed suitcase they just placed over the camera when the assi was distracted."

"That lousy creep… Notice how none of *his* gear went missing?" Buddy added in a voice dripping with derision.

"I don't know if you caught this at dinner," I said, trying to change the subject, "But Roger said without a camera we might as well consider it a wrap. I suggested we could try and rent one in Rome, but the way he hesitated, I get the feeling word came down from higher up to let us go."

Not exactly cheerful news in and of itself, the announcement did distract Buddy from his misery long enough to persuade him that passing out in the comfort of his room was preferable to a stone piazza.

The long drive home the next day was an eventful one to say the least, as Buddy continued to drown his guilt and sorrow with cheap wine. By the time we crossed the border into Austria, he'd managed to traverse nearly every emotion known to mankind. Rather than trying to alter the course he'd chosen, I remained silent, driving on into the night as he slid deeper and deeper into an incoherent stupor.

"You know what you can at least take some solace from?" I asked, fully aware Buddy was not in an understanding mood or state. "Imagine the look on the old couple's faces when they discover they've stolen one of the oldest cameras on the market.

CHAPTER 43

On the phone with Hitler

"*Hitler was not such a bad guy. As a boss, he was always fine to me.*" Finally something with a bit more substance, albeit a highly distasteful one. As it was, I couldn't imagine having accepted another "Dude" assignment even if it had meant a week's work on the moon... Well, perhaps the moon, but definitely not Mars which is where the guy who made this moronic statement must have been from. It was in the conference room of a four-star hotel in downtown Berlin, just blocks from where his former demented employer had dwelled and deviated, that this solicited and paid-for opinion was uttered; another example of the stuff spewed out to feed a public's enduring appetite for details of the WW II leader.

"I was Hitler's telephone operator, courier and body guard," Rochus Misch had explained, barely able to suppress his pride as he settled back in his chair to gather his thoughts and await the next question. Despite such a boast, part of Misch's polished routine was making it clear that he himself had never been a member of the Hitler Youth or Nazi Party. Once having established that fact, he moved on to revel in the recollection of his first, albeit distant encounter with "the Führer," all the while grinning from ear to ear.

"It happened in 1936 at the Olympic Stadium in Berlin," he recounted. "Hitler entered the packed stadium to thunderous applause. It was very moving and

I was there in the audience."

In the intervening period before Misch's next brush with the German leader four years later, he had voluntarily joined the SS and served as part of the occupying forces in Austria and Czechoslovakia. With the start of the war in 1939, he'd been sent on active duty to Poland, where he was severely wounded shortly after his deployment. Unable to return to service at the front because of his injuries, his superior had seen to it that Roche's name was registered for possible duty with Hitler's personnel corps of bodyguards.

"I was called for an interview in the Reich Chancellery in early 1940, after I had recovered from my wounds. Everything went very quickly. I was interviewed and then offered the job. It was only later that I found out Hitler had been standing behind an adjoining door listening to the whole interview."

As a member of Hitler's elite corps of bodyguards and service staff, Misch not only served as the Führer's telephone operator in the Reich Chancellery in Berlin, but also at the Obersalzburg, the Nazi leader's Alpine retreat above Berchtesgaden, Bavaria. He also claimed to have seen duty at the Wolf's Lair retreat near Rastenburg, East Prussia, and aboard Hitler's special train.

With what were clearly fond memories for him, Misch spoke of how it felt to be on standby twenty-four hours a day, in such close proximity to the centre of power.

"If we met him, we were not allowed to speak to the Führer unless spoken to. I was nervous about meeting him at first. Then one day I opened a door and there he was. He said something and that was it. From then on I felt better about the prospect of seeing him. He was not a monster. He was just an ordinary person."

"But what was it like to live and work in the Bunker near the end?" the producer asked.

"It felt as though we were already half dead. We were waiting for the end. It was like living in a morgue."

With the dual suicides of Hitler and Eva Braun on April 30th, 1945, and the extinction of Jospeh Goebbels and his entire family the next day, that is precisely what the Bunker became. Misch himself managed to escape from the underground refuge only to be caught by Russian troops a short time later. Confined to a Soviet jail for nine years, he returned to Berlin in 1953, and eventually established a painting and decorating firm. When the firm was sold in 1985, Misch entered what he initially presumed would be a quiet retirement. But as his fellow Bunker colleagues began to die off, more and more he became a sought after witness to the times. Designated as the last surviving witness to the final days in the Bunker in 2003, Misch saw a corresponding rise in the requests directed his way.

As interesting as it was to listen to Misch run through his litany of experiences, that feeling was matched by an equal amount of anger and frustration at the producer's failure to challenge Misch's basic premise that Hitler had been a "decent fellow." Unable to pose any questions of my own without incurring her wrath, at the end of the interview I simply exchanged a perfunctory "Auf Wiedersehen," as the two protagonists left to take care of financial matters.

"Can you believe that guy?" I said to Buddy as we broke down the set. "I half expected him to pull out a photo signed "To Mischie… your pal, Adolf."

"If this guy was really Hitler's operator, how do you think he answered the phone," Buddy wanted to know. "Most Germans answer with their name, don't they?"

"Hitler's House, or Der Bunker… Who knows? You should have asked him."

The subject might have ended then and there, had we not run into Misch a short while later, sitting alone in the hotel lobby. Presented with this unexpected opportunity, the temptation was too great to resist.

"Herr Misch, do you mind if I ask you a question?" I asked, taking his hesitant nod as a yes. "I didn't want to interrupt the interview upstairs, but the whole time you were speaking, I kept asking myself how someone can speak so favourably about a man who was responsible for so many atrocities? I mean as a member of the human race Hitler didn't even make it to the starting line."

Clearly not appreciative of such sarcasm, but aware he was somewhat stranded until he could collect his fiscal reward, Misch simply reverted to his standard line.

"Hitler was a good boss. I had no complaints. He treated me well. As far as his…"

"Excuse me, I'm not interrupting anything, am I?" the producer said, knowing perfectly well that was her intention.

"Not at all," Misch answered, rising to his full six foot two to greet her. Casting a steely glance in my direction, the producer casually handed Misch an envelope. Fingering its contents swiftly but thoroughly, he closed the flap, smiled and placed it inside his breast pocket. Thanking her with a handshake and shallow bow, he then nodded brusquely in my direction and walked out into downtown Berlin..

Much as it was for other former Nazis who evolved to become "Zeitzeuge" (witnesses to the time), marketing his war time memories had proven to be a lucrative sideline for Misch. Over the years he came to be exceptionally adept at the practice of giving interviews, but in 2013, at the age of 96, his trail of tainted tales finally came to an end.

CHAPTER 44

Terrible Tale of Twins

If nothing else, life as a freelance cameraman can at times be a world of striking contrasts. One minute you're facing adventure in the wilds of the Yukon, the next you're experiencing how the other half lives in Washington and New Orleans. Another day you could find yourself with a survivor of the Hindenburg disaster or part of a group chasing down Dracula's ghost in Romania. Within such a wide spectrum, there are of course a number of lamentable shoots, vivid reminders that television is by and large considered a medium, because it's rare that anything is well done. Every once in awhile, there's an encounter that simply stops you in your tracks, etching itself on your memory slate, making much of what had come before appear trivial or hackneyed. Würzburg was that kind of shoot.

Part of a planned series on the victims and relatives of the Nazi sterilization and euthanasia programs, it was in early October that we set off for the Bavarian city of Würzburg to conduct an interview with an eighty-one-year-old woman of Roma/Sinti descent. Gertrude's story, which would ultimately be housed in a permanent exhibition the United States Holocaust Memorial Museum was preparing on the racial policies of the Third Reich, began in the mid to late 1930's. It was during that phase of Nazi rule that she and members of her family had begun to notice their Jewish neighbours were leaving the community. While many had emigrated to what they hoped would be safer venues, as time went by it was more and more clear that those remaining were being rounded up and deported. Aware that their own heritage made them vulnerable to Nazi intentions to "cleanse the population," Gertrude's family had taken to keeping a low profile. Despite their precautions, at some point rumours began circulating that the Nazis were planning to see that all "gypsy" women were forcefully sterilized. Hoping to avoid such a fate, Gertrude, twenty-one at the time, persuaded an older friend of the family to get her pregnant. Able to conceal the pregnancy for four months, when it was eventually discovered, local authorities demanded that she attend a research institute in Würzburg for examination. News that she was expecting twins was immediately forwarded to Berlin where within days it reportedly reached the desk of Dr. Joseph Mengele. Prior to Mengele's transfer to Auschwitz in May of 1943, where his role in sending deportees directly to the gas chambers would earn him the moniker of "the angel of death," he had displayed a keen interest in studying identical and fraternal twins. Hoping to gain "access" to the expected twins in Würzburg, Mengele quickly sent word down the chain of command to assure that nothing "happen" to the mother and her unborn children. Following up on that directive, local Nazi officials informed Gertrude that if she agreed to give birth at the institute, where the twins could be examined by doctors, she and her extended family would be excluded from deportation to Auschwitz. Feeling she had little choice in the matter she reluctantly agreed. Directly after their birth, both infants were taken away and Gertrude was not allowed to see either of her newborn daughters for over a week. After that, she was allowed periodic visits, but never for any great length of time. Several months passed uneventfully until one day Gertrude arrived at the hospital to discover only one twin present. Questioning several sisters on duty as to the whereabouts of her child, she was met with an icy silence. Frantic to locate her missing daughter, she continued to plead for more information until one of the sisters finally relented, persuading the doctor on duty to "console" the distraught mother. Given no other details than that her daughter had died during an operation, Gertrude was taken to a room where the dead child lay in an empty bathtub, its head wrapped in a blood-splotched bandage. Half out of her mind with grief and anger, she attempted to leave the hospital with her baby but was stopped and sent home.

"Nazi promises had a habit of being hollow," the producer said quietly as the rest of us continued listening in stunned silence. "Many who protested lesser problems often ended up with a bullet in the back of the head or were packed off to the East. Why do you think you were allowed to confront the doctors without reprisals?"

"The local Nazis had simply been afraid of disobeying Berlin's ruling," Gertrude explained without emotion.

A week or so after the traumatic scene at the hospital, authorities finally agreed to allow Gertrude to have her dead child cremated. Fearing her other daughter was at risk of meeting a similar end, several days later, with the help of her father, she attempted to abduct the surviving child. The trio managed to make it as far as their home before the Gestapo caught up with them. Although Gertrude and her father escaped any direct retribution for their actions, the child was returned to the clinic and eventually transferred to another institution where Gertrude no longer had any opportunity to visit. Despite being subjected to a series of inhuman medical experiments at the hands of Nazi doctors over the next several years, the twin survived and was returned to her mother by the Red Cross shortly before the end of the war. In the interim Gertrude and her family had remained "untouchable" due to the enduring dictate from Berlin.

Having sat quietly in a corner of the living room during her mother's interview, Gertrude's surviving daughter, Marianne, now in her mid-sixties, agreed to a last-minute request for an interview. Speaking in a tone much softer than her mother, she recalled some of the experiments Nazi doctors had performed on her.

"They attempted to change my eye colour from brown to blue, by injecting a fluid into my eye cavity through the top of my skull," she calmly told the producer. Going on to explain that she suffered from a loss of balance from time to time as well as pains in her legs, she admitted she could not be certain, or prove, if those problems were directly attributable to her time within the Nazi institutes. As it was with many Nazi victims, such uncertainty allowed officials in the post-war German bureaucracy and political establishment to delay a decision on compensation for over thirty-five years. In the case of Gertrude and Marianne, it was not until the early 1980's that officials "determined" they should be awarded damages for their mistreatment under the NS regime.

"After all that happened to you here in Würzburg,"

the producer asked Gertrude, straining to maintain his composure as the interview slowly came to an end. "Why did you choose to stay here after the war?"

"I wanted to look those people in the face again," she told him matter-of-factly. "Some of the doctors who worked at the institute were guilty of crimes, but many walked away unpunished after the war. Some even resumed their work at the institute. They deserved to be reminded of what they did. When I see them on the street, I hound them just by being here."

Emotionally exhausted, yet inspired by the remarkable strength both women had showed in telling their stories, we packed up in silence. Once the equipment had been transferred to the car and the rearranged furniture returned to its original position, there was a chance to speak to Gertrude directly. Thanking her for sharing her story, I told her that if more Germans had shown one hundredth of her courage, events would have taken another course. With tears welling up, she simply smiled, took my hand in her hands and thanked me for filming it. At that moment, It took everything I had to keep from falling apart.

Several weeks later, the inner rage spawned by Gertrude's story was still burning intensely, spurring me to visit one of the former Nazi euthanasia centres. Situated on the northern perimeter of the Taunus foothills, eighty-five kilometres northwest of Frankfurt, Hadamar at first glance, resembled any one of a thousand picture-book villages in Germany. Unlike other towns however, it had been the site of one of six gassing installations the Nazis had established as part of their euthanasia program. Intended to help actualize their insane racial theories, the first order of business of the T4 program, as it was known, had been to identify all those who didn't match up to the Nazi ideal. The psychologically ill, the mentally deranged, criminals, confirmed alcoholics, the "socially alien," individuals deigned defective or "work shy," as well as those labeled Jewish half-breed children, all fell into the realm of T4's mandate. The facility in Hadamar had been highly "effective" in fulfilling T4's objectives, reportedly responsible for gassing over 10,000 people between January and August 1941. Even when the gassing was halted by an official order from Berlin that year, the killings at Hadamar continued for another three years, either through lethal injection or drug overdoses. By the time the Nazi reign of terror ended in 1945, over 400,000 people in the Third Reich had been killed or sterilized under the supervision of T4 officials in various centres. Those guilty of perpetuating such crimes tended to meet varying post-war fates. Amongst the hundred or so employees at the Hadamar "Tötungsanstalt," (killing centre) Dr. Adolf Wahlmann, a physician responsible for selecting victims, was tried, convicted and sentenced to death in 1947. That sentence was subsequently converted to life imprisonment in 1949, and in 1953 Wahlmann simply waltzed back into freedom. Pauleen Kneissler, a nurse who was convicted of having administered numerous deadly drug overdoses, was sentenced to three and a half years and released after serving one. Judith Thomas, a secretary in the administrative office, whose husband had been one of Hadamar's bus drivers bringing victims to the centre, claimed not to have noticed any of the deaths that took place. She was tried in 1947 and found innocent of being an accomplice to murder. The exceptions to the rule seem to have been Chief administrator Alfons Klein and head nurses, Heinrich Ruoff and Karl Willig who were tried, convicted and executed in 1946.

To this day, the buildings of the former "killing centre" still occupy a dominant position in the town. Given its location on the slopes of the Mönchberg, the credibility of former residents who claimed the "work" within its walls had largely gone unnoticed by the populace, remains highly dubious. Since 1983, a portion of the institute has been converted into a museum commemorating the victims. Placards detailing the procedures of the T4 program are displayed in various rooms along with photos and names of some of those who suffered under it. Nothing however, prepares one for the feelings induced by standing in the small, tiled room where 10,000 victims were gassed.

Following the disturbing experiences of Würzburg and Hadamar, the question of why I had chosen to live in a country capable and responsible for so many atrocities, returned with a renewed intensity. An answer was to emerge from a surprising source; a poster seen at a street demo held to protest against the propensity some Germans have towards "Fremdenfeindlichkeit" or Xenophobia. Carried aloft by one of the participants, its simple message was, "Ausländer herein, lass die Deutsche nicht allein." (Foreigners, do not leave the Germans alone)

Maybe that's why I'm still here.

CHAPTER 45

A Death Wish

"You know something?" Buddy had blurted out, just after we had crossed into Belgium at a speed considerably higher than the allowed limit. "We are so damn lucky. We get to travel all over the place, see all kinds of things, meet interesting people... and to top it off, get paid rather handsomely for it as well."

"Uh, huh," I said, briefly putting down the book I'd been reading. "In case you haven't noticed, we've been doing this for over ten years. What's with this sudden desire to wax fondly?"

"I don't know what made me think of it just now, but it's true. It's such a privileged lifestyle," he continued. "If we had to die tomorrow, I could easily say it's been a great life."

"What do you mean 'we' Kemo Sabe? Is there something you're not telling me? You don't have any sort of last minute urges to swerve into oncoming traffic or anything do you?"

Fortunately he hadn't and didn't, but the sudden outpouring of "foolosophical" renderings was a reminder that my own sense of gratitude hadn't always been what it might have. After all you'd have to be pretty dense not to appreciate the gift of extensive travel, the opportunity to be creative as much as time and script allowed, and all the while getting paid for it.

"But don't you think it's all relative," I said to Buddy after several minutes of afterthought.

"How so?"

"For sure it can sometimes feel like we're on an extended vacation, but we both know the job isn't always all it's cracked up to be. It may sound glamorous to be traveling to Paris or Brussels or who knows where else in Europe, three or four times a year, but what's so glamorous about filming at a sewage treatment plant, or a sausage factory, even if they're in Paris. And besides, you know as well as I do, you have to be careful talking about our travels so you don't come across as some sort of braggart."

For the moment, the Paris examples were enough to take the sheen off Buddy's golden memories, and for the next few miles he remained quiet.

"But you have to admit, we've had our fair share of interesting and humorous times over the years," he said, breaking the silence.

"That I give you. But we still have a ways to go to beat the one you told me about having with Ted."

The incident I was referring to, stemmed from the early 1990's, several years prior to Buddy and I having met. Back then he had joined ranks with an old school buddy from the States, and set up shop as a production company just outside of Hamburg. In the first few years the business had done reasonably well. Things had begun to change however, when Ted grew tired of life behind the camera and developed a hankering to step into the producer's role.

"He was always a bit of a cheap bugger," Buddy had explained. "I remember one time we got a call from a client who was looking for a field producer as well as a camera crew. It was supposed to be a simple sit-down interview, so Ted figured we could do it alone. He would take over as the producer and at the same time save money by not hiring another cameraman."

"But I'm not a cameraman," Buddy had protested, when Ted informed him of his new proposed role.

"Hey, don't worry about it," Ted had assured. "I'll set up the shot. All you'll have to do is keep him in frame. It'll be a snap."

Assuming the situation could easily be mastered, Ted had brushed aside the fact that their control monitor had not been working for some time, leaving the camera viewfinder as the single source of reference. On the day of the shoot, Ted took extra efforts to assure that everything was under control.

"Once I set the shot and lock it down, all you'll have to do is pan left or right to keep him in frame. That doesn't sound so complicated does it?"

As luck would have it, the interview was with a well-known sports star, one of whose biggest fans just happened to be Buddy. Already familiar with Buddy's wide-eyed innocence in certain situations, I had had no trouble envisioning the transfixed face of a six year old in awe, as he continued to tell the story.

"The guy was incredibly interesting," Buddy had recalled. "I just got so caught up in what he was saying, I forgot what I was supposed to be doing."

Revelling in the success of his first interview as a producer, Ted didn't bother to check the footage before rushing off to a colleague's studio. Seated in a darkened control room with the client, the pair had watched the screen with anticipation as the interview began. Five minutes in however, Ted couldn't help noticing that the talking head he had so carefully framed, had started to slowly drift to the left hand side of the screen. Muttering quietly to himself, "pan with him, Buddy... Pan with him... Pan," Ted looked on in horror as the face continued to slide until all that was left on screen for the remainder of the interview was a talking ear. Buddy had smiled as he described Ted's arrival home that evening at their shared apartment.

"He came in, threw the tape on the kitchen table and stormed into the living room without a word. I followed him in to ask what was wrong."

"I've never been so humiliated in my life," Ted said angrily, while pouring himself a stiff drink. "What was the matter with you? Why didn't you pan with him? For the last twenty minutes all we had was a bloody talking ear. What could I say to the client? 'Excuse me, my partner is a lunatic.' I was mortified. Thanks a bundle pal."

Needless to say it was Buddy's last assignment in such a role and a few months later he and Ted decided to go their separate ways.

And so it was with the warm glow created by that tale and other memories, that I leaned back to enjoy the miles still separating us from yet another adventure in the Belgian capital.

"Thank you man," I said, before returning to my book.

"Thank you for what?" Buddy asked with a puzzled look, as we swung into the exit lane leading to the Ring Road.

"Just thanks...just plain and simple, thanks... And do me a favour eh. Stay on this side of the road."

CHAPTER 46

A Memorable Exit

Perhaps because the descent had been a gradual one, the point of no return had slipped past largely unnoticed. People on the periphery had been able to see it coming more objectively than myself, issuing warnings for months, if not years, that the firm was stumbling towards an inevitable and ignominious end. For a variety of reasons, I had chosen to ignore the counsel, rationalizing that the time freed up by diminishing bookings could be put to good use by continuing research for a planned book.

After the co-operative endeavours of almost fourteen years, the final decline began with a call for a two-day shoot in Essen and Düsseldorf. Just prior to that, recent incidents had resulted in my having issued warnings to Buddy that he could no longer count on me as "his cameraman" unless he sought help for his problem. Once it became apparent that the ultimatums were having little effect, a line in the sand needed to be drawn.

"I'll work with you on one condition," I told him over the phone, on a Friday evening before the scheduled shoot. "You have to promise to stay on the wagon before the shoot. That means nothing at all over this weekend."

Perhaps because both of us knew there was little way I could monitor or enforce such a demand, Buddy had quickly agreed.

The first day of shooting at a high-tech factory in

Essen went smoothly, and there was no reason to believe it wouldn't continue to do so in Düsseldorf. To ease the pain of an early call time, we decided to drive the short distance to the city on the Rhine that evening, hoping to relax and enjoy dinner at the hotel restaurant before calling it a night. With just one interview scheduled for the next day, the tentative plan was to finish early enough to avoid the horrendous rush-hour traffic known to plague the Düsseldorf-Cologne corridor.

During the drive to the company headquarters the next morning, the producer, who had flown in from London to conduct the interview, briefly outlined the theme before reminding us that we needed to get an exterior shot of the building provided there was a break in the rain. Two hours later, we were about to call our interview partner to a fifth-floor conference room when a sunbeam suddenly appeared through a narrow slit in the drawn curtains. A quick glance outside confirmed it was destined to be a brief performance.

"Grab the camera and let's get the shot while we can," the producer ordered. Cutting myself free from the tethering cables, I negotiated my way through a forest of lights and flags and headed outside with him. It was one of those lucky breaks that occur from time to time. Literally seconds before the rain resumed, the requested exterior was "in the can." As the elevators doors opened at our floor, we were startled to see several people rushing past. Stepping out into the foyer, we noticed that six or seven people had gathered around the entrance to the conference room. The cause of the commotion became evident as we squeezed past the group to see two men crouched over Buddy's prostrate figure on the floor.

"What happened?" I asked, assuming Buddy had somehow stumbled over a cable and hit his head against the conference table. As the two men parted to offer a clearer view, I was stunned to see spittle frothing on both sides of Buddy's mouth, his hands tightly clutching a cable to his chest as his whole body convulsed. Not having a clue what to do, I initially just stood there stupefied. After several seconds, out of some misplaced instinct, I simply bent down and took the cable out of his hands asking, "What's going on? What are you doing on the floor?" Primed by years of previous antics, it had yet to register that Buddy was no longer of this world.

"Is he an epileptic?" one of the two men wanted to know.

"If he is, it's news to me," I answered, as the spasms continued. It was only when I managed to take hold of his weaving head that I saw the faraway look in his glazed eyes.

"Has somebody called an ambulance?" I asked.

"One is already on its way," a female voice near the doorway answered. Less than ten minutes later a pair of burly, heavily-equipped paramedics stormed off the elevator and into the room. As one bent down to make an initial assessment of the situation, I caught his attention long enough to quietly pass on my opinion that for all intents and purposes, Buddy was an alcoholic. As a result, the first medic immediately exchanged a set of code numbers with his partner, as they proceeded to stabilize him. Once they had placed him on a gurney and wheeled him out the door, the show was over and the crowd dispersed to return to their work cubicles. Still in a mild state of disbelief at what had just taken place, I slipped into automatic pilot, re-setting the camera and attaching the cables before even discussing whether the interview could still be conducted.

"Are you sure we can still do this?" the producer asked skeptically.

"We can at least give it a shot."

"What about your colleague?"

"I don't know what to say. I don't think there's anything we can do for him right now. Have to wait and see what the people at the hospital say."

Despite having to concentrate on monitoring both sound and video, my thoughts did not stray far from Buddy and the conviction that I had just witnessed the demise of the company.

Once the interview was finished and I was packed up and ready to leave, the secretary who had escorted us to the conference room several hours earlier approached me with an update.

"I just received a call from the hospital. Your friend has been admitted and doctors have recommended he stay in overnight for observation."

"Did they say what was wrong with him?"

"They wouldn't give me any information other than that he's been given something and is now resting."

Convinced it made little sense to try and visit Buddy if he'd been sedated, I made my apologies to the producer and client and took my leave. Once out on the crowded autobahn, the scene from the conference room replayed itself again and again, until it finally dawned on me that the probable cause of Buddy's collapse was that he had actually lived up to his promise. As excessive as I suspected his daily intake had been over the last few months, there had likely been enough alcohol in his system to tide him over the weekend. One didn't have to be a doctor to realize that by Tuesday, his body had simply gone into withdrawal, his brain cells screeching for their customary nourishment. As critical mass was reached, the lack of alcohol had likely triggered an epileptic fit of sorts and he'd simply keeled over. Equally disturbing was how quickly it had all unfolded. Prior to exiting for the exterior shot, Buddy had seemed and acted completely normal. Ten minutes later there he was thrashing around like a newly caught fish in the bottom of a boat.

Silence reigned over the next two days and it wasn't until the morning of the third that a friend of Buddy's rang up with details of what had taken place in the interim. Rewinding the tape, Richard explained that when questioned about his medical insurance at hospital admittance, Buddy had bluffed his way in with a story about a misplaced health insurance card. Sensing it was only a matter of time before staff discovered his ruse, the next morning he had disconnected himself from his intravenous drip and simply vanished. Despite his condition, he'd somehow managed to find his way to the main station and caught a train home.

"He showed up at my place two nights ago and has been here ever since. He's going back to his place this afternoon."

"How is he? Did he explain what happened?"

"He's feeling better but hasn't said much. It's pretty clear he needs help."

Dismayed at how far things had gotten and my own role as an "enabler," I waited until that evening before calling. Deep in denial, Buddy started off by jokingly suggesting the incident had been a onetime event, likely caused by a lack of food.

"I'm fine now," he maintained. "Can't wait to get out on the road again."

"Considering all that's happened," I told him. "I think the best thing you can do is to go back to the States and seek help. As far as I'm concerned our work together is finished."

A full month would pass before all arrangements could be made for Buddy's departure. Several days before his scheduled flight, he called sounding a trifle less than sober. Assuring me that everything was "great," he made a last-ditch attempt to salvage the unsalvageable, opining that putting an end to such a successful team was "crazy." I let him rant for a few minutes before ending the conversation with the offer of driving him to the airport.

"I'll pick you up at 8:00 a.m. Please be sure you're ready."

It was one of the few occasions in fourteen years, that he was on time. In spite of the underlying significance of the situation, neither one of us had much to say on the drive to the airport. With no spaces available in front of the departure terminal, I pulled alongside a row of parked cars, thinking I would let him off before heading to the parking garage. Just as we'd finished loading his luggage on to a cart, someone emerged from the terminal and climbed into the car just in front of us.

"Hang on," I said to Buddy, leaving him temporarily marooned with a stack of suitcases. "Let me grab that space so I can come in with you."

No more than a few minutes had passed since our arrival, yet when I jumped back in the car and turned the key, I was greeted with dead silence. Several more attempts produced similar reactions. After pushing the car into the empty space to await a tow truck, Buddy and I were forced into an awkward and hurried goodbye. Needless to say, it was an inauspicious, albeit symbolic end to a fourteen-year tour. Standing beside my crippled auto, I watched as Buddy moved across the roadway, turning to wave adieu before disappearing behind the sliding glass doors. Alone amidst the noise and commotion of a large airport, the final wave hit; that this time, he was gone for good.

CHAPTER 47

Land Mines

This was important stuff. My life could have depended on it. I should have been listening, but I wasn't. Instead my focus had fallen to a raucous game of soccer underway in an adjacent field. Able to risk only limited glimpses without incurring the wrath of the instructor, I had yet to grasp the rules of a game where there didn't appear to be any goals, no marked sidelines, not even a referee. To add to the melee, the opposing teams each seemed to have between thirty and forty players, all dressed in the familiar black-and-white uniforms of Cambodian school children. All the same, if whoops and yells were any indication, one had the impression that "herd ball" was a lot of fun despite the oppressive heat. As the game's momentum pulled players to the far side of the dusty field, my gaze drifted back to the base leader, just in time to see him turn away from a series of charts to face me. For a moment I was back in grade five Literature class, dreading I was about to be asked for a measured response to a question I hadn't heard. It turned out to be a false alarm, but just to be safe, I leaned forward in feigned concentration while taking another swig of much-needed water.

"Excuse me," I interrupted a few minutes later. "But why is there a mine detection base camp located right next to a school?"

Seemingly perplexed by the question, the former British army major yielded the floor to his colleague.

Dressed in an unofficial khaki uniform, with a shaved head that gave him an exaggerated military bearing, Franz was what one might have called, a bear of a man. He also happened to be the central figure of the film Conrad and I had come six thousand miles to shoot, the theme of which was to show how a former member of the East-German army had come to work for a land mine detection company, and how his young family dealt with the fact his occupation put him in danger all over the world. Franz's workplace that day happened to be a field station an hour's drive north of Cambodia's second largest city, Battambang.

"The population has learned to live amidst their contaminated country as best they can," Franz explained, picking up a pointer and directing my attention to a map. "Cambodia has between four and six million land mines scattered across its territory. Having a school next to a base camp is just a sign of their confidence in our work."

"But wasn't the school here first?"

"True," Franz replied, casting a *"who does this guy think he is?"* glance at Conrad. "Maybe I should just say they feel more at ease since they know we have worked to clear the area. They need this land so they can eat. And it's our job to make it safe... And now it's safe."

It was clear the game was over. The noise had subsided and players had disappeared back into a sun-bleached building at the far end of the field. Over on our side of the fence, a Cambodian assistant had taken over the podium, holding up a number of cards that now had my full and utter attention.

"The most critical sign is the red skull and crossbones," the man explained in accent-free English.

"Its purpose is to warn visitors of danger. Whenever you see this sign, do not enter the area for any reason. Go back in the direction you came or to an area you know is safe."

Asked to scrutinize several more signs before being directed to a table laden with protective equipment, we watched as a second assistant assumed command, to recite the rules that were to be followed when venturing into an area known to be mined.

"You must be dressed in a flak jacket and helmet at all times," he said, as other staff members fanned out to assist us in donning the safety gear. "Another important thing to remember is that your face visor must remain down at all times in the field. You are not to raise it until the team leader says it is safe to do so. That will be when you have reached the active base camp and not before. Is that clear?"

Conrad and I nodded, exchanging brief looks of bemusement at the sight of each other in full regalia.

"While proceeding to the camp, you are to keep the position assigned you," the instructor continued. "Follow the person ahead of you at a distance of approximately two meters. Under no circumstances are you to leave the marked route, which as you will see, will be clearly marked by red wires stretched along each side of the path. Any questions?"

A gulp of water, a private incantation or two, and we were off down the rutted trail. If I'd thought it had been hot during the lecture, it was nothing compared to being out on the trail in helmet and flak jacket. With the sole object in the sky having already nudged the temperature past thirty-three, there suddenly seemed the real possibility of passing out before reaching our destination. In an attempt to distract myself from the suffocating heat, one eye was kept glued to the heel of my predecessor, all the while wondering if the two-meter rule could actually have any impact when it came to limiting casualties. The other eye risked glancing out at a tiresome panorama of flat, uncultivated fields, interrupted occasionally by clump of bushes or small trees. The singular source of interest on the sun-scorched terrain was a distant, lone mountain, so out of place that one could have easily thought it had been dropped there by a clumsy deity. Oddly enough, what was missing that day was any feeling of danger. There we were, treading as close as anyone would ever willingly want to get to a live mine field, and yet there was no apparent sense of dread, which in some ways I suppose, was a danger in itself.

Twenty minutes and several litres of sweat lighter, our party of six reached the active staging area, just as the black walls of an imminent collapse had started to creep in along the edges of my peripheral vision. When permission was given to raise our visors, the top items on the agenda were to seek shelter in the shade of an equipment gazebo, secure a bottle of water, and find something other than my shirt sleeve to wipe away the streams of sweat careening down both sides of my face. Once freed of that salty veil, I happened to catch sight of a dark-green torso operating what appeared to be some sort of metal detector. Too far away for me to get a decent shot, I was about to move the camera to a better position when I felt a hand clamp down on my shoulder.

"Sorry," the base leader said, shaking his head. "Nobody's allowed closer than fifty meters to an active operator. You can shoot from here if you want, as long as you keep your visor down."

Far from thrilled at the prospect of re-entering that heat chamber, I nevertheless obeyed, following the action as best I could from that distance. Remaining at my side, no doubt to make sure I abided by the rules, the base leader began to explain the delicate procedures involved in locating and removing a mine.

"The worker only approaches as far as the red wire," he said, as we watched the man guide the detector in a sweeping arc several inches above the ground. The fact that its reach extended no more than two meters in front of him, was a clear illustration of just how slow the detection process was. "If something is detected," the leader added, "The worker will place a coloured chip on the spot where the signal is strongest. It doesn't happen often but sometimes a scanned area of as little as one or two meters can end up having several chips. That doesn't mean they're all land mines of course, but we have to act on the assumption they could be."

"And then?" Conrad asked, having moved up to join us.

"And then, another team will attempt to retrieve whatever is setting off the signal. But I can't let you film that. It would be too dangerous."

"Interesting stuff," I said to Conrad quietly, my voice echoing off the inside of the visor. "Might even be worthwhile if we could actually see more of what the guy is doing."

"Just get what you can," Conrad advised with a shrug.

With his explanation now complete, the base leader indicated it was time to head elsewhere. Trudging back up the path we'd just come down, we hadn't gone more than a hundred meters when he stopped to point out a pair of green-suited workers partially hidden in the underbrush. From this new vantage point we could make out a man and woman sweeping through long grass, with what we were told were high tech "weed-eaters." Faced once again with the option of filming limited action, the least I could do was assure the shot was sharp. Experience at the first location had shown that trying to focus with my visor down was virtually impossible. Aware that no broadcaster would accept such grounds for fuzzy images, I had resolved that problem by quickly lifting the visor to focus and frame, during the few seconds the base leader's attention had been drawn elsewhere. Confident no one had witnessed my previous transgression, I cautiously attempted an instant replay.

"Visor down," Franz suddenly ordered, in a tone usually reserved for domestic animals. With my visor already in the descending mode, I didn't bother to acknowledge his comment and simply continued to film. Seconds later there was another tap on my shoulder. Fortunately, it was only Conrad, directing my attention to yet another pair of workers on the opposite side of the path. Unlike their counterparts, this time there were no natural obstructions blocking my view of their actions. Quickly re positioning the camera, I instinctively moved to focus, but not before casting a furtive glance to confirm Franz's attention was momentarily occupied with other matters. But no sooner had my surreptitious move been completed, a voice boomed out above the whirring weed-cutters.

"That's it," Franz bellowed, before swaggering over to stand directly in front of the camera. "I warned you once. I won't warn you again. Visors are to be down on site, at *all* times. That is standard procedure. Stop filming."

It was a critical moment to say the least. With Franz the linchpin of the entire documentary, further antagonizing him would not have boded well for a smooth production. Confronted with potentially losing face, one way or the other, I stepped away from the camera, raising my hands in a mock surrender while curbing any rebuttal. Hoping to defuse matters, Conrad moved between us, his frown a welcome sign that he was as dumbfounded as me by Franz's outburst.

"What you choose to do with your life does not really interest me much," Franz snarled. "But today you are in an area under *my* control. If something was to happen to you on my watch, it would reflect badly on me and the whole organization. I am not about to let that happen, so I want you to pack up and leave the area immediately."

With the exception of two years in Navy League cadets at the impressionable age of fourteen, I'd never been much of a military man. Dealings with authority had generally swung between outright rejection and begrudging obedience. Despite such nurtured ambivalence however, I could see Franz had a point. Responsible for the safety of the entire troupe, he was not in the mood to tolerate violations, whatever their basis.

"It's okay," Conrad said to me in a low voice, as the group prepared to trek back to base camp. "I don't really need ten minutes of weed cutting anyway. But the man has a temper. Definitely something to keep in mind."

"Just how safe is safe?" I asked from the rear seat of

the Land Rover, once we were back on the road to Battambang. Recognizing the question for what it was, part curiosity and part ceasefire, Franz maintained a long pause before meeting me half way.

"A hundred percent," he answered, keeping his vision locked straight ahead.

"But how can you comb every square inch of an entire country and be sure you haven't missed something? That just doesn't seem feasible. What if someone is having a bad day, slacks off a bit and overlooks something. Who's to know, until one day?"

"Once we've designated an area cleared," Franz repeated firmly, "It is safe."

Sensing we had reached an impasse, I sat back in strained silence, gazing out at the passing countryside; blissfully unaware of how soon my theory was going to be tested.

We departed Battambang early the next morning, hoping to avoid the mid-day heat that had started its inexorable climb at 6:00 a.m.

"You know what that thing sounds like?" I said, breaking the tranquil that had endured for the first half-hour of the drive. "A garburator."

"It may be noisy," Franz snorted, gesturing to a cloud of dust that was trailing behind a passing car. "But that 'thing' is what's keeping us all from choking."

I couldn't argue the point. Ever since leaving Battambang the roads had been nothing short of lengthy dust factories. The confines of our Land Rover had offered *us* some protection against the massive amounts of dust being churned up, but the same couldn't be said for the scores of drivers and passengers on motorbikes, many of whom had resorted to wrapping scarves or surgical masks over their mouths and noses.

As we continued our advance into the countryside, I couldn't help but notice that nearly all the private dwellings we were passing, were perched atop wooden pilings set back ten or twenty yards from the road.

"These huts," I began, leaning forward as far as the seatbelt would allow.

"It's to protect against the rising waters in the rainy season," Franz interrupted, having anticipated the question. "When times are dry, it doubles as a shaded storage area."

A short while later, as my interest in the seemingly endless row of weathered domiciles was starting to lag, I spotted a brightly-coloured villa in their midst. A second appeared, followed by a third; sticking out like random gaudy baubles, only to be quickly swallowed up by the thick foliage lining the road. All of these two-storey, brick houses were set behind high-cement walls topped with strands of razor wire. But unlike their more modest neighbours, none showed any signs of being inhabited.

As difficult as it was to catch sight of anything at 75 kph, I continued to be fascinated by the extraordinary variety of passing vistas. Farmers in loose-fitting shirts and pants, topped with the familiar cone-shaped peon's hat, could be seen in unfenced yards, raking out mounds of chilli peppers to dry in the merciless sun. Other vignettes offered up brown-skinned youngsters at play, many unencumbered by clothing, as they scrambled amongst the lemongrass and palm trees. Further along, we came upon their elder siblings attired in white shirts and black pants or skirts, walking, cycling or balancing on the back end of motor bikes as they made their way to school. One such exodus, several kilometres long, ended abruptly at a walled-in courtyard, teeming with more black-and white-splotches.

Interspersed amidst this panorama of huts, villas, and schools were the roadside vendors. Many looked to be transitory, displaying their wares on makeshift stands crafted to the back end of a motorbike. More established merchants had arranged their multi-coloured goods on tables under rickety lean-to's, or had them spread out on the ground in front of their homes. No doubt forced to endure prolonged gaps between customers, many vendors appeared to be posing for a still life.

At some point, the paraphernalia of civilization gave way to large tracts of land stretching back to the horizon. Within them lay rice paddies in spectacular hues and intensities of green, sectioned off from each other by raised earthen embankments. Although it was neither harvest nor planting time, workers of various ages could nevertheless be seen toiling in the knee-deep, murky water, while solitary cows grazed lazily along the narrow pathways. Added to these compressed rural scenes were fleeting glimpses of young boys leaping from rocks or bridge abutments into the brownish waters of pools or creeks, in hopes of escaping the ever-present heat. Then without warning the fields receded and we found ourselves back in a channel of houses and trees, where long-skirted mothers came into view, frequently with child in arm, as they circled a large steaming pot in their front yards in preparation for the afternoon meal. It was nothing less than sensory saturation, an avalanche of impressions far too plentiful to be fully absorbed.

"We're heading for a disaster," Conrad announced a short while later, as another oncoming motorbike disappeared into the bulbous plume trailing us.

"What do mean heading?" I asked. "What would you call this dustbowl we're in?"

"No, I'm talking about the accident that took place a couple of weeks ago."

Events such as the one Conrad had referred to, normally didn't get reported beyond Cambodia's borders. The only reason this one had made international headlines was that thirteen lives had been lost in a single flash. As it had taken place within Franz's jurisdiction, he'd arranged for us to meet and speak with some of the relatives of those killed. According to Franz, the incident had involved a group of local chilli pickers returning home after a long day in the fields. They had been traveling in an open wagon pulled by a motorbike that was driven by a local man familiar with the area. The group had been on a safely marked route when they came to a point on the trail where it crossed over a small stream. As remnants from the recently ended rainy season had made passage at the crossing impossible, the driver had stopped to scout around for an alternative route. Believing that cow hoof-prints in the mud provided reasonable assurance that no mines lay in wait, he had eased his vehicle forward, straying no more than a few meters from the original path. Regrettably, what he failed to take into consideration was that while a cow was heavy enough to set off an anti-personnel land mine, its weight was insufficient to detonate an anti-tank one. To their tragic misfortune, a metal wagon with thirteen people aboard was.

After nearly two hours of bone-jarring travel, we finally pulled into a small village, that at first glance resembled a deserted movie set, complete with dust whirlpools and tumbleweeds chasing each other down a dirt street. It was also home to an abandoned stone fountain, long since incapable of offering relief from the heat. When our Cambodian driver stopped to ask directions, I used the opportunity to get out and stretch my legs. Save for a familiar looking kiosk or two, there was not a lot else to see. Stirred by the sight of a potential customer, one merchant began vying for my attention by franticly fanning his arms. Not in the market for any brightly-labeled packages of dish detergents, cooking oils or American snacks, I merely nodded hello and refrained from going anywhere near his stand. I was about to saunter off in the direction of the fountain when a curt honk summoned me back to the truck, only to learn we'd somehow missed our turn-off. Fortunately, we only needed to retrace a "dustance" of 300 meters before stopping alongside a wooden lean-to, one hefty breeze from collapse. Despite our reduced speed, the trailing cloud managed to briefly engulf the group of wide-eyed children sitting out front. As we disembarked, Conrad mimed that he wanted footage of the dozen or so smiling faces. Unlike in other parts of the world, where once having spotted a camera, youngsters would have immediately started waving and clowning around, this group of fledglings sat in utter silence, watching me set up beside the truck. Meanwhile, Conrad, who'd been off in a discussion with Franz and a local man, returned to inform me the woman we'd come to interview was in fact here at the kiosk. Using the camera lens to discreetly investigate, I found her seated in the shadows amongst a group of middle-aged women. What set her apart from the other inquisitive faces was a hollow, blank stare that bore straight through the lens and into the back of my head. Rising up with a start, I caught Conrad's chin with my shoulder as he leaned over to confirm that the woman in the viewfinder was indeed the mother of one of the victims, and grandmother to the small boy squirming on her lap.

Once it had been determined that the interview would be conducted at the woman's home, I was sent across the road to scout out a location. There didn't appear to be anyone in the yard as I approached with a combination of respect and curiosity. Calling out to no response, I ascended a short wooden ladder and poked my head through the open doorway. A quick survey of the sole room, basically the size of a small single-car garage, made it apparent there was no need to venture further. Divided in two by a pair of blankets draped over a rope, the room's grey, rough-hewn walls and floor simply made it too dark to shoot in. Still atop the ladder, I was suddenly besieged by images from another world; seeing myself wandering through a familiar house, flicking a light switch here, running a tap there, turning up a thermostat before grabbing a snack from the fridge and settling down in front of the television. I was yanked back to the present by the realization that most of the residents of this dwelling would likely never experience such creature comforts... ever.

Having set up in the dirt yard in front of the hut, we were about to begin the interview when the grandmother beckoned a young girl sitting on a nearby stoop, to join her. Holding a framed photo of her deceased mother, the young girl stood motionless as the older woman, - the restless three-year old still in her arms, -solemnly related her tale. Unable to hear what the translator was saying to Conrad, and not understanding a word of Khmer, during the ten-minute interview my thoughts were shadowed by a deep sense of embarrassment at the immense opportunities afforded us by the mere accident of birth.

"There's one more place I think you should see before we head back to Battambang," Franz said, as we watched the woman and her grandchildren turn away to avoid the dust blown up by our departure. The accident site was not far and within fifteen minutes of more grime-coated foliage, we had arrived at a plateau overlooking a broad plain. To no one's surprise, there in the distance was yet another solitary mountain. In an attempt to raise the somber mood present since leaving the village, Franz decided to explain the origin of these isolated peaks, as we unloaded.

"Five thousand years ago," he began, "Cambodia had yet to exist. The Mekong delta was much further north… somewhere up near the border to Thailand. Over time, the tons of silt washing downstream from the Himalayas gradually forced the seawater to recede. The flat fertile plain left behind is now Cambodia. Peaks like the one out there had simply been islands in the former sea."

The geography lesson was brought to a sudden end when Conrad called out.

"Out there in the valley. Can you get it?" he said, pointing to a small vehicle approaching in the distance.

As I scrambled to set up, Franz added to the pressure by announcing that the advancing vehicle was the same type as the one that had been involved in the deadly accident. Making the moment even more poignant, was the fact it was full of men, women and children, all smiling and waving as I panned and let them slip past out of frame.

Following another short safety lecture, the three of us set off down a narrow path. Once again the scenery was less than breathtaking, comprised mostly of empty scrubland, hyphenated now-and-then by a small cultivated field. As we continued to walk, it didn't escape me that there were no red strings anywhere to be seen. It wasn't until we had looped around a rudimentary animal compound, home to several skeletal cows and a few ornery goats, that I caught a glimpse of the familiar red skull and crossbones. Such reassurance, however, was short lived, as seconds later, Franz directed us off to the right, away from the signs. Saddled with both camera and tripod, keeping pace with the other two was becoming an effort. Just as the gap between us was getting large enough to warrant a shout, Franz and Conrad paused at the crest of a small hill. Joining them on the summit, I looked back to see our Land Rover in the distance, a reminder of how close the victims had been to safety that day.

"I want you both to stay here while I check out the area," Franz ordered, as we watched him descend to a dry-creek bed and walk the short distance to the edge of a small crater.

"I thought he said something about areas being safe once cleared."

"Don't bother mentioning that again," Conrad warned, as Franz waved the all clear to advance. Stumbling through a brief performance of, "After you… no after you," which ultimately would have been of no consequence if a mine had been present, we proceeded with caution. Setting up on the edge of a crater I estimated was three to four meters across and two meters deep, we listened as Franz explained how the initial retrieval team had secured the area.

"It's standard procedure to first confirm the site is safe. In this case it was even more vital, considering they discovered a second unexploded anti-tank mine not far from the original blast."

"That's information I could have done without," I mumbled to Conrad, as we both looked down into the shattered earth. With Frank's explanation done, an eerie silence descended, broken only by the rustling of dried corn stalks in a nearby field. I felt a chill rattle down my spine when Conrad directed my attention to a twisted mass of metal lodged on a ridge ten to fifteen meters away. From that distance, the blue-coloured object looked more like a piece of abstract art than any recognizable mode of transportation. Zooming in however, revealed it to be a gruesome symbol of the power that had ended thirteen lives.

"It's almost the same time of day as when the accident took place," Franz told us, glancing at his watch. Up until then, his choice of words hadn't really bothered me. But there at the site, it was irritating to hear Franz still refer to it as an accident. Staring at the residue in the pit, which included a few empty water bottles and an overturned flip-flop, my thoughts drifted to the lengthy chain of those who were responsible for our being there; infantrymen, officers, military leaders, politicians, advisors, bureaucrats, lobbyists, arms dealers, defence contractors, sales reps, manufacturers, assembly line workers, parts suppliers… all testimony to the fact this had been no accident, but rather a crime.

*

On our last full day in rural Cambodia, we once again found ourselves in uncharted territory, this time headed for a recovery base north of the city of Pailin. Unlike the scrub-filled plains we'd seen on previous outings, here, barely fifty kilometres outside of Battembang, the terrain started to sprout batches of isolated hills, the odd one decorated with a golden temple spire poking through the thick carpeting of trees. Save for the odd construction site, where entire sections of road washed away in the rainy season were being replaced by Chinese roadworks companies, the drive went smoothly, allowing us to arrive on the outskirts of Pailin earlier than scheduled. First impressions suggested the region was not as poor as others we'd seen and a quick look at the guidebook explained why. Precious gems, timber and rice were what accounted for the area's wealth, a fact the Khmer Rouge had not overlooked when looking for ways to keep their struggling revolution alive in the early 1970's. Although most of the mines had long since been exhausted and timber and rice production severely curtailed by the number of land mines in the area, something was still keeping this town of 23,000 relatively affluent. But whatever it was that residents were doing to earn their livelihoods, there were not many of them out doing it that day. With no thriving markets, no bustling crowds, and no chaotic traffic to deal with, our progress through Pailin was swift. But no sooner had we left the town limits, the paved surfaces gave way to a familiar teeth-rattling ride.

"We're entering an area known as K5," Franz told us, pointing to the adjacent fields and the dark forests of the Cardamon mountains off in the distance. "It's a strip thirty kilometres wide, and it runs all the way from the Gulf of Thailand up to Laos, a distance of between three and four hundred kilometres. It's the former front line between warring factions, the world's longest minefield and one of the most dangerous places on the planet."

"If this place is so saturated with mines," I began. "Where the heck do you start to de-mine, if there is such a word... I mean won't it take forever to clear that much land?"

"More like forever and a day," he answered. "Some people estimate it could take 10,000 years to make Cambodia completely safe again... But you need to start somewhere."

The thought of possibly having to live with the threat of land mines for ten thousand years suddenly sparked an idea.

"Why don't they re-plant some of the recovered mines in the backyards of company executives responsible for their manufacture and sale?" I whispered to Conrad, when Franz was absorbed in conversation with the driver.

"Do me a favour and keep Plan B to yourself," was all he said.

Although the camp turned out to be less than ten minutes from Pailin, our arrival was delayed by several minutes as the driver struggled to park the truck into perfect alignment under Franz's discerning eye.

"Remember your visor," was the sum total of Conrad's advice, as we climbed out to be greeted by the camp leader, another former British military officer. Short and squat, with a rigid manner that suggested he was also a stickler for order, Gerald welcomed us with a hearty handshake and smile before guiding us to a nearby gazebo; glancing over his shoulder to make sure the vehicle had been parked to his liking.

Already old pros in the safety lessons department, it was not long before we were tramping down a dirt track bordered by ripening corn fields. Thanks to the dips and swells in the path, thirty something heat, and a full load of equipment, sweating and wheezing were once again part of the routine.

"You sound like our air conditioner," Conrad said with a smile, as he stopped to let me pass.

"Tell me about," I mumbled. "I could do with one right about now."

This latest round of torture lasted for around twenty minutes, ending as we veered off down a narrow path that offered the promise of shade.

"Another five minutes and I would have evaporated," I told Conrad, as we reached a green field tent at the far end of a charred ravine. "I've got so much salt on me, it feels like I just came out of the Dead Sea," I groaned, as permission to raise our visors was given and we slumped down on a bench in the cooling shade. Hoping to compensate for the loss of fluids, I grabbed a bottle of water from a portable ice box, making sure the only parts of me moving were my throbbing temples.

"Well gentlemen," Gerald announced, springing to his feet after what was much too brief an interlude. "We should get a move on."

Despite having spent the full ten minutes doing nothing other than breathing, it took a gargantuan

Land Mines | 445

effort to get me to my feet again, and an even larger one to not sit back down again and order a mojito. But somehow automatic pilot kicked and I slowly followed the others back up the path. As the group continued to wind its way through what had become thick underbrush, I could see Franz and Gerald conferring up ahead. Although not close enough to hear what they were saying, their gestures were a vivid reminder that certain people can exude a military presence without ever opening their mouths.

"Gentlemen," Gerald barked, raising his hand to bring us to a halt where two paths intersected. "You are about to have the pleasure of filming the removal of a live mine. But first, I want you to wait here while Franz and I inspect the site."

"Just exactly where is this live mine?" I whispered to Conrad after noticing there were no reassuring red wires anywhere in sight.

"I'm sure we'll find out soon enough, one way or the other," he answered in what I thought was extremely poor taste.

Meanwhile, Gerald and Franz, who had stopped some twenty to thirty meters in front of us, beckoned us to approach. As we moved up to join them, I was somewhat alarmed to see two brown cylinders, the size of soda cans, lodged in the earthen wall of a hole at their feet.

"These mines are of Chinese origin," Gerald informed us. "When activated they will spring out of the ground before actually exploding."

"What do you mean 'will'?" I asked, acutely aware that we were in the middle of the Cambodian jungle, and miles from any medical assistance. The location seemed the last place one would ever expect to find a land mine, making it the perfect spot to lay one.

"They are capable of taking out everything within at least a five-meter radius," Gerald concluded.

Having seen quite enough of the ordinance up close, I was pleased to learn filming would only be allowed from a much greater distance. Once we'd moved back to a safer location, it was agreed that Franz would operate our second camera to obtain the close-up footage of Gerald actually extracting the mines. My job was to capture the backs of the two distant figures hunched over an unseen hole, an assignment I felt completely comfortable with despite my lowered visor. As the action began, I suddenly found myself wondering how I might react if a muffled boom was to occur. But before I could speculate on the financial implications of owning world-exclusive footage, the entire procedure was over.

Back on the trail, I was able to catch Gerald's attention long enough to ask why mines weren't just detonated where they were found rather than risking their removal. Though his expression said otherwise, he made a concerted effort not to sound too patronizing.

"Sometimes we have no choice and have to detonate on site. But when ordinance is blown up on location, shrapnel will either contaminate areas already cleared, or add metal fragments to sectors yet to be scanned. That would increase our workload substantially."

In a scene reminiscent of the television series Get Smart, and its infamous 'Cone of Silence,' a good portion of Gerald's subsequent explanation was lost to the muffling effects of a lowered visor. What I did manage to retain was that whenever possible, workers would place detected ordinance in another hole lined with sandbags, before covering the devices with more sandbags and detonating them from a safe distance.

"The sandbags limit the explosion, directing it downwards where it can do less harm."

Back at base camp, with a renewed appreciation for all my extremities, I was busy loading the gear back into our dust-laden truck when the urge to whistle suddenly came over me. It was a revealing moment, as I never whistled... ever.

※

Anyone remotely familiar with the events that took place in Cambodia between April,1975 and January,1979, is aware of how the "killing fields" got their name. Consequently, it didn't require a huge leap of the imagination to figure out what was awaiting us later that day, as we passed through a controlled gate at the base of Phnom Sambeau mountain, on our way to what Franz had called the "killing caves." Skirting past a collection of abandoned market stalls, laid out in rows beneath a canopy of shadowing trees, we ascended a steep, winding road through the forest until arriving at a cement courtyard so disheveled, it looked like it had suffered from a recent earthquake. On the far edge of the courtyard, in front a derelict-looking temple, a paint-chipped statue of Buddha presided over a plain caught in the haze of a sinking sun. Other than a pair of saffron-robed monks crossing the plaza, the only visible activity was that of several merchants hovering at stalls along its border. Familiar with the area, having been there on several previous occasions, Franz quickly guided us to the path leading to the caves. A short walk later, we began our descent down a long cement staircase, to enter what looked more like a natural amphitheater than any cave.

"People were brought here," he began, as we reached rock bottom and stepped out on to the black-and-white tiled floor of a large grotto. "Purported enemies of the State, which given the circumstances at the time could have been just about anyone. They were tortured in the temple you saw back at the courtyard, before being marched up to that ledge," he said, gesturing to a nearby rocky overhang. "Then one by one, they were thrown down the shaft to their death. A subsequent government built this as a memorial for those who perished here."

For no conscious reason, I felt myself drawn to a shaft off to my left, where a collection of jagged boulders lay scattered along its lower contours. Although I was now a good thirty feet away from Franz, I was still able to hear him explain that more than 14,000 victims had met their fate not far from where I was standing. Although it was not forbidden to film in this sacred place, it nevertheless felt intrusive to be doing so. As a result, I attempted to document aspects of the shrine as respectfully as possible, all the while unable to escape images I'd previously seen at the Nazi concentration camp in Mauthausen, Austria. In that hell on earth, Jewish prisoners had met a similar end, flung to their deaths at the camp's notorious stone quarry. Several minutes later, Franz's resonant voice returned me to the present.

"They killed the adults here. Children, fourteen and younger, around a thousand or so... were thrown down another shaft not far from here."

Moving to the opposite end of the grotto, I caught

sight of a lone monk sitting cross-legged amidst an array of Buddhas and burning candles. There to guard the vestiges of those lost, he nodded knowingly as I moved forward to pay my respects. Accepting his offer to light a stick of incense, I was bending down to place the smouldering tribute at his feet, when distracted by a brightly-coloured cabinet, within which several dozen human skulls lay stacked on its open shelves.

After filming for approximately half and hour, we returned to the top of the stairs just as the evening's shadows were starting to edge their way across the checkered floor.

"Why here?" I asked in a low voice, taking a final look at the cavern below. "Why like this?"

"This was a holy shrine before it became a cemetery," Franz answered. "The Khmer Rouge knew that and used it as a final insult before sending people to their grave."

"And the method?" I repeated.

"As gross as it sounds, because it was practical. Simple as that. Practical buggers, the Khmer Rouge. Access was easily controlled so there were no witnesses. Throwing people down a shaft saved on ammunition and the need for burials. They used the same logic in the killing fields, except there, people were murdered with shovels, or had their throats cut with sugar cane leaves to save on bullets."

The sense of detachment with which Franz related this information was a stark reminder of how routinely such acts had been carried out in the name of the revolution. By the time it was over, some two million people, around 25% of the population, are thought to have perished.

"It's a real paradox to see these friendly, helpful people today," Franz mused aloud as we rejoined the highway for the drive back to Battambang. "Maybe that's why I don't trust a lot of Cambodians. They may smile all the time, but you never know what they're thinking."

Given that Franz and I weren't exactly cut from the same cloth, parting that evening was neither sweet, nor particularly loaded down with sorrow. Within the span of two weeks, we had somehow come to dislike each other with an intensity that probably surprised both of us. And yet, as I watched him climb into the Land Rover and pull away for the last time, I realized that a part of me nonetheless respected him for having chosen the line of work he did, even if I found out later that part of his duties during his tenure with the East German army, had included planting mines along the border between the two Germanys.

CHAPTER 48

Denouement in Davos

"You're only as good as your last shoot"... a Damocles sword that may have often sounded like a complaint, but was simply part of the package of being a freelance cameraman. Expected to be at the top of your creative potential each and every day, you were lucky if some clients, usually repeat ones, would overlook your inspiration level not being quite what it could have been. Others were not so forgiving.

In the daze and months following Buddy's departure, work had continued to decline. Unbeknownst to me at the time, a portion of that reduction could be credited to the impression he had left with some clients, not to mention his failure to pay a number of people for their services. Having been closely associated with Buddy for so long, it was inevitable that I be tarred with the same brush. But rather than sit around and stare holes in the sky over the loss of work, much of the time was filled with writing and editing a book I'd started years earlier. Such an endeavour however, needed financing and it was only by taking occasional larger shoots that the necessary funds were attainable. First and foremost amongst those shoots was the annual World Economic Forum in Davos, Switzerland, a rather odd source of revenue given my longstanding antipathy towards big business.

Considering the number of VIP's that invaded the

picturesque mountain resort each January, one of my first impressions was that security did not appear to be as vigilant as one might have expected for an international conference of its calibre. Having driven down from Germany the day before the conference was set to commence, we had arrived at the first checkpoint several miles outside the Davos' city limits, concerned we might be asked to tear apart our fully-packed car for inspection. But rather than being inspected, we were simply asked a few questions by a machine- gun-toting policeman, before being waved through.

"Hey, don't get me wrong," I told my two companions. "I'm not complaining. But didn't that strike you as a bit lax? I mean here we are in a car chock full of equipment, and nobody even bothered to check to see what was in here. They didn't even ask for our passports."

I had of course, spoken too soon. Less than twenty minutes later, there we were, standing in a long line-up inside a tent, waiting to undergo a rigid and lengthy security check that would include passport control, fingerprint scanning and car registration.

Operating out of a small two-camera studio we'd set up in a rented office in the centre of Davos, we started early each morning; remaining on stand-by all day, ready to conduct interviews with as many business leaders, political figures and celebrities the client could persuade to slip away from workshops and seminars. Against my expectations, listening to many of these high-ranking "players" expound on world events and issues, proved to be quite intriguing. Equally as interesting however, was observing how differently people conducted themselves before, during and after an interview. While some executives came across as "sympatico," greeting members of the crew and engaging in light banter, others remained aloof or spent time boasting of the accomplishments and quirks their rather privileged lifestyles offered. Whether it was flying a small plane onto a glacier for a champagne breakfast, comparing the size of one's yacht, or listing off the locations of their various homes, listening to these skewered versions of reality was like having someone describe life on a foreign planet.

The pace of work, however, was anything but stressful. With never more than twenty interviews spread out over four days in each of the years we covered the event, suspicions were raised that the whole venture had simply been staged to highlight the client's presence in Davos.

Quick to take advantage of the "free time" such a schedule provided, we strolled the crowded streets looking for recognizable faces, or explored the spectacular scenery along back-mountain roads, indulging ourselves in the fine Swiss restaurants and bars at our beck and call. As if those perks weren't enough, we also had the pleasure of being billeted into luxurious accommodations. Although the first year was admittedly a bit of a dud, spent housed in a hotel with no working wi-fi and paper-thin walls, the final years found us bedded down in a lavish four-bedroom apartment which reportedly cost the company thousands of Swiss Francs to rent.

But as all good things must, and do… Davos came to an abrupt end in 2015, thanks in large part to a defective camera, a dissatisfied client and a sullied reputation. With visions of coasting to a commensurate retirement now crushed, it seemed as good a time as any to pack up my stuff and leave the playing field. After all, I'd never really wanted my own business and all the organizational details that entailed, yet had increasingly found myself in such a role ever since Buddy's exit. Thrust back into the real world, it didn't take long for another cycle of "now what?" to take centre stage.

CHAPTER 49

Cacoethes Scribendi

It was only a few months into my mildly lamentable retirement, as I was reflecting on the pluses and minuses of the tumultuous trail known as my so-called career, that a comfortable melancholy settled in. Amongst the pillars of memory to emerge while in dry-dock, was the realization that I didn't miss camerawork in the slightest. Rather, it was finding a new direction that had become a priority.

As the weeks and months passed, it slowly started to dawn on me that the route lying in wait was one towards writing full-time. Having been prey to periodic bouts of Cacoethia Scribendi in the past, translated as either "the wickedness of writing" or "the insatiable urge to scribble," the biggest obstacle then and now, was determining whether talent and discipline were of sufficient quality and quantity for me to have anything to say, and say it well. It was while trapped within that fog of uncertainty, that a piece of advice, uttered thirty years earlier, came floating back.

"Write about what you know," a creative-writing instructor had told me; solid and sage counsel until you took into account that this same man, when asked why he had chosen to write, had blithely answered, "because I like to see my name in print."

The suggestion of whether it wouldn't have been easier to just become an ax murderer, had earned me a C in his class.

Over the years there had never been a shortage of inspirational advice on how to get off the proverbial fence. The French novelist, Gustave Flaubert, had claimed that writing is a dog's life but the only life worth living, while the Irish legend, James Joyce suggested that all one needed before setting out on a literary journey was cunning, silence and exile. Although influenced by such sensible guidance, it would ultimately take another recollection from the late 70's to finally end my inertia.

"You know what your problem is, don't you?" a friend had stammered, slamming his glass down hard enough to send a tongue of beer shooting out on to the table. "You think there's a purpose to all this."

My response to that late-night analysis was that it seemed one's duty and privilege to *find* a purpose. Three years into the trenches, I can't say for sure whether I've found it or not. What I can say with some authority at this point, is that writing is not for everyone. If I thought freelancing as a cameraman had been a precarious calling at times, it was nothing compared to the soaring and plummeting, not to mention breath-taking full-throttle straightaways of writing full-time. One might be well advised to note however, that there will be days when the system you are attempting to buck and examine will seem ready to rise up and swallow you whole, letting you occasionally feel wind from the wing of madness. Such days however, will pass.

But unlike their bygone counterparts, aspiring writers today must compete with the torrent of commentary gushing from social media sites. Faced with such a glut of information, the question has naturally arisen, "What's left to say that hasn't been said a dozen, a hundred, a thousand times already?" Probably nothing, but fortunately that wasn't a deterrent for me. After all, how many Canadians born under a prairie sky and the illusion they might have something to say, had the opportunities I did in Europe?

So ultimately, the question remains. Why settle for a desultory existence when life lies in the attempt? In the overall scream of things, if exploring your own potential is not enough incentive in and of itself, what is?

Acknowledgements

First and foremost, my deepest thanks go to Ingeborg and Ina, for their patience, tolerance, respect, feedback, encouragement and acceptance of my being invisible for months at a time.

A large dose of gratitude also goes to my old college comrade-in-arms, Larry Hicock, himself an author and film director, whose generosity, wisdom, and talented editing skills helped make this a better book.

I'm also grateful to the "guinea-pig test readers," whose feedback on selected chapters was not only helpful but free. So thanks go to Trish, Josanne, Marilyn, Dave, Jeannine and Felix.

Other books by same author

HÖTTLLAND

How and why an educated man
became and remained a Nazi

Why them? Why there? What caused a nation of 'Dichter und Denker' to be transformed into one of 'Richter und Henker'?

Höttlland attempts to answer those questions by examining the life and times of Wilhelm Georg Höttl, a former high ranking member of the Austrian SS. The trail begins in Vienna in 1915, moving up through a culture of envy, past people and events that influenced a young man to make a fateful leap aboard the Nazi bandwagon at the age of 19. Tracing his rapid advance within the 'seething ranks' of the SS, which saw him emerge as a heeded advisor in the SD intelligence apparatus at 24, Höttlland documents Höttl's involvement in various wartime intrigues that included everything from a counterfeiting operation, the kidnapping of Mussolini, the rescue of Hitler's art treasure, and the occupation of Hungary, to name just a few. With priorities shifting in late 1944, the book follows Höttl as he dons the mantel of peacemaker to confer with American officials about a separate peace and the sabotaging of the much feared 'Alpenfestung'. Arrested at war's end, Höttl diligently polishes his past to salvage a future, evading post-war justice by supplying interrogators at Nuremberg with detailed information on the inner workings of the Nazi intelligence apparatus, portions of which later help incriminate such former colleagues as Ernst Kaltenbrunner and Adolf Eichmann. Part I concludes as Höttl resurfaces in Austria in late 1947, ready to resume plying his wares with various agencies clamouring for intelligence under the gathering clouds of the Cold War.

(ISBN # 978-3-00-051567-5 Paperback)
(ISBN # 978-3-00-051566-8 ebook)

❊❊❊❊❊

Höttlland Part II
A Life after Deaths

"He was a very dangerous person....He only looked out for his own advantage. He was very crafty and impenetrable. You couldn't pin anything on him. But he was a swindler nonetheless." Edith Frischmuth (former member of the Austrian Resistance)

Unlike many Nazi colleagues whose careers finished at the end of a rope or in exile, the former Austrian SS officer and SD operative returns to Austria in late 1947, ready to embark on a series of equally opaque activities. Taking advantage of the rivalry created by the growing Cold War, Höttl resumes plying his wares, initially with the American Counter Intelligence Agency (CIC), and German based Organization Gehlen, and later with whomever happened to show interest. Eventually outed as a dubious source and cast back into the cold, he returns to his academic roots, founding a school and assuming its directorship, while managing to publish three stylized versions of his wartime recollections. Despite suspected involvement in the 'Ratlines', a mechanism set up to aid Nazi fugitives flee to safer havens, entanglement in a Soviet-American spy scandal, a death sentence handed down by a Hungarian court, and numerous demands to testify at the trials of former colleagues, including that of Adolf Eichmann, Höttl nevertheless slithers through the jaws of justice to emerge as a 'qualified Zeitzeuge', catering to an enduring media circus willing to pay for his flawed reflections right up until his final breath.

(ISBN # 978-3-00-051568-2 Paperback)
(Isbn # 978-3-00-054712-6 Ebook)

❆❆❆❆❆

CPSIA information can be obtained
at www.ICGtesting.com
Printed in the USA
LVHW041910090619
620661LV00001B/25